Theodicy

THEODICY
AND THE
POWER
OF THE
AFRICAN WILL

A PROGNOSTICATION
BASED ON THE
WISDOM OF OUR
ANCIENT AFRICAN ANCESTORS

DR. JOHNNIE CORDERO

BES PUBLISHING COMPANY

COLUMBIA, SOUTH CAROLINA

USA

THEODICY AND THE POWER OF THE AFRICAN WILL:
A PROGNOSTICATION
BASED ON THE
WISDOM OF OUR AFRICAN ANCESTORS
Copyright © 2017 by Dr. Johnnie Cordero

All rights reserved. No part of this book may be used or reproduced by any means, graphic, electronic, or mechanical, including photocopying, recording, taping or by any information storage retrieval system without the written permission of the publisher except in the case of brief quotations embodied in critical articles and reviews.

BES books may be ordered through booksellers or by contacting:

BES Publishing, Company

4204 Mandel Drive

Columbia, SC 29210

www.bespublishing.com

1-803-873-0039

Because of the dynamic nature of the Internet, any Web addresses

or links contained in this book may have changed

since publication and may no longer be valid.

The views expressed in this work are solely those of the author and do not necessarily reflect the views of the publisher, and the publisher hereby disclaims any responsibility for them.

ISBN: 978-0-9985041-2-4 (pbk)

Printed in the United States of America

Theodicy

DEDICATION

To my children

Troy, Kellie, Rameses, Kyphi, Elektra, Xavier, Seti,

Min, Petara, Karis and Sasha

CONTENTS

Preface vi
Introduction 1

SECTION ONE: THEODICY

Chapter One: Definitions 13
Chapter Two: Theodicy and Divine Justice 20
Chapter Three: Theodicy as Philosophic Discipline 27
Chapter Four: Theodicy as Divine Journey 36

SECTION TWO: CULTURE

Chapter Five: The importance of Culture 59
Chapter Six: Authentic Ancestral Culture 90
Chapter Seven: Stolen Cultural Energy 99
Chapter Eight: Scared Science 124
Chapter Nine: The New Culture Imperative 143

SECTION THREE: VISION

Chapter Ten: Triad of Visionary Power 157
Chapter Eleven: The Vision of the New Body Politic 180
Chapter Twelve: Critical Mass 185

SECTION FOUR: POWER

Chapter Thirteen: Power as Substance and Idea 197
Chapter Fourteen: The Temple as Power Generator 210

Theodicy

SECTION FIVE: THE PLAN
Chapter Fifteen: Developing a Plan of Action............233

SECTION SIX: LEADERSHIP
Chapter Sixteen: The Fundamentals of Leadership 267

SECTION SEVEN: THE POWER OF THE AFRICAN WILL
Chapter Seventeen: Will........................314

Chapter Eighteen: Toward New *Waset* 329

Epilogue 337

Appendix : The Night of the Teardrop 344

PREFACE

At a time before time began, when positive and negative forces commingled, nascent and undivided, in the infinite vastness that is the Mind of God, a teleological impulse, dynamic and unrestrained, gave birth to the desire that lies at the heart of creation.

In that vast and incalculable moment, recorded only in the collective consciousness that is God, the spark of creation ignited potential life through the agency of God's awareness of itself. In that sacred instant, that wedge of theoretical reality outside of existence, the thunderclap of time reverberated throughout the universe and engendered the alternation that is frequency, vibration, sound, light and life.

The feminine/receptive impulse, passive and robust, expelled from the reproductive organ that is the Mind of God was the Idea of worlds, the cause and potential of all that would live, breathe and procreate.

Time had been conceived, the Now made manifest, and the Idea of instinctive and conscious life had been born. The molecular marriage of carbon and hydrogen, energetically charged, built upon itself the infrastructure that skeletalized life. The One became Two. Atom by atom the elaborate prison of the soul was constructed following the invisible axes of the cube, the divine proportion of the Golden Mean and the architecture of an infinite universe.

Thus was born the womb of pleasure whose aide-de-camp is desire and whose offspring are the twins, affinity and attraction, who full grown are rut and love.

In the newly engendered womb a microscopic egg bore not only the fabric and form of the physical world and its inhabitants, but also the positive and negative forces that are

Theodicy

the unremitting agents equal in stature, complicity and power, in the mysterious conspiracy that is life.

At the instant of the conception of time, at the moment of the dawning of the first day of the world, a seed power lay dormant in silent wake and readiness against the day when a thought in motion would impel them to vie, in bitter and interminable contest, for the ruler ship of humanity and the future of life. Thus was born the cyclical, compelled necessity --*Theodicy*.

Theodicy

INTRODUCTION

THEODICY AND THE POWER OF THE AFRICAN WILL, is a product of a lifelong search for answers. It is also the response to the call of the *Intelligence-Of-The-Heart*. It is an amalgam of empathy, frustration and disgust. Let the reader be warned that the ultimatum contained in its pages is not tempered by polite words fashioned to soothe political or religious sensibilities. Only those who seek knowledge for the sake of enlightenment need proceed.

I do not claim to be anything other than a displeased and displaced member of the human race. I do not claim divine inspiration although it is true that my association with *Oudja* enables me to see things, in the broad sense, that perhaps others, unfortunately, do not.

I am a Black man, descendant of African nobility brought to these shores proud prisoners of war and reduced to abject slavery. As such I am born into the hell that is this European dominated world. My experience in this land of progressive slavery has not, with the exception of interactions with family and friends, been endearing. I readily acknowledge the existence of a bias against the hypocrisy of this country that masquerades as democracy. I have compensated for my bias by stating it foremost and prominently. I alert the reader that her analysis will be the more scrupulous and exacting. I do not hide the bias I wear it as a badge of honor.

This is in my view a thoroughly racist and condemnable society. Its touted contributions to civilization and human progress are belied by its festering underbelly of poverty, racism and wholesale environmental contamination. The obscene wealth of the few juxtaposed against the poverty of the many speaks volumes about its true cultural tendencies and moralistic pretensions.

Those who proclaim that European civilization is the greatest in history do not know history and, apparently, have a limited capacity for objective analysis. When the value of this country's technological advancement is viewed against the backdrop of nuclear proliferation in the passage of a mere two centuries plus of existence, the term greatest seems hollow, underserved and certainly premature.

The reader is cautioned that this is not a scholarly work. Nor is it intended to be one. It is not written for the jaded academic whose imprisonment in academe has desensitized him by removing his antiseptic objectivity.

This is a prognostication. It is written for the layperson who is in search of answers and who breathes the fire that is the affinity of Critical Mass.

This is a diagnostic view of history seen through the mind's eye of an ancient people whose perspective is foreign, but by no means inferior, to that of the European. The distinction is more than semantic, it is revolutionary because it predicts a necessary, unavoidable, imminent and radical change. Admittedly, that which is revolutionary is often considered subversive.

This work will be inspiring to some and unsettling to many. I accept both extremes as inevitable and desirable. My hope is that the work will engender critical thinking and the genuine pursuit of *Oudja* by, and in, a people who have too long been devoid of both.

It is my confident belief that this humble offering will focus attention on the crucial need for cultural and spiritually based leadership. I also predict that it will help initiate a new vanguard who will spearhead and compel cataclysmic change in order that our children and our children's children will have authentic opportunities for advancement and prosperity worthy of the glorious history that is their and our true ancestral heritage.

This work focuses attention on the fact that our children are now grist for a massive prison system that is the legacy and natural outgrowth of past slavery; on our communities that are the concentration camps of the present and that promise to become the death camps of the near future.

I implore the reader to face the fact that in our misguided pursuit of the "American Dream" we abandoned and taught

Theodicy

our children, by our example, to abandon our Authentic Ancestral Culture. Our children's inexperience and lack of sophistication, born of our own, makes it virtually impossible for them to recognize that pursuit of the American Dream is tantamount to acceptance of second-class citizenship and the subjugation it demands. They are unaware that White supremacy and Black subjugation are symbiotic realities and have always been the pillars of the American Dream.

I predict that this work will be immediately branded "racist". This likelihood is disturbing because of its inaccuracy but only mildly so and not nearly enough to deter me. Let me state for the record, however, that there is but one race --the human race. The proof of the fact, as if proof were needed, is demonstrated by the ability of human beings to procreate regardless of epidermic hue. All so-called distinctions are unimportant.

The unfortunate reality, however, is that racism (more accurately White supremacy) does, in fact, exist and holds sway over the minds of a great many otherwise intelligent people. This dismal state of affairs is the legacy of the Piscean Age . I did not create it, I and all members of the human race are inheritors of its diseased mentality. As devastating as the power of White supremacy has been to humanity's quest for universal peace and prosperity we are still witting or unwitting transmitters of its viral mentality. Live it we must; to expose it we are duty bound. In the end though, its days are numbered by the movement of the *Wheel of Time*.

Not all Whites who read this book will forgive me. But those who are sincere will understand and accept this treatise for what it is -- a prognostication that bodes ill only for those who are themselves bearers of ill will and of whom many are anticipated.

It should be borne in mind that as a prognostication this work is only subversive if it proves to be accurate. If it is not accurate there is no need to worry. If it is accurate there is nothing that can be done to stop it.

This work attempts to accomplish five primary objectives. First, it seeks to reconcile the seemingly contradictory notion of the existence of divine justice with the reality of the unjust, centuries-long exploitation and demoralization of the African people deliberately at the hands of the purportedly just and god-fearing European.

In this context the specific question addressed is how a just god who allegedly answers prayer could permit the atrocities of the African slave trade, and all that has followed in its wake, to be visited upon a people who, for all intents and purposes, have been peaceful, non-aggressive and devoutly religious?

The implications of the question are immense. They point to an anomaly that has been, for too long, disregarded. African people, including African Americans, have for centuries, placed their faith and their fate in the hands of a god who boasts proudly of his jealousy, capriciousness, vengeance and ultimate incomprehensibility. And who condones slavery, racism and sexism when he does not command them.

The anomaly lies in the fact that despite this the African people, African Americans included, have never seriously contemplated the possibility that by calling on the gods of those who have enslaved us that we have received the divine justice of a capricious, vengeful god who condones and commands the very acts of which we complain. Astonishingly, continued mistreatment and cyclically renewed assaults on the meager gains we have made has only caused us to intensify our entreaties to the gods of those who have enslaved us. The result has been that we have perpetuated the vicious cycle of abuse, neglect and unanswered prayer.

The second objective of this work is a functional outgrowth of the first. In order to reconcile the contradictions mentioned above, the concept of Theodicy, that is the proof of the existence of divine justice in the face of the apparent contradictions, the term must be defined in a way that logically accounts for them.

Theodicy

Specifically, this work posits that divine justice exists, is perpetually operative; and can be clearly observed by the enlightened eye and the curious mind. Moreover, the work further posits that the perpetual operation of Theodicy is cyclical and as such may be predicted with logical, quasi-scientific accuracy.

The third objective is perhaps the most important. It seeks to set forth elements of the imminent, radical change predicted by the movement of the Wheel of Time. The Wheel of Time being the mechanism by which Theodicy and its divine justice are unfolded.

The elements of the predicted radical change are cultural, political and religious and like clouds that precede a thunderous storm, gather on the horizon causing the atmospheric change that brings fear to men and disorder to the complacency of life. Simultaneously, the clouds carry the life-giving water that guarantees a new harvest that, in turn, guarantees another season of life.

The fourth objective is to provide African Americans with an understanding of the implications of Theodicy, the movement of the Wheel of Time and the cultural/political chain reaction that will follow in its wake.

It is posited that the Wheel of Time will foster a political climate and cosmic atmosphere that will be propitious for the ascendency of an African power to the center stage of world affairs.

Specifically, the work focuses on the mechanics of the change and the level of consciousness that must be attained by African people in general and African Americans in particular in order to derive maximum benefit from it.

The fifth and final objective of this work seeks to set forth the framework for a return to our Authentic Ancestral Culture. It is posited that such a return will attract, focus and dispense the cultural energy necessary to raise us from a dead level to a living perpendicular and guarantee that our children will not only survive but prosper and assume the mantle of world leadership to insure that they and humanity in general will not perish from the face of the earth.

The secondary objectives of this work are also compelling and must not be overlooked. These are three in number and together they dictate a compelled necessity that requires our immediate attention.

The first directs our attention to the undeclared war against the African people that seeks daily to destroy our families and render us incapable of launching a counteroffensive against what can only be described as planned genocide.

The second is the necessity for us to understand power, develop a plan of action and train the leadership to meet the conditions imposed upon us by the state of undeclared war.

The third objective is to lay the foundation for a dialogue that will bring together those who breathe the fire and form them into a Critical Mass that will spearhead the return to our Authentic Ancestral Culture and usher in the New Age of *Hapy*.

Theodicy and the Power of the Will is divided into seven sections. Each deals with a topic that is an essential element of Theodicy. As Theodicy is the central theme of this work each of the essential elements must be understood in order for the reader to comprehend the key indicators of the coming age as well as the mechanism and operation of the *Wheel of Time*.

Section I examines theodicy as a concept. It notes the triune nature of Theodicy as Divine Justice, Philosophical Discipline and Divine Journey.

Chapter One of this section sets forth the sometimes unique definitions of key terms and concepts that must be fully understood, in advance, for Theodicy to be understood.

Chapter Two explains the concept of Theodicy as Divine Justice and sets forth a framework for the assertion that Divine Justice does, in fact, exist and is operative despite the existence of negative circumstances that would seem to argue persuasively against such existence.

Chapter Three looks a Theodicy as a Philosophic Discipline. It holds that Theodicy is also an academic undertaking that examines the most basic question whose answers have been sought by all people through all the history of human consciousness. It is posited that in this respect Theodicy represents a movement toward a higher consciousness. This higher consciousness represents a quantum leap in understanding of the central questions that will re-orient our thinking toward the accomplishment of the primary objectives of the New Cosmic Age.

Section II is a pivotal section. It defines culture and examines its importance to the overall scheme of Theodicy and the survival and prosperity of African Americans. The section also looks closely at the related concepts of Culture Shift, Cultural Rebirth, Authentic Ancestral Culture and Cultural Energy.

Chapter Five defines culture as the Technology of Survival and examines its connection to religion, political power, prosperity and self-determination. It seeks to demonstrate that culture is everything and that a people cannot prosper unless they know and abide by the dictates of their unique ancestral culture.

Chapter Six asks and answers the all-important question of who our ancestors are and what is our Authentic Ancestral Culture. The chapter further indicates the ancestral culture that is best suited to serve the cultural needs of Africans in general and African Americans in particular. This chapter is crucial to the inauguration of the New Age of *Hapy* and must be considered carefully and objectively.

Chapter Seven introduces the concepts of Cultural Energy, Cultural Hegemony and Cultural Deprivation. To illustrate the theft of African Cultural Energy it reviews the original source of ancient wisdom and its transmission to the West via the ancient Greeks whose plagiarism of African source material is legendary.

Chapter Eight is dedicated to Sacred Science, also known as the Science of Tehuti. This source of ancient wisdom covers the First Principles of our Authentic Ancestral Culture and represents the fundamental teachings upon which the first great civilization of the world was built. The chapter also serves to illustrate how culture is employed as technology and how the appropriate technology in trained hands insures not only survival but prosperity as well.

Chapter Nine, the last chapter of Section II, frames the New Cultural Imperative whose implications are profound and whose message we ignore at our peril. This chapter is necessarily foreboding because it discloses the uncomfortable possibility of a final settlement of the problem of America's "internal enemy" through a planned genocide of the African American population. The case for this extraordinary prediction is established by the realities of the African American condition that are self-evident to honest observers of that condition.

Section III is entitled Vision. It introduces the Triad of Visionary Power embodied in the concepts of *Oudja*, *Critical Thinking* and the *Intelligence-of-the-Heart*. These concepts comprise the fundamental components of vision, a technique without which the people will surely perish. The chapter also introduces the ancient belief in the Ancestral Stream that finds its origin in the Cosmic Ocean that contains all things and from which all things emerge.

Chapter Ten defines *Oudja*, the ancient Kemitic word meaning clarity of vision and the first requirement of visionary power. It next presents the dire necessity for Critical Thinking among African Americans in order that we may analyze the ever increasing volume of information, much of it intentionally false or useless, with which we and our children are bombarded daily.

The Intelligence-of-the-Heart is another Kemitic term that is introduced in Chapter Ten and which directs us to the inner way of knowing that speaks to us directly, without dilution, distraction or interference. It also notes the source of this wondrous way of knowing that is to be found in the

Theodicy

Ancestral Stream wherein are found the vital, collected wisdom-knowledge and cosmic energy of our ancestors, the ones who have gone before.

Chapter Eleven deals with the vision of the Political Being. It covers both the method of seeing the Political Being and what it sees. The Political Being is defined as the New Body Politic whose existence requires a collective mind and spirit.

Chapter Twelve gives birth to the Political Being. In this chapter the concept of Critical Mass is explained as is its importance and connection to Theodicy and power. The calculation of the precise numbers required to attain Critical Mass and the cultural/political chain reaction that it will engender, is revealed in the understanding of the Divine Proportion.

Section IV is an in depth examination of power as both physical power and idea. This section serves to focus the reader's attention on what power is and the important role it plays it dictating the circumstances and conditions of our lives. This section also looks at the Temple as powerhouse and God as power.

Chapter Thirteen defines power as substance and idea. It notes that power is neutral and expansive and that it will work for any master. It introduces the concept of power units and discusses political power, the power process.

Chapter Fourteen is employed to explain the concept of the power generator. It demonstrates that the appropriate power generator for African Americans is to be found in the model of our ancient Temples constructed to focus and dispense the power of the *NeTeR NeTeRu* as well as transmit the teachings of our Authentic Ancestral Culture. The chapter also looks at the history of the ancient Kemitic Temple as the epicenter of our quest for survival, prosperity and high civilization.

Section V is dedicated to the Plan. It embraces the mechanics of developing a successful plan of action, as well as the fundamentals of leadership. The section cautions that the plan must always precede the leadership and that the failure to plan has been, for African Americans, a very costly omission.

Chapter Fifteen sets forth the elements of the successful plan of action and looks at the Internal Intelligence Function, Strategy, knowledge and the use of Symbols and Symbol Systems and introduces Bes our ancient symbol of childbirth and war. The chapter does not provide the plan but merely serves as a primer for the development of the plan.

Chapter Sixteen sets forth the fundamentals and qualities of leadership and examines the concept of war and the war against the African American family as well as the concepts of Illusory Leadership, Redundant Leadership and Multiple Centers of Control. The chapter closes with the analysis of the concept of the Rise of the Black Messiah and its connection to African Power.

Section VII is entitled the Power of the Will. It informs us of the latent and unlimited power of our will and illustrates the connection between it and the cosmic age. It explains the nature of the will that the Age of *Hapy* will evoke and how it will mold the consciousness of our people to permit them to take advantage of the benefits inherent in the new age. The chapter also looks at the eternal symbol of the power of the will and the power it contains to inspire and uplift.

Chapter Eighteen is the final chapter that takes us Toward New *Waset*. *Waset* is the Kemitic name of the ancient city referred to by the Greeks as "Thebes of the Hundred Gates". It is the place where our greatest achievement occurred and the place to which the world came to learn civilization and paid tribute for the privilege. The chapter includes a brief history of *Waset* and notes that our resurgence has always been launched from the south and posits that *Waset* is a picture upon which our collective mind's eye can focus as the destination toward which Theodicy and the Wheel of Time are moving.

The Epilogue brings the reader full circle and weaves the numerous strands together in a fabric of understanding. The picture painted is variously grim, foreboding and

Theodicy

inspirational. This work does not attempt to present the fullness of Kemitic culture, history or achievement. Sacred Science is merely alluded to. This is done for two reasons.

First of all no single volume work could even scratch the surface of our ancestral culture and second our history is still unfolding. Scholars have spent entire lifetimes dedicated to a single aspect of the achievements of our ancestors. As to Sacred Science, suffice it to say that the substance of it may not be written and may only be divulged to the initiated and then only from mouth to ear. The reader need only remember that all roads lead to Kemit and to speak of the dead is to make them live again.

SECTION ONE:

THEODICY

CHAPTER ONE:

Definitions.

This work seeks to establish a dialogue on a subject perceived by the author to be one of vital importance. The perceived importance of the subject dictates that a level of precision must be sought that will insure, as far as possible, that the dialogue progresses toward resolution and enlightenment, expeditiously. It's objective, in a word, is communication.

Communication is the transmission of ideas from one mind to another and whose ultimate objective is the attainment of mutual understanding.

The relative effectiveness of communication is directly related to the level of prior agreement on the definition of the words used to convey the ideas. Perhaps the greatest obstacle to communication then is the failure to define, in advance, the terms used.

The reader is cautioned and implored to be certain that she understands each word used in this work and that she does not proceed until an unknown term has been defined.

There are also terms used in this work that are unique and essential to the understanding of the overall theme of Theodicy and the broader message it seeks to convey. Because of their importance these essential terms are defined by way of preamble.

THEODICY

The word theodicy derives from the Greek *theosdike* and means, literally, god justice. The word originally described a system of natural theology that sought to explain how and why evil was able to exist on God's watch. Theodicy consists, therefore, in the attempt to vindicate God for allowing evil to exist.

For the purposes of this work theodicy shall have three distinct definitions. The first two are conventional, the third is not. The first conventional definition of theodicy is the vindication of divine justice in the face of the existence of evil. In this respect this work seeks to demonstrate how and why African Americans may logically continue to maintain faith* in, and reliance on, the ultimate reality of divine justice in the face of the unbroken history of oppression and atrocity perpetrated against them over the entire course of their unfortunate contact with the Caucasian and his tripartite system of political, economic and theological White supremacy.

On this level this work seeks to re-introduce the essence of our Authentic Ancestral Culture to a generation increasingly disillusioned with religion and enamored of individualism. The work further attempts to show that it was not the inadequacy of our culture, but rather, the abrupt abandonment of it in a forced culture shift that has forged the shackles of our current and historical oppression.

It should be noted at this juncture that religion is related to culture. It is, in fact, the deification of culture.* Theodicy must be understood then, as the vindication of our Authentic Ancestral Culture in the face of the historical record the evil of our past and present subjugation.

The second conventional sense in which theodicy is used defines it as a philosophic discipline that examines the nature of God, the government of God and the destiny of the soul.

The third sense is unconventional and, admittedly, new. It consists in a play on the word theodicy that permits a meaning not found in the etymology but that is suggested by the word itself. The third meaning is, therefore, symbolic.

---

* Faith is defined in the African sense of the belief that something will occur in the future based on its having occurred in the past and not the western meaning of a belief in things unseen or belief not based on logical proof or material evidence.

Theodicy

The word theodicy suggests a phonetic contraction of two words: *theo* meaning god and *odicy* which is homonymic of the word odyssey indicating an intellectual or spiritual journey. In this unconventional sense then theodicy shall mean a spiritual journey that by its natural operation vindicates divine justice. In this sense the fabled wanderings of Odysseus are brought to mind vividly. In the Homeric epic the storyteller recounts the journey of the Greek hero after the fall of Troy. For Africans of the Diaspora the millennia since the fall of our Authentic Ancestral Culture represents a spiritual, cultural wandering in which we may be likened to a collective, befuddled Odysseus. The effect of this aimless, unguided wandering has been a spiritual, intellectual fatigue, vulnerability, disorientation, disillusionment and sustained powerlessness. The acceptance of this symbolic meaning of theodicy is pivotal to the further understanding of the impending culture shift that will mark the return to our Authentic Ancestral Culture which is itself part and parcel of the vindication that theodicy seeks to explain.

It must also be understood that although theodicy may not logically be divorced from the study of God, and its relations with humanity or effect on the universe, it is also true that the theological underpinnings of theodicy are those of natural theology and not an alleged divine revelation.

Theodicy or god justice, is a system of natural theology that posits the existence of Divine Justice. It acknowledges the presence of forces that seem to frustrate that justice. It holds that Divine Justice and evil are compatible if not mutually dependent.

Theodicy seeks to explain, to vindicate, to justify the peculiar brand of justice called divine. The existence of evil on the other hand, seems to undermine any claim that such god justice may have to the admiration, respect or allegiance of humanity.

Theodicy is a proposition and an explanation. It attempts to make comprehensible the great paradox that underlies humanity's love/hate relationship with religion and its related confusion over the concept of god.

As used in this work theodicy also reveals an impending crisis. African Americans are on the brink of a sea change. The instability of our collective political and economic affairs indicate the necessity for abrupt, decisive, radical change. Without such change the hostile forces arrayed against us and the intense state of their opposition will consume us and our children.

Theodicy explains why and how this state of crisis, of danger and opportunity, is inevitable and predictable. It introduces us to the Wheel of Time and the concept of Divine Journey, as well as the ultimate destination of that journey.

The intense state of opposition is operative at two levels. One is the general, or global application and the other as it applies to African Americans in particular. One indicates the looming possibility of global destruction. The other foretells the possibility of the deliberate extermination of the Black race. Both may be avoided by the timely implementation of a master plan that embraces a return to our Authentic Ancestral Culture and the First Principles of Survival instructed by it.

THEOLOGY

In modern parlance the word theology has come to mean the study of god and relations between god, humanity and the universe. But the word itself is said to derive from the Greek meaning discussions of god. In the Latin, however, the word meant the study of heathen gods, specifically, giving the word an historical frame of reference.

Above all, theology is a brand of philosophy and derives from philosophical teachings that were, themselves, derived from discussions of god. Theology is most accurately defined, therefore, as a brand of philosophy that deals with the teachings of the heathens derived from their discussions about god. It should be remembered here that a heathen is an unconverted member of a people or nation that does not acknowledge the God of the Bible. Heathens are, in a word, pagans. Pagans are persons who are neither Christian, Muslim or Jew.

Theodicy

NATURAL THEOLOGY

Natural theology is the study of god based on the study of nature and without aid of a professed divine revelation. The definition links natural theology to the so-called pagans who studied nature to ascertain the characteristics and attributes of god.

In their naturalistic approach the pagans assumed that god existed and was the power that undergirds the universe. They also assumed that that incomprehensible power was constrained by and could be known by the universal laws created by it and by which it and all things were eternally bound.

Theology and natural theology are combined as the foundation from which the quest for theodicy is launched. These concepts relate that the study of god, central to the understanding of divine justice, is properly governed not by the pronouncements of prophets who profess to have been specially selected by god to direct messages for promulgation to the masses, but by the observation of natural phenomena. This approach has always been the mainstay of so-called heathens and pagans. It is to be noted that Africans, prior to their unfortunate contact with the Caucasian were proud, dignified independent and civilized, pagans.

PROGNOSTICATION

Prognostication is best understood as the act of predicting something that will occur in the future and that can be verified by subsequent observation. There are three senses in which the term is used scientifically. The first is deductive and refers to a predictive process that moves from known to unknown facts. The second deals with the process that posits predictions about that which will occur in the future based on recurrent, consecutive events of the past. The third sense is commonly understood as prophesy and involves the prediction of the future under the influence of divine guidance that is accomplished by so-called prophets.

This work is primarily concerned with the second sense of the term and claims no connection or dependence on the third whatsoever.

The prognostication in this work is, in one sense, sidereal, that is based on the observation of the stars and in the other, on the recorded wisdom of our ancient ancestors and is properly called cultural prediction. It is little different in method and result from a prediction of the number of automobile accidents to occur in the United States in a given period of time.

Prognostication has found its way into virtually all cultures. It is a method that enables societies to prepare for the future with some measure of accuracy, in spite of its characteristic uncertainty. It is also a useful, even invaluable tool when used to encourage and assist favorable outcomes and to prevent disadvantageous ones.

Although it is not claimed that this prognostication is strictly scientific it does partake of scientific method and to the extent that it does it may be classified with statistics and probability theory. Like scientific predictions in general it is based on a theory and evidentiary findings that are material to the verification of the theory postulated. In this work the basis is group characteristics, historical events, cosmic influences and past trends used to predict future cultural and political developments. In this regard two methods of cultural prediction bear mentioning: extrapolation and correlation.

Extrapolation is the method by which the future growth of a particular group is predicted based on its growth in the past.

Correlation is a method that makes predictions based on demonstrated connections between events occurring sequentially but within a discrete group.

Prognostication is neither new, nor foreign to science. The methods and concepts that underlie it are, routinely accepted in the academic and scientific communities. It is also true, however, that prognostication is capable of causing

Theodicy

that which it predicts. In this respect the author can only hope that this work will serve to hasten that which it predicts.

As used in this work prognostication is to be understood as a forecast of the course of human events. The basis of the forecast is the knowledge accumulated from our past in combination with the philosophy of our ancient ancestors from which predictions about the future can be made. We cannot plan for the future without knowledge of our past. Since all knowledge of the future is, at best, speculation the key to future planning is prognostication.

CHAPTER TWO:

THEODICY AND DIVINE JUSTICE

It is the premise of this work that a divine, universal justice, of sorts, exists. It is described as a movement analogous to the movement of a wheel that is inherent in the natural order of existence and serves to perpetually re-adjust and balance the opposing forces of NaTuRe.

Divine, universal justice is here posited as not only discoverable but comprehensible as well. Because it exist5 without apparent concern for human delusions about right and wrong it has no need of a supreme being to effect its purposes.

It is as a result of the se arch for divine, universal justice that humanity has created a being of like form and temperament to control that which appears uncontrollable. But the notion mandates a reason and justification for that which seems so imperfect in a world presumed to be created and governed by a perfect being. Of course such a notion also requires a being of intellect. Vengeance, deceit, duplicity and jealousy are attributed to a supreme being because they are first characteristic of the human mind. It follows that that which controls moral and natural evil must be, itself, evil in some measurable way.

This seemingly intractable problem, an apparent quirk in the divine plan, is known as the problem of evil and is reconciled here, perhaps for the first time, by Theodicy.

Though not a well-known term theodicy is certainly not a new one. The term has been used since the 18th century when it was coined by the German philosopher, Gottfried Wilhelm Leibniz. According to Leibniz, the world is the result of a divine plan and evil is a necessary ingredient of that plan.

Over time theodicy has come to be defined as a system of natural theology aimed at vindicating god in ordaining and permitting natural and moral evil to exist. The term is used in this work in a unique sense that must be understood and

Theodicy

accepted at the outset. The definition here expands the term in a way that permits divine, universal justice to not only be vindicated but also to be explained and predicted.

This divine or universal justice, this god justice, is here posited as pre-existent, cyclical and perpetual. As such it easily lends itself to accurate prediction when its cycles are recognized and understood. It is in this sense that theodicy relates to a fundamental dilemma confronting African Americans. We are a people who pride ourselves, simultaneously, on our faith in god and his divine justice in spite of our seemingly perpetual status as second-class citizens in a society in which all men are purported to be created equal.

Theodicy seeks to justify god for allowing evil to exist. It implicitly asks how it is possible to arrive at a concept of justice, let alone divine justice, when evil increases its power generationally? The question is, admittedly, perennial. Ironically, it is asked most often by those who are simultaneously convinced of the existence of an omniscient, omnipresent and omnipotent Supreme Being who is said to rule the universe from his heavenly abode.

To philosophers the question is known as the problem of evil; to the religious it is simply the devil's handiwork; to the a theist it is the smoking gun of god's non-existence; to the agnostic it is irrelevant. The question, however, begs an answer --Theodicy provides it.

Theodicy asserts first, and boldly, that divine, universal justice exists, and second that it can be justified despite the apparent existence of evil. That the concept is paradoxical when viewed, as it must be, against the backdrop of human history and its record of incessant brutality, carnage and gratuitous violence, is conceded. The enigma lies not in divine universal justice but in its current, accepted definition.

Divine justice is popularly understood as the method by which the Supreme Being rewards or penalizes the actions of his necessarily inferior creatures. The definition is based on premises that obscure rather than elucidate. The popular definition of theodicy implies that (1) a Supreme Being exists; (2) that the said being is a male; and (3) that he is capable of rewarding or penalizing human behavior. If reward is understood as something given in return for good or evil, done or received, the one who rewards would also, as a matter of course, be required to discern between good and evil in order to determine if and when reward or penalty is appropriate in a particular case. Such a being must, therefore, be rational and cognitive. In short, the being who is the divine in divine justice must be human or humanlike.

Second, and equally problematic, is the implication that good and evil are, in fact, quantifiable. The implication compels further analysis. Let us begin by conceding that that which is deemed evil by one group of persons may not be universally accepted as such. Discernment of what is objectively and universally good or evil is therefore, an exercise in futility. Concepts such as objective good and evil have no substantive meaning. Good and evil are wholly matters of perception, interpretation and acceptance. Examples of the virtual impossibility of discovering objective good and evil are legion. Perhaps the best among these is the controversy surrounding the taking of a human life whether by euthanasia, homicide or government administered capital punishment.

Whether we speak of capital punishment or murder (assuming for the sake of argument that there is some difference between the two) it is a human life that is extinguished. Yet, the former is deemed acceptable or non-evil while the latter is condemned as *malum in se*. This apparent contradiction is often justified by the notion of necessary evil, that is, evil that is good under the circumstances. It follows that the taking of a human life it not always evil and may sometimes, as in the case of self-defense (legally termed justification), be good.

Perhaps the most revealing example is the Supreme Being's inability to decide if the taking of a human life is evil. In the Decalogue the Judeo and later Christian Supreme Being prohibits killing. Yet, while punishing Moses for slaying the

Theodicy

Egyptian, he commands Joshua and his tribes to swoop down on Canaan and murder every man, woman and child in order that the chosen people can inhabit the Promised Land. This is, of course, no more than god-directed genocide. To call it war or even holy war does not lessen its murderous impact. In the same context the awarding of medals to soldiers for murder in time of war, or the consecration of battleships and atomic bombs does not magically or religiously transform the taking of a human life into something benign.

It is apparent that the current, accepted definition of divine justice seems to prevent rather than assist the understanding of the concept of theodicy. If the term is re-defined, however, comprehension may follow and a once enigmatic concept becomes lucent.

Theodicy is the vindication of divine justice in the face of the existence of evil but it is much more. Understanding of the term further depends on the meanings of the individual terms divine justice, vindication and evil, all of which are necessarily subsumed in the concept of Theodicy.

DIVINE JUSTICE

Divine Justice is best defined as non-judgmental justice or justice without judgment. It consists in the corpus of universal laws that derive from NaTuRe and which are binding on the actions of all living things. It is also readily discernible in the universal laws discovered by the scientific disciplines of physics, biology and chemistry, among others.

The concept of Divine Justice is also noted in the law of physics that states that for every action there is an equal and opposite reaction.

It is also a concept symbolized by the wheel. Like a wheel that elevates and casts down, in natural succession, theodicy is neither human nor intelligent. It is feasible, therefore, to posit the existence of divine, universal justice without the resort to the dubious notion of an intellectual, human Supreme Being.

Divine Justice is, therefore, the orderly, predictable consequence of actions. It is comprised of both action and reaction. It is non-judgmental because it operates strictly according to self-contained, pre-existing laws from which it is incapable of deviating, and without moral regard to the actor or the nature of the act. Once set in motion by willful, instinctive or natural act, its return and completion is inevitable.

VINDICATION

The concept of vindication adds to the confusion. Vindication means justification. mere attempt to justify or defend the wanton, indiscriminate destruction and senseless violence of animals (including humans) and natural forces is itself an illogical, contradictory application of the word.

An allegedly rational and compassionate Supreme Being cannot be justified if he is responsible for all the heinous acts attributed to him in biblical text and religious lore. The notion of human justice will not permit us to vindicate a human being for such acts. Much less can we do so for a Supreme Being whose postulated existence means, if nothing else, that he is prevented from exhibiting the frailties of his necessarily inferior creatures.

The understanding of theodicy is only complicated by the definition of vindication as justification. If, however, divine justice is understood as non-judgmental and orderly consequence of actions, it is justified and vindicated, *ipso facto*.

EVIL

Evil, when viewed in the context of theodicy, is the most difficult meaning to accept. This is because it is hopelessly subjective. It is further complicated by the fact that it embodies morality as a part of its meaning. Morality is, perhaps, the most subjective word in the English language.

Evil is defined as that which is morally bad or wrong, wicked, depraved or simply immoral. Morality is that which is "right"

Theodicy

and "good" as those terms are defined by some unnamed group of people.

Morality is most often used in the context of sexual conduct. Sexual conduct is, if anything, divergent. That which is accepted as normal sexual behavior among the members of one group may be deviant to another.

In some societies polygamy and/or polyandry are acceptable. In others monogamy is the only acceptable method of cohabitation. In some societies a female virgin is ostracized and a poor choice for marriage, while in others the non-virgin invites spinsterhood.

Matters of evil and morality turn not on what is intrinsically right or wrong, good or bad, but on the subjective view of a particular group of people. Evil and morality are, therefore, the result of historical and cultural factors having nothing to do with right or wrong.

As regards the Supreme Being we must conclude from this that in order to discern the subtle nuances and gradations of what is morally bad or evil he must be capable of thinking.

This apparent dilemma is not, however, intractable. We need only re-define evil. If evil is understood as the distortion of fact we are able to understand how it can exist in the presence of divine, universal justice.

It has been said that the lie is the essence of evil. When the lie is understood as the intentional distortion of fact for the purpose of taking unfair advantage of another, evil is seen to be a purely human characteristic and invention.

The lie includes the act of intending to deceive, which is perhaps as odious as the accomplishment of the actual deception. Intention both wills the act and makes it evil. Deception is a conscious behavior pattern. Evil, therefore, can only be the act of cognitive beings. Although deception has been observed in primates as well as humans, it is only malicious in the case of the latter. Malicious deceit is manifested in the ability to appear to be one thing while actually and intentionally being something else for the specific purpose of taking unfair advantage of another. Malicious deceit is impossible for animals other than humans. It is also impossible for a Supreme Being who does not think.

Having re-defined divine justice, vindication and evil we are compelled to arrive at the following conclusions:

(1) divine justice is the orderly, non-judgmental and predictable consequence of prior actions whether the actions are willful, instinctive or natural;

(2) divine justice is set in motion by universal and unalterable laws best understood as cause and effect;

3) the divine in divine justice is not a rational, cognitive, substantial or material being who can, in any logical sense, be held responsible for the wanton acts of intellectual beings or the mindless catastrophes NaTuRe; and

(4) the existence of evil as the distortion of fact is perfectly consistent with the simultaneous existence of divine justice.

Theodicy

CHAPTER THREE:
THEODICY AS PHILOSOPHIC DISCIPLINE

As philosophic discipline theodicy examines (1) the NaTuRe of God; (2) the government of God (theocracy); and (3) the transmigration of souls (metempsychosis).

THE NATURE OF GOD

The attempt to determine the NaTuRe of God is perhaps one of the oldest pursuits of intellectual humanity. It may have been that pursuit that gave rise to consciousness and set the limits of intelligence between man and beast. This is not to say, however, that individual people have not answered questions about the NaTuRe of God to their own independent satisfaction.

In the ranks of such people were the ancient Kemites (also known as the Ancient Egyptians) who concluded millennia ago that God is the active power that produces and creates things in orderly and regular recurrence.

In short, they concluded that the NaTuRe of God was best described as NaTuRe. From this foundational belief arose the concepts of cause and effect and the Double Law or Two Truths.*

The ancient Kemites understanding of this active, creative and regularly recurring power is the foundation upon which the concept of Theodicy, as used in this work, rests. An in-depth analysis of the NaTuRe of God is beyond the scope of this work. Suffice it to say that the Kemites maintained that the *NeTeR NeTeRu* (literally God of Gods) was the power that created the world. It was believed to have no further contact with humanity and, remains eternally hidden because

---

*The Two Truths or Double Law, in its most basic form, states that all facts, statements, assertions, laws, observations and realities implicitly state the simultaneous existence and reality of its opposite.

incomprehensible. The Kemite understanding of the NaTuRe of God is fundamentally and undeniably African. It is diametrically opposed to the NaTuRe of God promulgated by the European. To the Kemite the *NeTeR NeTeRu* is unintelligent and insubstantial. It pre-exists all things. It is the creative power at the origin of all things, but it necessarily exists outside of time and beyond the limited and finite comprehension of humanity. To the Kemites, indigenous Black Africans all, the notion that the NeTeR NeTeRu could be directly communicated with was pure insanity. That humanity could, by prayer or entreaty I cause it to act according to their whim or in defiance of its own universal and unalterable laws was utter nonsense unworthy of serious contemplation. The NeTeR NeTeRu was neither he nor she. It was not animal, vegetable or mineral and certainly could not speak, think or intervene in human affairs. To these ancient people the *NeTeR NeTeRu* exists because every effect must have a cause. The *NeTeR NeTeRu* is, therefore, a necessary postulate whose existence is affirmed not only by our own existence, but also by all that exists.

THEOCRACY

The popularly accepted definition of theocracy is government by God. The definition is illogical and misleading. It is also uniquely European. Its insufficiency consists in the implicit notion that God can institute and maintain a government. In order to do so, we may agree without much argument, that God would have to be an intelligent being capable of thought and communication. Apparently, the definition says more about the mind-set of the people who accept it then it does about the concept it claims to define. Such a definition is possible only if God is anthropomorphic. That this concept of God currently holds sway over the minds of many of the world's otherwise intelligent people does not change the fact. It follows that if God is not a person it cannot be capable of governing in the sense intended by the word government.

Government is the control, management and administration of a political unit. It is also the system or policy by which the political unit is governed. This systematic control, management and administration requires a person or persons to effectuate it. If God is not a person it cannot govern. There can be no government by God. How is it possible then that the longest lived and most stable form of government in human history has been the theocracy? The answer, again, is found in the definition of the term.

Theocracy is not government by God. It is government based on spiritual principles, sacerdotally administered. The difference is more than semantic. Since God cannot administer and manage a political unit those who actually do so only claim to do so in God's name. Human beings are, if nothing else, frail and given to avarice and animal passions. When they act in the name of God they attribute their necessarily imperfect actions to God. When man is greedy, God is greedy. When man is irrational, so is God.

It is because of the historical and blatant abuses of a particular religion that theocracy has received such a bad name. The historical disdain attached to the word theocracy is linked exclusively to European churches, specifically

Catholic and Protestant churches. But these were not theocracies, they were churches of men grown politically powerful and arrogant in that power. These men were immeasurably strengthened by a book whose accepted interpretation was determined by whose army was the strongest, or whose indulgences were the most liberal. As a result of this unfortunate historical experience and long periods of indoctrination we have become conditioned to believe that religion and government, like oil and water, do not mix.

The popular political maxim that elevates the separation of church and state to a first principle of liberty is essentially, if not exclusively, European and of very recent origin. The First Amendment to the United States Constitution proclaims freedom of religion and erects, at least by judicial interpretation, an impenetrable wall of separation between church and state. Although the Constitution speaks of religion it declares a separation between church and state not religion and state. This too is a distinction worthy of elaboration.

The word church refers, exclusively, to a Christian spiritual body. It follows that the separation alleged to be so essential to democracy is a separation of government from Christianity. It is axiomatic that the need for such separation could not have existed before the Christian church.

The fear and disapproval of theocracy arises then, from the combination of an inaccurate definition of the word and the historical abuses* at the hands of European Christian churches, both Catholic and Protestant. That such abuses have served to undermine the legitimacy of the concept of theocracy is logical and inevitable. But the abuses are not

---

*The selling of indulgences; the Inquisitions; the Crusades; the condoning of slavery; sanctification of the annihilation or extermination of numerous peoples around the world. The full scope of Christian church atrocities is beyond the scope of this work.

attributable to God. The separation of church and state means the Christian church and state do not mix. In this regard we need only look at the political trend of the United States since the birth of the Moral (Christian) Majority and Republican (Christian) Right.

We must be careful not to throw the clean baby out with the dirty bath water. Let us look, instead, to the ancient concept of theocracy to understand what it meant before it was bastardized by the Christian hordes.

THE ANCIENT CONCEPT OF THEOCRACY

As an ancient concept of governance, theocracy was not dependent on the will of priests or a hierarchy of ecclesiastics. Theocracy was, quite simply, political government based on the universal and unalterable laws of NaTuRe, administered by elders.* Theocracy was the application of Sacred Science** to the lives and fortunes of the nation with emphasis on the fundamental concept of universal responsibility implied by the law of cause and effect.

In ancient theocracy the governing principles of universal law were applied, with precision, to the overall planning and implementation of programs and goals that were deemed beneficial to the people as a whole. The policies emphasized cooperation over competition while individualism was subordinated to the needs of the entire populace. Work was a necessary requirement of group survival and prosperity and personal satisfaction lay in the ennobling accomplishment of a task well done. Of necessity a division of labor, based on the needs of the society and the innate ability of individual citizens was implemented. This method permitted any person with talent to rise to his or her own greatest possible level of achievement. In this way, a person of meager beginning and humble circumstance had

---

*The word priest literally means elder.

** The Science of Tehuti see Chapter VIII

unhindered access to any profession or occupation for which he or she was suited.

Perhaps the greatest testimony of the efficiency of theocratic governments is their longevity. The longest lived civilization in ancient times and to the present day was Kemit, popularly known as ancient Egypt. Historians remain baffled in their attempts to explain how the ancient Kemites were able to maintain such a high level of civilization under a governmental structure that unified secular and spiritual affairs. More perplexing to those who have attempted to unravel the mystery is the fact that periods of instability, always of brief duration, were marked by the departure from that form of government while order only returned when theocratic government was re-established. It is indeed remarkable that Kemit never experienced revolution or popular uprising by its citizens in the more than 4,000 years of its recorded and unbroken history. Kings and priests came and went, only adherence to the universal law of Sacred Science and the theocratic government remained. Theocracy was the golden thread that maintained continuity and longevity and kept the present informed by the past.

These facts indicate that theocracy, when understood as governance based on universal law and spiritual principles, is not only feasible and desirable, but also represents the most successful form of government in human history.

This uniquely African concept required a government based on spiritual principles and administered by persons specially selected and rigorously trained to govern. All proclaimed leaders including the king were merely titular. The European bastardization of and debasement of the concept gave the world sovereign immunity, papal infallibility, the divine right of kings and chattel slavery.

Theodicy

METEMPSYCHOSIS

Theodicy is a philosophic discipline that seeks to determine the destiny of the soul.* Metempsychosis or the transmigration of the soul is the ancient theory that solves the mystery of the ultimate destiny of our spiritual and energetic essence. The Kemitic theory of metempsychosis asserts that the soul's fate is to pass into and thereby animate another body after the death of the one it presently occupies, if it fails to free itself from the Path of Asar on the day of the Weighing of the Soul.

Metempsychosis is based on the further theory that the soul is energy and that which animates all living things. As such it is the part of the *NeTeR NeTeRu* that resides in all living things. The soul is, therefore, the energy or power that is God and which animates human beings.

The verification of the theory of metempsychosis is found in the now well known, and accepted Laws of Thermodynamics.

Thermodynamics is a branch of physics that deals with the transformation and conversion of energy. The name, appropriately enough, derives from the Greek words therm, meaning heat, and *dynamikos* meaning power.

The First Law of Thermodynamics (also known as the law of the conservation of energy) states that energy cannot be created or destroyed. It may, however, change from one form to another and the transformation is reversible.

The Second Law of Thermodynamics (also known as entropy) is a qualification on energy transformations. It states that in any energy transformation a part of the energy is converted to heat. The amount of energy is always constant, but a part

---

*The Kemites were the first to posit (1) the existence of the soul; and (2) that the soul is immortal.

of it cannot be used for work. The second law holds, therefore, that energy, as a result of transformation, is always diminishing.

According to the Laws of Thermodynamics, energy can and does transfer from one form to another, but it cannot be either created or destroyed and that it decreases within a system as a direct result of transformation. The laws also hold that where there is energy there is heat.

By contrast the ancient Kemitic theory of metempsychosis posits that the soul is energy and that energy is transformed at the moment of death to ultimately enter another body. The source of that energy, the *NeTeR NeTeRu*, is the source of all energy. That energy exists, is always the same and cannot be created or destroyed because it always existed and always will exist.

The Law of Entropy holds that energy diminishes in the process of transformation. It follows that energy use causes energy to be converted or transferred and therefore decreased in the body that uses it. The total depletion of energy, therefore, is, decay and death. Death is literally the depletion of energy sufficient to sustain life. It also indicates the presence of energy in the human body by virtue of the presence of heat that radiates from it. Of course, a corpse is cold because its energy, or divine essence has departed. This occurs in two ways: either the energy allotted for the particular lifespan has been used, or the body has been, in some way, damaged to the extent that it can no longer contain the energy.

The destiny of the soul then is governed by the law of physics* pertinent to the transformation of energy. It should also be noted here that destiny is best understood as destination. The destiny of the soul is to return to its place of origin. Its destiny, therefore, is its destination.

Whether metempsychosis is proven to be an accurate explanation of the destiny of the soul is irrelevant and need not detain us here. The important thing for this stage of our

Theodicy

analysis is that the second component of Theodicy as philosophic discipline is satisfied.

CHAPTER FOUR:

THEODICY AS DIVINE JOURNEY --THE WHEEL OF TIME

In its symbolic meaning theodicy implies a divine journey that is the vehicle of divine, universal justice. As a traveling from one place to another, a journey connotes distance and time.

The postulated divine journey is the precessional movement of the stars through the houses of the Zodiac from a specified point and return to that point. The distance traveled is that necessary to traverse each of the twelve houses. The time is that of the cosmic year of 25,920 calendar years.

The theory of Theodicy as divine journey is best symbolized by the movement of a wheel. As the wheel journeys from one place to another it simultaneously elevates one part of its circumference as it casts down another. In the natural course of its operation the wheel suggests both continuity and stability by its turning, while also suggesting instability of its individual parts as they repeatedly rise and fall. In the context of theodicy the wheel is to be understood as that of human history and affairs. The Wheel of Time is divine, universal justice in action. It is the movement of time that elevates and casts down in regular succession as it moves toward its destination.

Time is itself a concept that can be viewed in several ways. In the popular view time is understood as a real entity that seems to have movement and as such is the manifestation of the forward motion principle. The forward motion principle dictates that all life activity is teleological in focus, always moving forward, never backward. By this principle the phrase "time marches on" is quite accurate. But time can also be divided into past, present and future. Of course, there are those who consider such calibration a mere human convenience. In this regard the ancient Kemites recognized the ever-present moment. This concept is best described that as the "now". By their reckoning any other calculation of time is illusory because we always exist in the now. The past

Theodicy

is the memory of now, while the future is the possibility of now. Nevertheless, the time that we experience is always now.

Time is most often understood, however, to refer to measurable time. That is time based on some recurring phenomenon. Astronomers in ancient Kemit concluded, and their modern day counterparts agree, that the most reliable recurring phenomenon is the motion of celestial bodies. The notion of time, therefore, derives from the observation of the motion of bodies through space. The accuracy of the measurement is reason the sun and fixed stars provide the most accurate gauge of time and the hallmark of the forward motion principle. Time reckoned by the motion of the stars is called sidereal time and that based on the sun is known as solar time. Both are theoretically based on the concept of movement in circuit, hence the Wheel of Time.

Careful observation of the movement of the Wheel of Time permits the determination of its direction, the speed at which it travels and the estimated time of arrival when its destination is known.

Like the wheel, the Divine Journey, and by extension divine, universal justice are each predict able. It is in this sense that Theodicy may be seen as a key indicator of possible future events. Theodicy, therefore, implies the Divine Journey of human history and affairs toward a specific destination.

During the course of its journey the Wheel of Time, by its movement, facilitates the rise and fall of individuals and nations alike. Those who find themselves riding the crest of the wheel today need be mindful of the fact that the selfsame movement will ineluctably and predictably cast them down as they are replaced by others whose immediate past, also by operation of the Wheel of Time, has held them at the bottom of human affairs for a time.

The concept of theodicy as it relates to the Wheel of Time is not new. It has been recognized and relied upon, in another guise, in oriental societies for millennia, To the Chinese and the Japanese it is known as the *Mandate of Heaven*.

The Mandate of Heaven is a concept that is, at once, political and religious. It is an ancient theory that holds that the ruler is able to rule because he has received the mandate of heaven. More precisely, it implies that some heavenly power granted his authority to rule. Conversely, his authority and power ended when he lost the mandate. An emperor who abused his authority would necessarily upset the balance of NaTuRe, and *ipso facto*, cause the mandate to be removed. But even the positive ruler who did nothing to abuse his authority could lose the mandate for reasons totally unrelated to his reign.

The Chinese believed in a NaTuRal pattern of 500 year cycles.* These cycles were discovered by observations of celestial bodies and the interpretation of the meaning of various planetary relationships. This approach was philosophically possible because they believed that heaven did not rule NaTuRe but was part of NaTuRe. This distinction was recognized in ancient Kemit and was less clearly defined, if it existed at all, in European religious and philosophical concepts. It should also be noted that the Chinese had an essentially agricultural civilization that would make them extremely sensitive to cycles and seasons.

The Chinese also recorded that there were certain signs that conclusively indicated when the mandate had been or was about to be removed. Among these were the occurrence of floods, earthquakes and other NaTuRal disasters. Also significant was a marked change in the thinking of the people that caused them to shift their allegiance from one leader to another. In this sense it was *the will of the people that evidenced the grant or removal of the Mandate of Heaven*. But the change in thinking of the people was effect of and not the cause of the loss of the mandate. It was, therefore,

---

*The 500 year cycle was represented in ancient Kemit by the *Bennu* bird who sets itself on fire every 500 years and rises renewed from the ashes. To the Greeks it was known as the Phoenix

Theodicy

the celestial milieu that evoked the new and potent will of the people.

Finally, certain conditions precedent were necessary for the change, which is really a cultural-political shift, to take place. There would have to be a political crisis; an alternative leadership; and a precipitating event. Perhaps the best modern example of this concept is the rise of Mao Tse Tung in the 1940's. The people believed that the mandate have been taken away from the current leadership and given to the communists. But it was their will to revolution and their willingness to endure hardship that made the greatest and most radical cultural revolution in history possible.

The Chinese belief that governments that lose the mandate deserve to be, and ultimately will be, overthrown by the new holders of the mandate and that the shift happens cyclically, NaTuRally and predictably and the signs of the loss of the mandate are to be discerned by celestial observation, is little different than the concept of Theodicy and the Wheel of Time advanced in this work.

The recurring celestial phenomenon upon which Theodicy and the movement of the Wheel of Time, and to a lesser extent the Mandate of Heaven, and their predictable effects on human history and affairs is based is known as the *Precession of the Equinoxes*.

THE PRECESSION OF THE EQUINOXES

There are those who will reject the concept of prognostication out of hand. They will do so because of its historical connection with mysticism and prophets. This is, perhaps, as it should be.

History records an abundance of individuals whose proclamation of the advent of a New Age was more an attempt to enrich their own coffers than true messianic vision. Other prophets have honestly believed their own message but were simply mistaken. That the masses have been deceived, misled and fleeced demonstrates the pitfalls of gullibility. The fundamental and universal law of regular, cyclical and predictable change remains, however, unimpaired. Skepticism is the antidote for gullibility. It is not a substitute for investigation.

All living things progress on a continuum that encompasses birth, growth and ultimately, death. All living things manifest independent movement. The universe, apparently, has independent movement. The universe can, therefore, be said to be itself a living thing. Life cannot come from non-life. Life exists in the universe, therefore, the itself must, again, be alive. As a living thing the universe is subject to the same cycles as all other living things.

Ancient astronomers recognized and recorded the law of cyclical renewal that they found written on the heavens. These ancient stargazers, over long periods of time, observed that the stars appeared and disappeared only to reappear in the same place in the heavens regularly and therefore predictably. They also noted a correlation, in some cases, between the reappearance of certain stars and the occurrence of certain significant events.

The ancient Kemites of Africa's Nile Valley, now universally recognized as the first to recognize such celestial connections, noted the seasonal changes, so important to the science of agriculture that were heralded by the appearance of certain stars. These cyclical reappearances permitted, over time, the establishment of an accurate

Theodicy

calendar and other time reckoning devices that provide order and assisted the advance of civilization.

In time Kemitic astronomers, perhaps as a separate branch of their Sacred Science, began to intuit or read more abstract correspondences and influences that seemed to accompany the cyclical changes. On the basis of empirical data regarding human NaTuRe they concluded that with each occurrence the universe itself underwent a process of change that in turn created a new and different cosmic milieu that colored everything in it. It was also theorized that if one could accurately determine the cosmic milieu that was attendant upon the coming age, one could also foretell, not specifically but generally, that which could be expected to transpire during the period in question. These erstwhile astrologers, using the recorded observation of their sister astronomers could then, upon the basis of their star records, in combination with the political, economic, geological and atmospheric history of the country and its people, predict the NaTuRe of the coming age.

The concept of cosmic ages was, in turn, based on the theoretical division of the heavens into twelve imaginary houses or signs lasting thirty days. Astronomers also noticed that the Earth had not only daily and annual rotations, but also a cyclic wobbling in its axis of rotation. This third motion of the Earth is now known as the Precession of the Equinoxes, in which it appeared that the Earth shifted in relation to the solar system. As a result, the vernal equinox, one of the two annual periods when the length of day and night is approximately the same, appears earlier ,and earlier, that is precessionally, in each house of the Zodiac over time. Because of this precession the vernal equinox appeared to move from one house to the one before it approximately every 2,160 years, taking 25,920 years to complete the circuit. This was known as the Cosmic Year.

The Kemites believed that the passage from one house to another was always marked by political, economic, geological and atmospheric change and that the influence of the prior milieu began to dissipate while the new was ascendant.

This precessional shift required change in the theological emphasis and therefore occasioned the dismantling of old temples and the disregard of the service of former NeTeRs and the erection of new temples dedicated to different NeTeRs whose influence was thought to color the coming cosmic month. The Ritual of the Divine Cult* and the theological teaching were necessarily modified to reflect the anticipated shift. For this reason theological teaching was not static but vital, transcendent and reflective of the current age and its people.

Perhaps more importantly, the shift required modification or alteration of the master plan for the emphasis, direction and accomplishment of the collective goals and objective of the nation. This re-dedication and renewal of national focus and will carried with it the implicit acceptance of that which the New Age dictated. This self-imposed re-orientation motivated a complete change in emphasis of government and sacred endeavor as well as the will of the people generally.

The concept of theodicy as a divine journey and a key indicator of future events is amply illustrated by the Precession of the Equinoxes. The Wheel of Time that it demonstrates predicts dramatic change and cosmic upheaval with each precessional movement. We stand poised on the

---

*The Ritual of the Divine Cult refers to the ritual practices observed by the priests of Kemit and performed in the sanctuary of the temple at sunrise, high noon and sunset, daily. The practice duplicated what had been done by their, and our ancestors on the First Day of the World and which were believed to be efficacious in maintaining the order and regularity of the universe as well as the life, health and strength of the nation. The ritual included the Ancestral Cult which paid homage to the memory of our ancestors whose intercession with the "Hidden One" was considered absolutely essential to national survival, order and prosperity.

0

cusp of a new age. We stand at the threshold of a new era when the influence of the old age dissipates and the effect and power of the new age increases.

The future is a possibility even if the possibilities are infinite. It is determined by foresight, accurate present information, preparation and the power of the will. It is dependent on what we think and do -- now. As the future becomes the now we must learn that the decisions we make today mold our future, and to a large extent, dictate decisions that will be made tomorrow.

Preparation for the New Age, then, will require familiarity with its characteristics and appropriate change or modification of our focus to achieve harmony with its anticipated cosmic ambiance.

Theodicy contemplates familiarity with the characteristics of the age and appropriate modification of the cultural, political and economic factors to accommodate, direct and derive the greatest benefit from the cosmic milieu that will mark the age. In order to do so let us look at the anticipated character of the coming age.

THE AGE OF *HAPY*

Theodicy informs us that the Divine Journey of the Wheel of Time dictates the speed and direction of human history and affairs. This precessional movement, the circuit of which is the span of nearly 26,000 calendar years, is called the Cosmic Year, and is comprised of 12 cosmic months of 2,160 calendar years each. Each of the Cosmic Months are subdivided into three decans of 720 years each. By this reckoning a day is 72 years, an hour 3 years and 18 days to the minute. Each of the cosmic months in the cosmic year are designated by a dominant constellation whose influence colors the month by giving it a distinctive character and quality.

In ancient Kemit the constellation that governed each cosmic month was referred to as the Great *NeTeR* of the Cult. The word cult, as used here, means the observation and veneration of the principle or ideal characteristic of the age which the Great *NeTeR* betokens. Again, each age is a cosmic month.

The influence of the Great *NeTeR* of the Cult registers its effect not on individuals, as modern astrologers would have us believe, but on the cosmic milieu.

In ancient Kemit the cosmic milieu was called the Nun. The Nun is best understood as the cosmic ocean that surrounds the universe and in which the universe and everything in it is submerged. It is the cosmic energy upon which the Great *NeTeR's* influence acts, and through which human affairs are affected by any change in the *Nun*. The Great *NeTeR* of the cosmic month colors the *Nun* and the *Nun*, in turn, colors everything in it.

The change in the *Nun* is effected by the precession of the equinoxes. Such change represents a true metamorphosis. It is a seemingly magical transformation marked by radical change in character, condition and function. The change is so radical as to be akin to the metamorphosis of a caterpillar to a butterfly or a tadpole to a frog.

Each Great *NeTeR*, itself the purest of energy, has a vibration peculiar to it alone. This vibration, or moving back and forth rapidly, is characteristic of all energy and all life.

It is, functionally, the heart beat of the *NeTeR* that dictates the speed and rhythm of the age.

Because of the ancient Kemitic connection between the heart and intelligence* the Great *NeTeR* of the Cult also

---

* This was known, in ancient Kemit, as the *Intelligence-Of-The-Heart* and was understood as the inborn intelligence in human beings that was the only source of direct knowledge, unimpaired by the distorting and inherently unreliable

dictates the intellectual orientation of the age that is manifested by and through instinct in animals and intuition in humans. It is by means of this transcendent, direct intelligence and way of knowing that the message of the age (itself an energetic impulse) is received and utilized to modify the direction and orientation of government, spiritual endeavor and personal ambition in harmony with the ambiance of the age.

We stand at a unique moment in the history of humanity. We are at the end of the Age of Pisces and the beginning of the Age of Aquarius. We are also at the end of a cosmic year and the beginning of a new one. This unique confluence of energy will focus such great power in one place, at one time, that the possibilities are staggering to imagine.

It is anticipated that this build up of energy will force a quantum leap to the next level of consciousness, intelligence and spiritual understanding. Greater energy means greater vision.

The quantum leap will represent the advent of peace and tranquility not experienced in the world since the close of the Age of *Amun*. Those who believe that such a prediction implies that humanity has only to wait for the change and

have no responsibility to assist the change are sadly mistaken.

Tranquility and peace imply freedom from disturbance and the absence of hostility. But these admirable conditions would necessarily exist in the absence of the sole source of disturbance and hostility in the world, humanity. The anticipated tranquility and peace of the new age also imply the possibility of the extinction of humankind as the method by which such conditions will prevail.

We need only consider the rate of nuclear proliferation throughout the world to see the real possibility of nuclear

---

reason based exclusively on input from the five senses. It was the sixth sense.

holocaust. The coming age indicates, therefore, that there exists the possibility of occurrence of one of two precipitating events that will usher in the beginning of the age. One anticipates the quantum leap to the next level of universal consciousness that will undermine and dispose of hostility and disturbance. The other will obliterate the cause.

The coming age is widely referred to as the Age of Aquarius. The word Aquarius has two meanings. One refers to a constellation in the equatorial region of the Southern Hemisphere; the other refers to the eleventh house and sign of the Zodiac.

As a constellation whose location is the equatorial region of the Southern Hemisphere it indicates the focal point of the energy of the age and the section of the Earth from which the energy will be dispersed. It also reveals that the emphasis of the age will be on that area of the world. Put another way, the energetic movement of the age will be from north to south.

As the eleventh house or sign of the Zodiac it refers to Aquarius as the Great *NeTeR* of the Cult that will color and influence the age to come.

The word Aquarius comes from the Latin *aqua* meaning water, the sign of Aquarius refers, specifically, to a water bearer. No satisfactory explanation has ever been given as to why Aquarius referred to water bearer or why its astrological symbol (≈≈≈) is the same as the Kemitic hieroglyph (≈≈≈) for water. The answer, once again, is to be found in the records of ancient Kemit.

In ancient Kemit, in the Temple of Dendera, there existed a Zodiac carved into the ceiling. On it the sign now called Aquarius was clearly depicted as a *NeTeR* holding two vases from each of which pours a stream of N symbols (the same symbol as the sign of Aquarius) said to represent water. The Kemitic name of the *NeTeR* is *Hapy* it is also the name of the Great *Neter* of the Nile river and the name of the river itself. The name Nile is Greek. This *NeTeR* has been depicted in the same way from prehistoric times.

The *NeTeR Hapy*, was always depicted as carrying two water vessels from which it poured out the water that overflowed

Theodicy

the banks of the river and marked the beginning of the new year. Of course, the overflowing of Hapy; meant abundance, tranquility and peace by virtue of the harvest that was sure to follow.

In all royal processions, from the remotest times, this *NeTeR* proceeded both the king and the priests as the precursor of both political and spiritual authority and authenticity.

The name water bearer can only refer to who was literally the bearer or carrier of the water that caused the inundation and marked the beginning of the year. Moreover, the astrological symbol of Aquarius is actually two Kemitic n's that spell Nun. As previously noted the Nun was the cosmic ocean and relates to so-called water that the water bearer carries to a cosmic connection. It should also be remembered here that astrology was originally the interpretation of cosmic or celestial influences.

The name water bearer, therefore, precisely represents the sign of Aquarius, but only when its Kemitic origin and connection to Hap;· is recognized. It follows that we must turn to ancient Kemit to discover the meaning of the Age of Hap} and to predict the character of the coming age as well as the influence it will exert on human affairs and the course of world events.

THE ATTRIBUTES OF *HAPY*

It has been said that "Egypt is the gift of the Nile". More accurately, "Kemit is the gift of the *Hapy* ". It is for this reason that *Hapy* was regarded by the Kemites as the source of all good fortune, wealth and success. It was out of this life-giving water that the *NeTers* and all created things arose. In this way was identified with all the *NeTeRs* from the remotest times. Because *Hapy* was identified with all the *NeTeRs* as the source of their origin all of their attributes were believed to be first contained in it.

Hapy was also the *neter* who could not be sculpted in stone, to whom service could not be rendered, and whose place of residence was unknown. Having all the powers of the *neters* and pre-existing them having all the powers of the *Neter Neteru* or God of Gods.

European Egyptologists proclaim that *Hapy* is a man with breasts that represent fertility. Although it is true that *Hapy* is invariably depicted with upper torso naked and ample, pendulous breasts, the conclusion that it is a man is not so easily reached.

If a person were to view a human being naked from the waist up and the person viewed had breasts, would the viewer conclude that a male or a female had been seen? The answer seems too obvious to state.

n all fairness it is true that *Hapy* is always depicted with a beard, clearly indicative of a male. The beard is the false beard of Kemitic royalty. In this regard we may recall Pharaoh/Queen Hatshepsut who was indisputably a female but who was also depicted wearing a false beard. While a false beard does not necessarily indicate a man, pendulous breasts are uniquely descriptive of the female. The logical conclusion is that is a female rather than a male. In our attempt to reconcile this apparent contradiction regarding the gender of *Hapy* we must consider the possibility that it has the characteristics of both genders.

Theodicy

First we must consider that is not a human being. It is a symbolic representation of a spiritual concept. It is an energetic impulse, It is a force, a power. It is also the source of all power and energy, and as such is, of necessity, both positively and negatively charged. What better way to symbolize such a notion than as a *NeTeR* with attributes of both male and female.

Second, we must consider the possibility that *Hapy* represents an hermaphroditic *NeTeR*, that would give the coming age the characteristics of both male and female simultaneously.

Interestingly, the term hermaphrodite comes from the Greek story in which Hermaphroditus, son of Hermes and Aphrodite became united with the Nymph Salmacis as one being. The story goes that Hermaphroditus, the beautiful son of Hermes and Aphrodite, spurned the affections of a nymph named Salmacis who prayed that they would become one for all eternity. One day the unsuspecting Hermaphroditus swam in Salmacis' spring and the two became one being with characteristics of both male and female.

Hermes was the Greek version of Tehuti, the Kemitic *NeTeR* of divine intelligence. Aphrodite, his lover, is believed to be the Greek version of a Kemitic *NeTeR* of fertility who was associated with new growth after the flooding of *Hapy*. Once again our intellectual pursuit leads us back to ancient Kemit in order to elucidate an obscure concept. Apparently, all roads lead to Kemit.

An hermaphrodite is the offspring of divine intelligence and beauty. Interestingly, the conjoining of the two takes place in water. No better symbol of the Age of *Hapy* could be devised. It should also be noted at this point the use of the term hermaphrodite in the science of botany. When flowers, themselves universal symbols of beauty, are hermaphroditic they are termed perfect flowers.

These considerations compel the likelihood that *Hapy* is a hermaphroditic *NeTeR* and its influence as Great *NeTeR* of the Cult will be that of peace and tranquility by virtue of the cessation of hostilities between male and female now referred to as the "Battle of the Sexes".

We may also take note of the fact that in the Age of Amun/Aries the influence of Great *NeTeR* of the Cult was matrilineal while during the Age of Pisces under the influence of Christianity it was patrilineal. Under the matrilineal age peace prevailed. Under the patrilineal the hallmark of the age has been war and environmental pollution. What better way to return to peace and tranquility than to join the matrilineal and patrilineal as one in the water of *Hapy*.

The Age of *Hapy* will be influenced by the joining of both masculine and feminine energies, influences and NaTuRes. This amalgamation will necessarily require a wider social acceptance of groups who are now ostracized because of sexual preferences that represent what are now termed "alternative lifestyles".

In the Age of *Hapy* society will begin to understand that the sexual drive is a force that manifests itself through attraction. But, and here is the key, the attraction is a direct result of the spirit or sacred essence of the person.

The sacred essence is both male/initiative and female/receptive, with one or the other in a dominant position. In some cases they are evenly balanced and neither dominates. It is also possible for a male dominant spirit to be imprisoned in a female body or a female dominant spirit to be captured in a male body.

This seeming misalignment of spirit with body is only apparently so. Spirit is attracted to spirit regardless of the body in which the spirit finds itself resident. This is spiritual affinity and is related to spiritual partnership, that is, the repeated reappearance of spirits, in tandem for the purpose of fulfilling karmic responsibilities assumed together in former lives. Since the spirit does not reproduce or procreate it is not involved with sexual or material attraction.

Theodicy

The Age of *Hapy* will permit spirits to find each other and fulfill their destinies without societal condemnation or interference. Admittedly, not all such relationships are spiritually motivated. These are explained by the concept of bio-sexuality that will also manifest itself in the coming age.

52

Theodicy

BIO-SEXUALITY

Bio-sexuality is sexual attraction that is biological rather than gender driven. It is also intimately linked to the concept of beauty, that we have seen is a characteristic of the age.

Sexual attraction in humans is essentially visual and is stimulated by the appearance of the human form. It is the human form, itself obviously material, that motivates the act of mechanical reproduction. It is the appearance of the body, its physical form and contours that attracts.

If sex is understood as copulation, the attraction is not sex, even though sex is the end result, it is beauty that is attractive. A beautiful form is a joy to behold. Of course, beauty is in the eye of the beholder. But once the standard of beauty is reached attraction follows.

A rose is beautiful to both men and women without regard to its gender. The determining factor, upon which both men and woman agree, is its inherent beauty. A beautiful woman is beautiful to both men and women. A beautiful man is certainly beautiful to women, but he is also beautiful to men --whether they admit it or not.

Beauty is a pleasing quality associated with harmony of form or divine proportion and is that which stirs a heightened response of the senses and of the mind at the highest level. Bio-sexuality is the recognition of that fact.

The Age of *Hapy* will witness an increased understanding and acceptance of the concept of bio-sexuality. This will not interfere in any way with the reproductive process upon which the survival of the race is dependent. The birth rate will not decline though it may level off. Because of the sexual influence of the age the cure for Acquired Immune Deficiency Syndrome (AIDS) will be discovered.

The Age of *Hapy* is also the period of time during which he life-giving cosmic water which has been severely polluted during the Age of Pisces will be refreshed and rejuvenated. In order for the age to be one of peace there must be a corresponding power to insure it.

The power of the age will derive from our ability to summon the *NeTeRs*. In the Age of *Hapy* they will manifest all around us as the life-giving waters begin to flow abundantly. The Age of *Hapy* will also be an age of unimaginable prosperity because the cosmic influence of *Hapy* will he analogous to the period of overflowing of the great river *Hapy* when new life, renewal and abundance begin. It will be a time o f celebration of the new and bountiful age.

It may also be observed that because of the progressive decimation of the ranks of African American males of reproductive age as a result of mass incarceration and planned prevention of births, polygamy and/or polyandry will become necessary during the coming age.

Polygamy is here understood as the sharing of seed necessary to increase the number of males until relative parity is reached with females in the African American population. In like manner, a reversal in the numbers to a disproportionate level wherein males outnumber females would require polyandry or the sharing of eggs for the purpose of reproduction.

It should also be noted that the concept of polygamy is a time honored and well respected tradition in parts of present day Africa. In certain parts of non-Islamic Africa, polygamy is practiced and interestingly it is instigated by the female and cannot, in any event, exist without her approval. It is not considered adultery, is not perverted or in any way frowned upon. It is the decision of the woman to share her husband and her household with another woman. Not surprisingly, the man can reject the offer because he does not feel himself capable of carrying on an intimate relationship with more than one woman.

The point is that to the African mind there are many reasons why polygamy is acceptable and desirable. It is never taboo.

The above are basic observations about the Age of *Hapy*. We have previously mentioned, however, that the cosmic age is characterized by certain occurrences based on the celestial

Theodicy

influences unique to the particular cosmic month. The Age of *Hapy* is no exception.

Each cosmic age is influenced by its ruling planets and its complement. A ruling planet is one that is believed to exercise the greatest influence over a particular house or sign of the Zodiac. A complement, in the zodiacal sense, is the opposite house or sign to the one that is ascendant and that balances, rounds out and completes the influence of the whole. The cosmic milieu of each age is comprised, therefore, of the dominant house and its complement.

Hapy's ruling planets are Saturn and Uranus. Its complement is Leo. Let us look briefly at the anticipated affect of these on the coming age.

SATURN

The influence of Saturn is said to be characterized by sobriety, prudence, good sense, dependability and patience. It is recognized as being connected to both time and agriculture. Saturn is best understood, however, as the ruler of change and the governor of organization. Saturn also governs the will.

As the ruler of change Saturn evokes the sudden and violent change that brings things into existence abruptly as a result of activities and associations that are apparently unrelated. It oversees change and the new realities that invariably result from change.

As the governor of organization Saturn is said to rule every organization from the lowest organism to the governments of nations and multinational corporations.

From these facts it may be concluded that the influence of Saturn as joint ruler of the Age of *Hapy* will be felt as a sudden, perhaps violent change that will result in the organization of new associations and new governments.

Uranus

Uranus is the planet that is believed to govern originality, independence and that which is beyond human understanding. It governs insight, particularly regarding the laws of NaTuRe. This insight is understood as occurring in periodic flashes that are seen as revelation or inspiration on matters relevant to the useful arts. Its relationship to electricity and energy have been frequently noted as has its influence on inventors and thereby inventions.

Uranus is also the planet of revolutionaries. When the flashes of insight occur, like lightning, they can undermine or destroy that which has been constructed and seems stable. In this sense, Uranus governs removal of the old for the specific purpose of enabling the new to manifest. Like revolutionaries it influences resistance to the status quo and seeks to subvert and undermine its previously unchallenged authority.

Uranus is also a higher octave planet that effects regeneration by shifting to a higher level of consciousness thereby causing the equivalent of a quantum leap.

According to Greek mythology, Uranus was the husband of Earth who was overthrown by his son Saturn. Therefore, Uranus and Saturn as co-rulers of *Hapy* indicate that the age will be one of initial and mortal combat of men or ideas, that will result in the destruction of the old and reconstruction of a new era of government based on a higher level of consciousness and transcendent will guided by the intuition that is the *Intelligence-Of-The-Heart*.

THE COMPLEMENT OF HAPY

Each cosmic age has its complement. A complement is that which completes or brings something to perfection. The complement of the cosmic age is its opposite house or sign and that which influences, balances, rounds out and completes the cosmic milieu that is the dominant age. The age is, therefore, colored and influenced by its complement.

In the famous zodiac of Dendera the complement of *Hapy* is depicted as a reclining lion. The complement of Aquarius is Leo, the lion. The lion has, since ancient times, represented courage, strength, majesty, royalty and above all leadership.

Theodicy

It is for these reasons that the lion is frequently referred to as the "King of the Beasts".

In ancient Kemit the lion was called *maa*, a word that has the cognate meaning of to see, or vision. The lion is the one who provides leadership. Leadership is, in turn, closely related to vision. Vision is only effective if it is clear. The Age of *Hapy* will be one of tranquility, beauty, peace and prosperity by virtue of the superior leadership and *Oudja (clarity of vision)*.

It seems evident that the Age of *Hapy* will witness a resuscitation of the ancient Kemitic culture that gave civilization to the people of *Hapy* Valley through the profound knowledge of Sacred Science and strict adherence to the necessities of the cosmic age in which they lived. By doing so they focused the radiant energy that breathed life and prosperity into individuals and the nation of Kemit alike.

When all of these varied but interrelated aspects of the corning age are considered the certain key indicators become apparent. Clearly, the Age of *Hapy* will be marked by the following:

(1) a profound cultural, political, religious shift; (2) the shift will be marked by a quantum leap to a higher level of consciousness that will release the energy necessary to foment and ferment radical and immediate revolutionary change;

(3) that the cosmic milieu of the age will be characterized by beauty, visionary leadership, cessation of hostilities between men and woman and emphasis upon child nurturing and protection;

(4) there will be a re-orientation and re-focusing of the energy of the milieu from Eurocentric to Afro-centric thinking that more closely mirrors the fundamental characteristics of the age;

(5) because the focal point of this energetic reorientation is to be the equatorial region of the Southern Hemisphere it presupposes a world enlightenment through the African dialectical approach; or

(6) there will be a total destruction of humanity, in which case, peace and tranquility will prevail by virtue of the absence of the human factor.

In short, the Age of *Hapy* will mark the resuscitation of ancient African culture as the dominant world-view. Because the African perspective has remained essentially dormant for the duration of the Piscean Age and the cultural shift will, of necessity, include a return to our *Authentic Ancestral Culture*.

The quantum leap that will mark the Age of *Hapy* is, in effect, both a shift in culture and the cyclical rebirth of dormant culture.

Theodicy

SECTION TWO:

CULTURE

CHAPTER FIVE:

THE IMPORTANCE OF CULTURE

Culture is a ubiquitous phenomenon. Its impact and influence are, in a word, pervasive. Few areas of life are untouched by culture, directly or indirectly. Its ramifications are often so subtle that the connection between it and virtually every aspect of our lives and fortunes is frequently overlooked. Culture forms an all-embracing web that is sometime so finely spun as to be all but invisible. Like the web of the spider its strength is indeed remarkable. Because of this, the importance of culture is widely neglected or woefully misunderstood. This fatal misapprehension carries with it the unmistakable portent of the lingering, debilitating bondage of mind and body of those who fail to perceive its importance. For on the road to civilization and national identity, culture is everything.

Culture is, first and foremost, the technology of group survival. It is a developed and evolved technology that consists of all the tools used by the group., including everything from farm implements like the digging stick and plow, to implements of war like the shield, *assagai* and the drum. This technology of group survival also consists of intangible tools such as words, values and ideas. As such it comprise actions, thoughts, emotions and all communication skills deemed appropriate by the group and which serve to distinguish the group and their behavior from that of others.

Culture is also the system by which a society provides its members with the things they need to survive and as such implicates political considerations arising from the evolution of government which is a necessary development in the transition of society into civilization.

Culture is the vehicle by which a people are enabled to keep in constant contact with their ancient ancestors and drink from the cup of their collected wisdom. It is culture that permits them to see the world through the seasoned eyes of their ancestors while tapping the unlimited power of those who have gone before.

Theodicy

Culture is that which answers the core set of fundamental questions whose answers determine the survival and prosperity of the group. The questions are universal. It is the answers that distinguish one people and their culture from another.

Culture begins as a loosely defined set of group behaviors that represent the folkways of the ancients that provide resistl:JJJ:1.ce to sudden change and a sense of order. It is these folkways that sustain a people through the generational vicissitudes of life in an increasingly hostile world. It provides the same type of stability to a group of people that instinct provides to the lower animals.

Culture develops through a variant of natural selection whereby methods that have proven to be effective in dealing with the problems of life and survival are informally codified by the group and earmarked as necessary components of survival.

Culture is, therefore, a system and a technology of survival comprised of the dominant ideas, knowledge and sentiments that permit solitary individuals to survive and thrive as a group. These group ideas consist in notions about everything from agriculture to weaponry, to the roles of men, women and children. They determine what shall be the diet staple and who, if anyone, shall lead and who shall marry whom. These rules based on collective experience, are specific to the group and exist across the spectrum of race and geographic location.

When in the course of time this set of ancient, shared prescriptions become linked to the wisdom of those who went before they become ancestral. The imprimatur of ancestry is perhaps the single most important aspect of culture. This is because of the comparative importance of ancestors to the functioning of societies. Authenticity and legitimacy are inextricably linked to the ancestors. All societies venerate ancestors. From the Founding Fathers of America to Jesus, Abraham and Muhammad, all are ancestors.

In a state of NaTuRe, long before the acknowledgement of the existence of gods, we knew only our parents whose formidable and apparently unlimited power and intelligence gave us our first glimpses of the supernatural.

Our parents, and by extension those who were responsible for our care and nurturing, were our first gods. It was, after all, they who towering over us seemed to know our every thought and desire, who answered our entreaties and protected us from the hostile forces that surrounded us. They provided food, clothing and shelter. It could only be they to whom we invariable turned in times o danger and need.

Then one day, suddenly and· inexplicably they, first one, then the other, fell to the ground lifeless, never to rise again. The ancient and now familiar despair and sense of hopelessness, though not recorded, remains universal and is experienced by the entire human family.

Almost immediately, these "primitives" were confronted with the simple imperative that life, even after the death of those on whose shoulders our very survival seemed to rest, must go on. Now bereft of the wisdom and guidance of our erstwhile gods, the realization was forced upon us that we had received a body of knowledge from our deceased parents by their word and example, that could be relied upon and utilized to guide them into an uncertain future.

We can speculate that shortly thereafter someone, perhaps everyone of a certain age, experienced a dream in which the deceased parent appeared alive and well, talking and instructing. The deceased parent had not actually left, but was accessible in another lace. The place was of location, but the lines of communication were still intact.

Parents, like all other human beings, are given to fits of anger and occasional irrationality as well as acts of kindness and love. It became apparent from this fact that it was advisable to court the benevolence of the deceased parents and to appease their wrath. To that end offerings were provided and rituals established to insure that the proper words and

Theodicy

gestures were used in providing service to the ancestors. The purpose of the service was not only to memorialize them but also to insure their intervention on behalf of their children when necessary to guarantee the survival of the group. This was, apparently the origin of so-called ancestor worship.* These same circumstances are likely to have given rise to the concepts of an afterlife, that is, an existence that transcended apparent physical death. And a physical place where such a life was lived, that is a place outside of time.

The body of knowledge, that corpus of specialized information, compiled by the ancestors, in all its varied aspects and nuances, is culture. Each accumulated body of knowledge was, and must ever remain, unique to the people and their descendants for whom it was accumulated, codified and preserved.

In time it would have become apparent that such an important and vital body of knowledge must be preserved for future generations if the people were to survive. The preservation of the information that is culture may also have been enjoined on the people through a dream.

In time it would have also been recognized that given the importance of the information to the survival of succeeding generations and the fact that it was the legacy of those who had gone before, and who had now acquired a special status that required offerings and ritual service, that it was the culture and the memory of the creators of information and the ancestors of the people that had to be sanctified.

This process of sanctification, perhaps better defined as the deification of culture, resulted in the establishment of what is now called religion. It is composed of the ancient beliefs,

---

*Ancestor worship is a misleading term because the word "worship" is of relatively recent origin, perhaps Old or Middle English. For Africans, the word translated "worship" is more accurately stated as "service".

mythology and ritual practices. Culture and religion, therefore, emerge from the same operative conditions and circumstances, congenitally joined, like Siamese twins.

Culture is, therefore, a stabilizing and cohesive force that binds together the people for whom it developed and by whom it is consistently applied.

Culture represents the true ancestral gift to posterity. It is the blessing of continuous identity, of genetic longevity and a return to ancient wisdom. Such wisdom is the fount of renewal and regeneration from which all people must drink to revivify their national character and soul.

From time immemorial it has been the return to cultural foundations that has marked the ability of groups to survive and prosper. Culture has, in this respect, functioned as a weapon against oppression and subjugation. It has proven to be both shield and sword, defensive and offensive simultaneously.

Culture is also a time capsule in which the future of a people is locked. A time capsule that contains a dormant energy of the past. It contains immense power that may used creatively or destructively.

Culture also creates national identity. Self-determination is impossible without it. People become a nation as a result of the existence of an underlying culture that has given them identity and cohesion.

The importance of culture must not be underestimated and it cannot be overemphasized. Its importance lies in its ancestral peculiarity and verifiable authenticity. For culture to uplift and transform it must be the Authentic Ancestral Culture of the people involved. It is that culture, and that culture alone, that raises culture from theoretical to practical value.

As we have seen, the coming Age of *Hapy* will bring about a culture shift that is the quantum leap in consciousness whose characteristics we must be fully apprised of in order to be the beneficiaries of its unlimited power.

Theodicy

THE CHARACTERISTICS OF CULTURE SHOCK

The sages of ancient Kemit predicted that a time would come when the *NeTeRs* would abandon the great and ancient Land of the Blacks.* They foretold that the land that was once the home of religion would be widowed of its *NeTeRs* and left destitute. They predicted the enactment of laws to forbid the people from adhering to the cult of their ancestors and enjoining them to serve the gods of other and foreign people. The fulfillment of that prophecy occurred about the time of the precessional movement of the Wheel of Time from the House of *Amun* (Aries) to the House of *Mehit* (Pisces).

We have seen that the apparent movement of the Sun from one house of the Zodiac to the next is marked by cultural, political and religious upheaval. The last precessional shift is estimated to have occurred between 50 B.C. and 139 A.D. Notably, that period was marked by the decline of ancient Kemit and the ascendency of the Cult of the Fish, also known as Christianity.

These contemporaneous occurrences represent the political and religious upheaval characteristic of a precessional shift. The nature of the shift was profoundly cultural and therefore represents a culture shift as well.

A culture shift is characterized by a change in the patterns of behavior of an entire group of people. More specifically, a culture shift is a dramatic change in the cultural beliefs of a people, *en masse*, at or near a precessional change of the equinoxes, resulting in the replacement of one core set of beliefs with another. The shift can be either assimilative or integrational.

Cultural assimilation occurs when one culture is substituted for another under circumstances where one culture replaces the other building or reconstructing a new culture upon the

---

*The name Kemit means the land of the blacks.

planned and completed destruction of the other. In this case the conquering cultural group will usually maintain and enforce some of the older cultural norms to insure some similarity and continuity. The conquering group will not, however, fully integrate or accept as equals the members of the conquered cultural group. The fact that the conquered group has given up its own culture and adopted that of the conqueror is unimportant. The conquered group will remain outcasts and pariah in the new cultural setting.

Cultural integration, on the other hand, involves the acceptance of and adherence to, the superior elements of the culture of the conquered group as an integral part of the new culture. Theoretically, this alternative implies a level of comparative equality between the two cultures that is recognized by the conquering group.

culture of the conquered group as an integral part of the new culture. Theoretically, this alternative implies a level of comparative equality between the two cultures that is recognized by the conquering group.

The culture shift marked by the precessional change from Aries to Pisces represented a classic example of cultural assimilation. The so-called Christie Revelation was literally built on the planned and completed destruction of the cultural and religious belief system of ancient Kemit. May of the beliefs fundamental to that ancient culture were simply appropriated and reintroduced to the unsuspecting under different names. These stolen fundamentals became the basis of the new cultural/religious system of the Western world. Of course, the ancient culture of Kemit was not credited for its contributions and was not recognized as equal to the new dominant culture.

The importance of the noted culture shift to our analysis is that it marked the shift from African cultural values and beliefs to European ones and also marked the political and economic decline of our ancient and displaced culture .

Predictably, a culture shift represents the change from one world-view to another. The world-view of a people is based,

Theodicy

to a great extent, on their physical environment. Environmental differences may be slight or dramatic. The most dramatic differences are between temperate and equatorial climates.

In the case of the temperate or northern climate the environment is, in word, hostile. In order to survive people must become vicious and competitive. Scarcity is a fact of life. Scarce resources dictated competitiveness in order to survive. The concept of the "survival of the fi.ttest" is closely allied to competitiveness. It is the stronger, most cunning and aggressive who survives. The necessities of a hostile environment engender a world-view that tends to see the solutions to life's problems in terms of aggression, hostility and the violent use of force.

By contrast, in equatorial or southern climates resources tend to be comparatively speaking, abundant. A people who find themselves bathed in perpetual warm weather, surrounded by abundant food and fresh water supplies are more apt to think of shared interests. The world-view of such people is profoundly different than that of people in temperate climates, and explains the diametrically opposed views.

On the one hand, the people from equatorial climates tend to view the world as paradise and its inhabitants as partner in what is essentially a cooperative, or share the wealth enterprise. They tend to see God or the Creator as a benevolent force that creates abundantly and moves on, always scrupulously adhering to its own discoverable universal laws.

In a state of NaTuRe, the people of temperate climate would necessarily tend to view the world as a dark, dismal place where only the strong survive and where the man of industry is a fool and the wise man merely takes what he wants. That approach breeds aggressiveness and extols violence as virtue.

Characteristically, God or the Creator will be seen by them as vicious, jealous, unpredictable, inscrutable, vindictive and mean-spirited.

When a culture shift occurs it amounts to the replacement of one cultural world-view for another. The most dramatic change takes place, of course, when the views are diametrically opposed. If the controlling world-view is one of competition and diminished spiritual involvement in the affairs of humanity, a capitalist society is the result. If the controlling world-view is one of spiritually guided cooperation the world-view tends toward a shared, social welfare society.

The last precessional shift from Aries to Pisces represented a shift from an African world-view to that of the European. But Theodicy teaches that the Wheel of Time is constantly turning, elevating and casting down, one after another, in regular predictable succession.

We are on the brink of a culture shift that will change the course of human history by changing the predominant world-view from the European emphasis on reason and competitiveness to the African view of based on a world community of shared interests marked by enlightened spirituality and respect for Mother Earth.

The Precession of the Equinoxes is invariably marked by cultural, religious and political upheaval. Politics and religion are both driven by culture. The precession from Pisces to *Hapy* (Aquarius) predicts, therefore, a culture shift that will carry political and religious upheaval in its wake. Both theological teaching and the direction and orientation of government will be modified to reflect the change. The old temples will be dismantled and new ones will be erected on the same sacred ground where temples have stood since the world began. The Ritual of the Divine Cult will remain but it will be performed in the name of the "Hidden One" whose attributes are reflective of the current cosmic color, vibration and note. A culture shift requires, therefore, a re-orientation of the emphasis of the culture. In extreme cases, it involves the return to a culture that has remained dormant or even one that has been declared "dead" by those whose interests are best served by its demise.

A BRIEF DIGRESSION ON CULTURE SHOCK

A shift in culture necessarily implies the replacement and displacement of a prior set of beliefs. Such a drastic change will entail, for some, confusion, surprise and perhaps deep-seated alienation. For many the new cultural norms will be as shocking and traumatic as that from being suddenly immersed in icy cold water.

The possibility of trauma should not, however, cause disillusionment or operate as a deterrent. In fact, the culture shock among African Americans will be minor when it is understood that the "new culture" is the explanation of what is now recognized as the persistent "Black or African perspective". The way we look at the world, even under the domineering, propagandizing, centuries-old influence of the European culture, is still fundamentally different and in most cases diametrically opposed to the way the European sees the world. Our view of the world is uniquely characteristic of the core African belief system handed down by our African forebears who came to these shores shackled and with nothing to protect them but their culture. That African belief system, hidden under a thin veneer of Christianity or other European value system, is the cause, justification and mainstay of the "Black or African perspective".

When we are forced to recognize and acknowledge the underlying premises and deep-rooted connections of our present belief system with that of our Authentic Ancestral Culture, the uniformity and continuity of purpose revealed will significantly limit the otherwise traumatic cultural shock that might be otherwise anticipated. The minor discomfort that might be caused will be outweighed by the benefit of the establishment of the cultural base from which we will launch our long-awaited *cultural rebirth*.

CULTURAL REBIRTH

The Precession of the Equinoxes indicates an imminent change in the cosmic milieu. The change will be marked by a radical, sudden transformation of culture, religion and politics.

Politics and religion are both behavior patterns that are constructed and governed by culture. Change, therefore, is dependent on the participation of human beings whose thoughts and activities will facilitate the transformation predicted by Theodicy. At the epicenter of the anticipated change is the re-orientation of the collective mind and will of Africans in general and African Americans in particular.

The preceding age, that of Pisces, has exacted a great toll on the consciousness of humanity and the Earth's physical environment. The Age of Pisces has made its dubious contribution to the world. Though its technological advances have been attractive, each has brought greater and seemingly intractable problems in its wake. It has interfered with the balance of NaTuRe and polluted Earth and atmosphere. It has poisoned the planet which recommending travel to other planets where it can continue its worship of the god of individualistic materialism. The introduction of the means by which all humanity may be destroyed by the press of a button is tis creation and legacy. Destruction of the rain forests and the introduction of lethal pollutants into the food chain is its trademark.

The fish is the symbol of the Piscean Age. The fish is also the sign of Jesus and Christianity, the dominant religion of the age. The symbol is actually two fishes swimming in opposite directions, one to the east, one to the west.

The fish is a most appropriate symbol of the age. It fouls its environment and eats its young.* Interestingly, the shark, the only true killing machine on the planet, is a fish. As we

---

* Ancient Kemitic priests were forbidden to eat fish for precisely those reasons.

Theodicy

witness the close of the Age of Pisces it is obvious that its symbol was selected with precision.

Theodicy predicts that the new age, the Age of *Hapy,* will rejuvenate and replenish the waters polluted by the Pisceans. The accomplishment of this seemingly impossible task is predicted on a cultural rebirth a fundamental, radical, sudden, perhaps revolutionary change in the thought and behavior of those who decide the fate of the planet. Whether the change in thinking is self-imposed or encouraged by external forces to strong to be ignored, remains to be seen.

The cultural rebirth will require two things: First, a general change in the consciousness of the people of the world who, as a result, will see further, expect and demand more from their leaders and themselves. Second, it will require the transference of the torch of world leadership from a European to an African world-view. The second requirement is directly related to Theodicy, the Divine Journey, the Wheel of Time and the plight. of Africans generally and African Americans particularly.

We have seen that the Age of *Hapy* will be one of peace and tranquility. But, the way those admirable states are obtained may not necessarily be peaceful or tranquil. It is the end result that characterizes the age, not the means.

Subsumed in this notion of an age of peace and tranquility are two further implications that we overlook at great peril to ourselves and our future. The first is that since the problem of the "internal enemy"* is one of paramount importance to the White supremacists who control the present political establishment, a tranquil world can best exist if that enemy is eliminated completely.

The second implication is that if those who create atomic bombs, chemical and biological weapons of mass destruction are permitted to continue on their self-destructive course, they will obliterate all humanity, in which case, peace and tranquility will, after a time, reign.

Historically, the only people who have been able to keep the world on a even keel have been those who have exercised a right brain approach to problem-solving. These are primarily African people. The hope of humanity then lies with the rise of Africa, birthplace of humanity and civilization, as spiritual and political leader of the world in the Age of *Hapy*.

The most likely place for this cultural rebirth to begin is not Africa, however. It is the United States of America, and among Americans of African descent. A brief elaboration is necessary in order to understand the importance of this fact.

African needs assistance. It is at once the richest continent on the planet and the least developed. Africa has few friends in the world. Unlike other nations she has no effective American lobby. More than 30 millions of her people are citizens of the richest, most technologically advanced nation in the world. Yet, they exert virtually no influence over American policy toward Africa. They are never consulted and actions adverse to African interests are not even considered as within the purview of African American interest, concern or expertise.

Politicians in the United States consider it political suicide to take, or even propose, any action that would affect the interest of the State of Israel without first consulting with the representatives of the American Jewish community. It should not be surprising that Israel receives, by far, the largest American foreign aid package of any country in the world.

African Americans, unlike Jewish Americans, are considered weak, political unsophisticated, disorganized and, therefore, powerless. Based on the number of African Americans alone Africa should have considerable influence in the halls of Congress and the in the White House. It follows that Africa cannot rise to a position of prominence in world affairs, one that accurately reflects her glorious history and her natural resources, unless and until, she has powerful allies in countries that exert international power and influence. But,

Theodicy

*See Chapter XII

this cannot begin to happen until African Americans control enough power to make it happen.

The rise of a powerful African American community whose will it is to force the United States government to provide assistance to Africa on a proportional scale to that provided to Israel will be the friend that Africa so desperately needs.*

The fate of the world is linked to Africa, whose fate is, in turn, linked to the African American communities of the United States where the interconnection between culture, religion, political power and self-determination must first be understood and then mastered.

We are compelled by the necessity of our current circumstances and the vitality of our glorious past to gather, with speed of urgency, the remnants of our Authentic Ancestral Culture wherever they may be found, and to forge from them the living organism that will activate the power of our collective will and manifest the imminent and unerring operation of Theodicy.

CULTURE AND RELIGION

We have seen that culture and religion emerge from the same operative conditions and circumstances and that they are congenitally joined. In short, culture and religion are flip sides of the same coin. Culture consists of the corpus of knowledge of the technology of survival compiled by our

---

*It should be remembered here that Africa is due reparations, as are African Americans, for the kidnap and enslavement of 100 million of her citizens. This massive, forced, illegal displacement of human beings, unprecedented in history, represents the single greatest unprosecuted, uncompensated crime against humanity. During the time of the barbarous, European enterprise not only were those kidnapped deprived of the value of their labor --Africa was deprived of her greatest resource, her people. While we

labored building the wealth that is America the resources of Africa were left undeveloped for want of labor.

ancient ancestors. Religion is the deification of that knowledge. Religion is a way of preserving the technology of survival for use by the future generations for whom it was gathered. Religion then is part and parcel of the most valuable bargaining chip in the game of power. We may call it the coin of culture. Although it is true that culture is the most valuable side of the coin of culture it is also true that there is no such thing as a one-sided coin.

Culture, as distinct from religion, was practiced in ancient Kemit as they way of life of the people, all the time. Religion, on the other hand, had a far more limited application in that it was practiced *on behalf of the people* by a comparatively small number of specially selected and trained persons. These persons, both female and male, were known as the "Servants of the *NeTeR*" and were given to duty and honor of performing the Ritual of the Divine Cult.

The servants were taught the ancient ritual practices for two reasons: First, the ancient ritual practices were enjoined on them by their ancestors and had been performed in the identical fashion since the "First Day of the World". Second, it was believed that the Ritual, based on precisely intoned incantations, using specially selected and prepared incense and sacred oils, and accompanied by perfect gestures, fashioned in accord with the universal laws of Sacred Science, was effective in maintaining *Maat*, the balance, order and regularity of NaTuRe without which disorder and chaos would reign. The performance of the Ritual of the Divine Cult was, therefore, the method by which the harmony of the universe and the prosperity of the people of Kemit was maintained.

The Service of the Great *Neter* of the Cult, which included service of the National Ancestors *(Asar* and *Aset)* was a matter of national rather than individual concern. The daily performance of the ritual, nominally by the king alone assured that the collective obligation to the *Neters* and the National Ancestors was carried out in regular and ancient

Theodicy

fashion, without the necessity for the people individually, to do anything.

The practice of religion was, therefore, national in scope and of little concern to the people generally, beyond the assurance that the Ritual of the Divine was being performed on their behalf. The proof of the proper maintenance of the ritual was, for the people, the existence of order and prosperity.

Popular, personal religious observances did exist, but these were the practices of individuals in the privacy of their homes. Service to one's lineal ancestors was an important matter to individuals and their families. As a result virtually all private dwellings were equipped with a shrine dedicated to the ancestor as well as the *Neter* of the particular tribe or clan to which the family belonged. The rituals performed in service of the ancestor or *Neter* or both was a time honored tradition that had been passed down from generation to generation in an unbroken cultural chain.

Culture and religion are interdependent. The relation is in many ways, symbiotic --each flourishing with the other. It follows that when culture is abandoned or destroyed the demise of its religion soon follows. Conversely, a people cannot long practice the religion of their ancestors in the absence of their ancestral culture. This is one of the reasons that conquerors have, with few exceptions, deemed the destruction of the culture of the conquered people to be an essential component of lasting domination and control. This military objection has always been accomplished by wholesale destruction of libraries, temples and other places of religious expression; murder or exile of teachers, priests, shaman, medicine men and griots; and the abolition of native songs, dances, languages, drums and ancient customs in general.

There is another way to look at the connection between culture and religion. Culture is like soil. In fact, the word culture is said to derive from the Latin *cultura* meaning the act of tilling the soil. Culture, like soil, is indigenous to a particular geographic area that is favorable to the growth of certain species of plants. These plants will thrive in the soil and will be generally less hardy or not grow at all in other soil. In this analogy culture is to be understood as the soil in which the seed of religion is planted and grows.

If the seed is planted in foreign soil it may suffer stunted growth, not bear fruit or not germinate at all. This analogy, simplistic as it is, provides a mental framework for understanding the profound implication of the connection between culture and religion.

Our people have been plagued by a recurring paradox. We are obviously a people of profound religiosity. We have far more than our share of churches, preachers and that old-time religion. We have prayed till our knees raw and our throats parched. We have made a joyful noise to the Lord that is deafening in its volume and intensity. We have called on Abraham, Isaac and Jacob not to mention Jehovah, Jesus, Muhammad and Allah. We have trekked to Jerusalem and Mecca. Still our earnest entreaties are unheard or unanswered. For all or religion we are still the most maligned and powerless people on the planet. This is not only a paradox, it is a paradox wrapped in an enigma.

As we embark upon the new millennium we must ask ourselves how is it possible for the most religious people to be apparently the least favored by God. In short, why are people who claim to serve a just and omnipotent god, powerless? The answer is not so hard to discern. It is found by analyzing the religion we profess and the fruit it may be logically expected to bear.

The religion we now profess grows strong because it is planted in the appropriate soil (culture). Though the fruit it bears is not what we desire or pray for, it is what can be logically expected. An apple tree does not bring forth bananas and we will wait interminably for the fig tree to bear pecans.

It may be difficult for many of us to accept, but the fact remains that the culture from which our adopted and initially forced religion grows is one of slavery, racism, sexism and

Theodicy

unspeakable violence. The specie of plant that thrives in it is reflective of that cultural soil. Its fruit is, and always will be slavocracy, White supremacy, female subordination and rampant, inexplicable aggression and violence.

The slave master and the slave both believe in and pray to the same God. The slave, as we might expect, prays for his freedom and that of his family. The slave master attends the same church, sings the same hymns and calls on the same God. Only the slave master prays for the continued enslavement, increased material and biological productivity of his slaves. If the slave is not freed we must logically conclude that the slave master's prayer has been answered and preferred over that of the slave. In any event, the slave's prayer has not been answered.

Let us disambiguate. The slave master's prayers are answered precisely because what he requests is that which is the natural and predictable fruit of his religion. The slave on the other hand, asks the fig tree to bear pecans. In short, the religion of the slave master cannot logically be the religion of the slave, especially when the two are of different and diametrically opposed cultures. The analogy applies where the religion of the slave master is Judaism, Christianity or Islam because they each advocate, practice or condone slavery in the name of their God.

On another important level religion, apart from its relationship to culture, is a method of communication with one's ancestors. It is based on the notion that one's lineal ancestors are predisposed to assist you to survive and prosper based on the blood of familial attachment. Therefore, any religion that incorporates the veneration of deceased human being, whether called God, or the Son of God or the last prophet of God, is by that fact alone, ancestral. We are compelled then, to ask whether a Jew or an Arab or Caucasian for that matter can be the ancestor of the African? If the answer is no, and it cannot be otherwise, how can we expect that ancestor to aid us if it is true that ancestors intervene on behalf of their direct descendants?

Simply stated our problem is that our religious fervor and devotion, though undoubtedly sincere, is hopelessly misdirected and confused. The results we seek are virtually unobtainable when we recognize and understand the NaTuRe of religion and its relationship to culture. We must remember that religion only flourishes, only brings forth good fruit, when it is planted in its own cultural soil. But, no matter what cultural soil it is planted in it will only bring forth the fruit of its seed. If you plant an apple seed the only thing you will get come harvest time, under ideal conditions, is an apple tree.

Theodicy

CULTURE AND POLITICS

If culture is ubiquitous it should not be surprising to find that it is also directly related to politics. Let us look at the connection between culture and politics.

This work predicts a return by African Americans to their Authentic Ancestral Culture that will create a cultural chain reaction that will result in the acquisition of political power commensurate with our numbers in the population.

It is a fundamental fact of life that all political activities and all political decisions are based on and informed by cultural considerations. Although it is true that politics can be usefully defined as the science of government, it is equally true that a particular government, the policies it enacts, the laws it promulgates and enforces, are a direct result of the customs, world-view, traditions and heritage, hence, the culture of the dominant political group. In this sense, it is the culture that informs the policies of the government as well as the views and perspectives of those who comprise the particular governing group.

It is now apparent that culture, religion and politics are intimately related. They form a triad of power whose existence has been a closely guarded secret. The existence of the triad has been ingeniously concealed by linking the word culture with the word cult and by popularizing the indefensible and defeatist notion among African Americans that you never discuss religion or politics.

As previously stated the word culture derives from the Latin *cultura*, which in turn derives from the Latin *colere* meaning to till the soil. The word cult comes from *cultus* meaning care or cultivation and was originally the past participle of *colere*.* Although the primary meaning of cult is a system of

---

Colere is also related to the English word wheel, perhaps from the turning of the soil in cultivation. The connection between culture and the Wheel of Time is uncanny.

religious worship or ritual (by which definition all religions are cults) it is the secondary meaning that is typically referred to when the word is used. The secondary meaning is a is a quasi-religious group, often living in a colony, with a charismatic leader who indoctrinates members with unorthodox or extremist views, practices and beliefs. The meaning is both derogatory and condescending. It invariably conjures the memory of Charles Manson, the Reverend Jim Jones and their ilk. It also implies that only orthodox views, practices and beliefs are legitimate. It follows that any group that is not mainstream is immediately branded as a cult which stifles its development before it can be tested in the crucible of ideas.

As to the ridiculous notion that it is somehow unwise to discuss politics or religion, the view is unfounded, defeatist and counterproductive, particularly for African Americans whose existence is lived between the rock of European religion and the hard place of White supremacist politics. It does not take a genius to understand that if the rule of never discussing these life threatening, progress inhibiting subjects is abided we forever remove from intellectual analysis and debate the two factors that most oppress us. By following such rules we also adopt a mind-set that effectively serves the interests of our enemies and obscures, to our pronounced disadvantage, the connection between culture, religion and politics.

Because politics is directly related to culture it is also related to survival and prosperity. Survival is merely the act of staying alive. It implies existing but not moving. Survival is, in a real sense, closely akin to stagnation. That which is stagnant has become foul and malodorous from standing still. The word stagnant literally means a swamp, a place that has become foul precisely because its water has ceased to move, to be active it is the place where the water of life stands still. It is with good reason that our ancestors admonished us never to drink from standing water.

Prosperity is the antithesis of survival. To be prosperous is to thrive, to make progress, to flourish. It is that which indicates advancement. Interestingly, the word derives from the root *orifa* meaning to seize. It follows from the above that an individual or group may survive and not prosper. Survival is not a guarantee of prosperity. The importance of culture is, once again, emphasized.

Culture teaches survival and defines prosperity. It sets and regulates the standard of accomplishment to which the people must collectively aspire and attain in order to thrive and flourish. It is culture that informs us of the difference between survival and prosperity. All things being equal it is politics that makes the difference.

We must not overlook the message implicit in the word seize which we have seen is the root of prosperity. To seize means to take forcible and legal possession of, or to take forcibly and quickly. By this definition at least one of the reasons for our inability to be prosperous in the land of our captivity becomes vividly apparent. We have failed to prosper because we have, among other things, failed to understand that prosperity inheres in the seizure of political power, forcibly and quickly. We have neglected to take forcible and legal possession of that which is our rightful share of the wealth of this nation and the world. One of the reasons that we have failed to do so is because we have not been taught and therefore have not learned the importance and function of *political culture*.

POLITICAL CULTURE

Political culture is the marriage of politics and culture. It is a separate branch of culture that deals exclusively with the acquisition of power. Like all culture it represents the world-view of a particular people, developed over time, and reverently handed down to succeeding generations. It represents the tactics and techniques, acquisition and control of power in sufficient amount to insure the survival and prosperity of a particular group of people. It is the corpus of knowledge, information and concepts of the group regarding the NaTuRe, properties and elements of power.

Political culture is historical and ancestral. In a state of NaTuRe it was confined to clan activities. As populations grew and sedentary existence flourished it was extended to new inter-tribal and national activities that required pre-set rules to insure order and efficiency. For this reason political culture became a form of initiation. The political initiation process would have had at least three characteristics.

First, it requires initiation into a general culture which would have been accomplished at the family level or in age-groups.*

Second, there would have been an initiation into political culture, at least for those who would someday rule, which would amount to an education in the science of politics.

Finally, there would have been the recruitment and training of persons for specific functions in the political system and the deployment of those so trained. In the most effective application of these principles the initiation into political culture would have occurred simultaneously with the initiation into the general culture.

Political culture is important to the understanding of Theodicy and power because there is a vital connection between general and political culture. It is the world-view of the dominant general culture, its values and beliefs, that the political culture strengthens and supports. To this end the education system always functions to maintain the cultural and political status quo.

When a political culture governs people of diverse cultural backgrounds it tends to develop an undercurrent of agitation that remains always just below the deceptively calm surface. This stems from the fact that while most people tend to view politicians cynically, they also believe that the political process works in spite of them. The agitation arises from the

---

* A group of persons of the same sex and approximately the same age who have been initiated together in the duties and responsibilities of tribal membership.

Theodicy

fact that within the society there is always another group whose tendency it is to develop a radical view and who believes that political change can only come as a result of violent upheaval. The agitation is similar to that produced by the tectonic plates of the Earth's crust. The plates rub against each other, below the surface, almost imperceptibly, until they cause an earthquake. The process is slow but the result is inevitable.

The United States of America is a political culture. African Americans are, by and large, descendants of American slaves who have been left stranded by time and technology. We are much like the appendix -- alive but in a state of atrophy because it has outlived its usefulness. We have learned to imitate American's general culture well. We have not mastered its political culture.

African Americans have come to believe, like most White Americans, that the system can be reformed and that the lofty pronouncements upon which it is based actually govern the distribution of power and privilege. This is perhaps understandable of White Americans who have seen their fortunes increase over the years and who have always had the reassurance that the people who were running things were, at least, of their "race".

In the case of African Americans the belief is preposterous despite the large numbers of us who profess to believe it. Logic would seem to dictate that African Americans, perhaps more than any other group of Americans, would be overwhelmingly in the ranks of those who hold the radical view and who believe that political change in America can only result from violent upheaval. This paradox arises from our lack of familiarity with the concepts of Authentic Ancestral Culture and its counterpart which may be called Authentic Political Culture.

Authentic Political Culture is the way of governance, the rules of government and the science of politics as developed by a specific group of people, over time, and handed down to succeeding generations to insure their political survival and prosperity. Having failed to understand the importance of Authentic Ancestral Culture we have likewise misapprehended the importance of Authentic Political Culture. The result is that we have been unable to understand the dynamics of the political culture in which we find ourselves.

The situation of the African American is also distinct from that of White Americans because we are a minority that cannot become part of the national political culture that dictates the rights and privileges under which we are forced to live. Our inability to do so is a direct result of the refusal of the dominant political culture to accept us as equals. We must, therefore, begin to think in terms of not only Authentic Ancestral Culture but also national political culture. It should be noted here that the nationalism and national political culture are not the same.. Nationalism is self-determination. National political Culture is the method by which nationalism is achieved.

A national political culture has two components. It consists in a professional political group. 1.) always relatively small, that promulgates the rules, and a significantly larger group who abides by the rules promulgated. The true distinction in the two groups is that the former is knowledgeable in the science of power while the latter is not. It is this passive arrangement that permits the development of the national political culture. Even when the larger group}i, is literate they tend not to involve themselves in the political process being satisfied with abiding by the rules promulgated by the "professionals".

Another factor is that the larger group is always a mix of persons from different backgrounds and degrees of political sophistication and involvement. The smaller group, on the other hand, is generally comprised of persons more nearly homogeneous in at least one characteristic, wealth. The effect of this is best illustrated by the bicameral system of governance employed in the United States.

In a bicameral system such as that in the United States, a larger body and a smaller body make the laws. But why, it may be logically asked, are two legislatures required? The

Theodicy

answer may be found in the history of the United States Congress.

The United States House of Representatives was referred to by the Framers of the Constitution as the "House of Rabble". The term is one of contempt for the masses or common people who would be represented there. The United States Senate, on the other hand, was to be the "House of the Aristocracy" the landed gentry.

The bicameral or two house system serves one purpose. It insures that the rich (always a minority) will have veto power over the ability of the poor (always a majority) to enact legislation that addresses their needs. Why else would a system be installed that requires that bills be passed in identical form by both houses before they may be forwarded to the president to become law? Of course, the notion that the rich will ever agree to provide meaningful assistance to the poor sufficient to lift them from their poverty is utopian at best and preposterous at worst. Moreover, it is this same mix that determines such fundamental matters as what makes government lawful; what power may leaders and their delegates lawfully exercise; how citizens may or may not organize in opposition to their leaders; and how power is transferred. In each of these categories those who rule (politicians are literally rulers) have a vested interest in insuring that the lawful government is favorable to their present and future interests; that leaders shall have virtually unlimited power that is, in appearance, limited; and that the transfer shall be carefully controlled.

In a political culture where the political initiation process is separate from the general cultural initiation, a class of professionals known as politicians arises. These soon become defenders of a vested interest in their privileged positions and lose sight of their sworn obligation to those who they profess to represent. This further exacerbates the inherent agitation in the political culture. Since they will forever be at odds with their constituents, the longer they hold office the greater the distance between them will become.

Political culture also serves the purpose of defining how and when power may be used within the group and within the community of nations. Because political culture is a body of ideas regarding power, it must include power messages as the core of its language.

Power messages are the words and symbols that instill the belief in one's ability to excel by virtue of the connection to a glorious past and the vision of a prosperous future. They are based on the achievement of our ancestors who fought and succeeded. When these are combined with Authentic Ancestral Culture, power or some healthy concept of it is instilled congenitally.

It follows that in the case of African Americans the most favorable situation would be one in which our Authentic Ancestral Culture and our National Political Culture become melded in the New Body Politic. These fundamental principles must be taught as one and from the inception in a learning environment developed by African Americans and taught by African Americans. By so doing we develop responsible social beings who are also political beings trained and experienced in the technology of survival and the science of power.

In our quest to understand the importance of culture and its connection to Theodicy we have looked at the many ways culture affects virtually every aspect of our lives and fortunes. We must now look at what may be the most important connection, that which cements culture to Theodicy. Let us look at the concept of *self-determination*.

Theodicy

CULTURE AND SELF-DETERMINATION

Self-determination is the will of a living organism to survive by growth and reproduction. In terms of Theodicy self-determination is the will of the people to survive, grow, reproduce and prosper free from the external constraints imposed by any authority they do not respect. Self-determination is, in the political sense, nationalism.

NATIONALISM

Nationalism is, of course, based on the concept of nation. The word nation means *to be born* and claims the original meaning of *people born in the same location*. The term has long since lost that restricted meaning and is now expanded to mean a group of people who have come together on the basis of shared beliefs, common racial or ethnic characteristics, and whose first allegiance is to the group exclusively.

It is important to note that the nation need not currently exist. It is the will to create the nation that marks its birth. By extension then, the coming into existence of a group of people who on the basis of shared beliefs, such as an Authentic Ancestral Culture and common racial characteristics is technically the birth of a nation.

Nationhood, the state or condition of being a nation, is marked by objective and subjective characteristics. Among the objective characteristics are common culture, history, political and economic structure. The subjective characteristics include consciousness, and will. Subsumed in these subjective characteristics are the notions of *national character, interest and security*.

OBJECTIVE CHARACTERISTICS OF NATIONHOOD

For the purposes of our analysis common culture is to be understood as our *Authentic Ancestral Culture*, that stabilizing and cohesive power that is required before a people can truly become a nation.

A common history is the shared memory of the people. It is the foundation of collective consciousness. It is the foundational information upon which the people rely to construct the fabric of their present reality. It is the memory of our ancestors, that is the memories accumulated by our ancestors.

Common political and economic structure is dictated by the place in which the people find themselves at any given time. It is also the anticipated political and economic structure.

Common political and economic structure is dictated by the place in which the people find themselves at any given time. It is also the *anticipated* political and economic structure.

SUBJECTIVE CHARACTERISTICS OF NATIONHOOD

National character refers to the combination of qualities that distinguish one group from another and may include dress, a unique lifestyle and world-view. It is necessarily fashioned by culture.

National interest is simply that which the group concludes is in its best short and/ or long term interest.

National security is the ability of a group to protect itself from danger, whether the source of the danger be internal or external.

People are not born with a sense of nation. It is a product of the system of learning and communication. Once learned it becomes a cement, a cohesive that bonds people to a commonality of purpose and will. So too the concepts of national character, interest and security created, as they must be, by the inculcated sense of nation, help to form the people into a purposeful, determined and goal-oriented group reality consisting of a group field*, and known as a body politic.

The concept of nation or nationalism, also relates to politics and political power because the nation it seeks to create is always a political establishment. It is for this reason that the

---

*A group field is the vital force at the center of the national consciousness created by the power of the collective will.

concept of nationalism has always been viewed as subversive when championed by a separate group within a larger society. Nationalism is seen as revolutionary when its goals include re-distribution of economic wealth, reparations for past injustices and true economic and educational opportunity.

Nationalism naturally embraces not only political self-determination but also cultural self-determination. Herein lies the unbreakable, unalterable link between culture and self-determination. *Cultural self-determination must precede political self-determination* because it is the foundation upon which nationalism is erected. Once again, we see the importance of culture to all the undertakings contemplated by any group that values prosperity more than mere survival.

Nationalism, or collective self-determination then is the collective will of a specific group of people, initially comprised of the CM*, who have committed themselves to the establishment of a specific nation-hood that derives from a specific Authentic Ancestral Culture. Ultimately this nationalism, self-determination and collective will focuses and directs the loyalty, allegiance and commitment of all the body politic, not just the CM, on the task of cultivating and nurturing the seed of self-determination into its only fruit, an independent nation respected and feared among the nations of the world.

Having examined the importance of culture and its connection to religion, politics, prosperity and self-determination we are compelled to seek the Authentic Ancestral Culture that is best suited to provide the foundation of the cultural revolution carried on the Wheel of Time and delivered in the Age of *Hapy*.

---

*Critical Mass. Defined as the minimum number of persons necessary to sustain a cultural/political chain reaction. See Chapter Twelve.

CHAPTER SIX:

AUTHENTIC ANCESTRAL CULTURE

The importance of culture is its stabilizing and cohesive effect its power to mold individual units into a cohesive whole and provide racial, cultural and national identity to people who have lost their sense of kinship.

Culture is specific and peculiar to the group of people by whom it is developed. The effectiveness of a particular culture, that is its power to affect the survival and prosperity objectives of the group, is identified to, and compatible with, the historical will and spirit of the group exclusively.

History teaches that to the extent a people have lost, abandoned or have been forced to depart from their own culture they have, over time, perished completely or ceased to exist as a separate and distinct people within the family of nations. Similarly, those who have adopted the culture of others have, almost without exception, remained outcast, disrespected and suspect minorities among the people whose culture they have sheepishly embraced.

History also reminds us that those people who have jealously guarded their culture and consistently adhered to its prescriptions have maintained their identity, self-determination and political power.

Acts of assimilation or acculturation are, therefore, acts of surrender to the collective will and culture of others the;·, demonstrates a dangerous weakness in the collective will of those who do so. Those who abandon the mandate of their ancestors and abdicate their responsibility to avenge the deaths of their ancestors, represent the weak link in the cultural chain that is our connection, our lifeline to the unlimited power of our ancestral past.

It must be remembered, however, that even the damage done by numerous past acts of surrender and weakness are not irreversible. History is replete with examples of people who have re-discovered, revived and resuscitated their ancestral culture. Each of them have used their quest for group identity, collective self-determination and political power. In fact, the groups who have adhered to their Authentic Ancestral Culture have historically exercised political and economic power disproportionate to their numbers.

These facts raise two pivotal questions the answers to which will direct the search for the Authentic Ancestral culture of the African American. First we must determine who, in fact are our ancestors? Second, what were the components of the culture of our ancestors? Both questions acknowledge an implicit requirement of verifiable authenticity and antiquity.

WHO ARE OUR ANCESTORS?

The question is straightforward enough. Yet, it is complicated by the fact that our people, perhaps unique in the world, have suffered the adverse effects of a centuries long cultural deprivation resulting from the systematic theft and concealment of our cultural energy. The adverse effects and potential obstacles they present are not insurmountable. The task is both imperative and possible of accomplishment. We have been left one clue that has not, and perhaps cannot be obliterated. Let us begin with what we know.

We are African Americans, that is Americans who recognize that their forebears were born on the African continent. Some of us are descendant of American slaves. These facts give us our start because they are the first key to rediscovery of our Authentic Ancestral Culture. Put another way, we agree, virtually unanimously, that we are of African descent. We are, therefore, connected by blood, to the people of the African continent. We are a product of their history, their thought and their collective consciousness. It follows that Africa is, unquestionably, the birthplace of our most ancient ancestors who would have been the possessions of the technology of survival that was intended to be passed down to us and for our benefit. It follows that Africa must be the place where our Authentic Ancestral Culture is to be rediscovered.

The implications of this re-discovery must not be underestimated. Our ancestors, those who went before us, were African and partook of all things African. They would have 'raised us as Africans, steeped in African tradition, had we not been violently and forcibly removed from their nurture and loving care. WE could have spoken an African tongue, seen the world through African eyes, held African philosophical and spiritual beliefs and served an African God.

We are an African people. We are not Asian, although Africans may be found in Asia and have lived there before the Asians. We are not Arabs, although Arabs may have African blood. We are not Hebrews, although the Hebrews may have resided in Kemit for centuries. Weare displaced Africans. We are confused, de-culturized victims of centuries of unrelenting, intense psychological warfare, aimed at obliterating our connection to and identification with our ancestral culture. Not, it must be emphasized, for the purpose of easier assimilation into the dominant culture because that culture has no place for us and never will, but for the purpose of insuring that we remain, for as long as possible, a battered, listing, wind tossed, rudderless ship of state without direction or destination. Despite this we are still and will forever remain, African people. Our ancient ancestors are and can only be Africans. Our ancestral beginnings, our cultural base can only be found in Africa -- the land of our ancestral birth. Oh, Mother Afru-ika, we look to you as the beacon whose resplendent light will guide us home.

WHAT IS THE AUTHENTIC CULTURE OF OUR ANCESTORS?

We state categorically and without fear of contradiction that our ancestors were Africans. The implications of this profound statement is that our Authentic Ancestral Culture is that of the African people. Of this we are certain and will never be dissuaded.

We anticipate the argument that we have been too long removed, anonymously, from our homeland to be able to determine from what tribe or clan we descended. And that without such knowledge we are hopelessly incapable of

Theodicy

arriving at an acceptable conclusion regarding our Authentic Ancestral Culture. We note at the outset that such argument, no matter how presented, is spurious and unacceptable. The argument is as treacherous as it is inaccurate. It is fundamentally flawed because it mistakes individual tribal custom for African culture.

The diversity of the African people is well known even if somewhat exaggerated. But, the multiplicity of African tribal groupings is immaterial. Tribal numerosity is irrelevant when the objective of the analysis is the determination of the core teachings that comprise the authentic, foundational cultural beliefs underlying all African custom.

Prior to the unfortunate arrival of the Arabs and Europeans, Africans adhered to a core set of beliefs that comprised their culture. This set of beliefs can be found among virtually all tribal groups, and forms, in turn, the course of our Authentic Ancestral Culture. The origin of these beliefs may be ascertained with precision. Let us fully understand the purpose of our search for Authentic Ancestral Culture in order to assist us in the attainment of our goal.

It is conceded that the importance of culture is its stabilizing and cohesive effect on a specific group of people . It is also conceded that the group cannot become empowered without st ability and cohesion. These concessions render the purpose of the search self-evident. They also compel another.

In our search we must look for the authentic African culture that has attained the highest degree of success in the accomplishment of the goals of culture. These are, survival, prosperity, stability, cohesion, longevity and civilization. It seems too obvious to mention that it would serve little purpose and would be counterproductive and illogical to emulate any African culture th had not attained the highest degree of success.

Since culture is itself the outgrowth of an evolutionary process, the highest state to which the ancestral culture has evolved would be that which is the most worthy of emulation. The begged question is whether there is a culture, African in origin and of ancient beginnings, whose success, gauged by its material and spiritual accomplishments and which contains the fundamental components of ancient African culture generally, has evolved so far beyond others as to be the epitome of all cultures that partake of the erstwhile fundamental components?

If such a culture may be distinguished it is axiomatic that it, more than any other, must be the superior candidate to accomplish the overall objectives of culture as applied to the group of African descendants whose cultureless, hence powerless condition (culture is also a power) among peoples and nations of the world is sought to be remedied.

To sum up, we have found that our ancestors were undoubtedly Africans; that these our ancient progenitors subscribed to a core set of fundamental beliefs that evolved over millennia and which comprised the traditional, indigenous culture which remained pure and consistent from one tribe to the next.

We must next determine if a superior candidate having all the above mentioned qualifications does, in fact, exist. By our definition there is only one candidate that fulfills all of the prerequisites. It is found where it flourished for untold millennia among the Nilotic people known as the Kemites, popularly known as the ancient Egyptians. These people, an indigenous, Black, purely African people, attained a level of civilization through the consistent application of their unique culture that remains unsurpassed in the annals of time.

It should also be noted here that Kemit was an indigenous African culture that acknowledged its ancestral roots were to be found in the bamboo forests of equatorial Africa. The descent from and debt to the *Twa* people was duly enshrined in their recorded history. The civilization of Ethiopia was contemporaneous and may have been a forerunner of Kemit. Other examples of refined African culture such as Kush, Axum, Songhay or Timbuktu are noteworthy and laudable. Their accomplishments are certainly important but remain insubstantial when compared

Theodicy

with Kemit. Before there was a Songhay or a Timbuktu there was "Thebes of the Hundred Gates"; before the cathedrals of Europe and the minarets of Mecca there were the towering pyramids of Giza. The Sphinx, silent watchman over our ancient history and treasures, has stood his vigil so long that its date of origin cannot be fixed.

The people of Kemit stated that their ancestors came from the forests at the foothills of the Mountains of the Moon (the Ruwenzori Mountain Range in present day Uganda) in South Central Africa. They stated that these people traveled down the great river *Hapy* and finally settled where the river deposits its rich alluvial soil and creates an agricultural paradise.

This glorious, ancient African culture, once deified became the forerunner, either directly or indirectly, of all the major religions of the world. The teachings of her ancient priests and the example of her system of governance gave Greece its philosophy and Plato his Republic. Pythagoras, after twenty or more years of study, was awarded the theorem that made him famous. Hippocrates found his oath there; the Masons and Rosicrucian's their secret doctrines; the Jews, Christians and Muslims found their amen and no person can contemplate the Creator without the framework of her spiritual concepts. She is the birthplace of writing and paper, the home of medicine, chemistry and physics. The first armies to conquer the world marched to the beat of her sacred drums and under the standards of her African Gods and Goddesses. She was the first superpower in recorded history and vigilant protector of women and children.

It is posited here, unabashedly, that a collective return to that culture, modified to suit contemporary standards, and the cosmic ambiance of the new age, will permit a renaissance of our former glory and our ancient birthright as the spiritual and intellectual leaders of the world. Clearly, the importance of agreed ancestral identity as the initial step in the journey toward the resuscitation of our Authentic Ancestral Culture warrants further examination.

The key word in the concept of Authentic Ancestral Culture is ancestral. The word ancestor derives from the Latin and means one who goes before. Long before Latinium existed, however, the ancient Kemites too understood the concept of the ancestors or those who have gone before.

The ancient Kemitic word for ancestor was tepia. The word derived from tepi meaning first, best leader, chief, captain, and governor. To the Kemites the one who goes before is the leader. The word *tepia* meant the beginning of things and old primeval time. To the ancient Kemite then, the ancestors were not only those who had gone before in time, they were also the best leaders.

of agreed ancestral identity as the initial step in the journey toward the resuscitation of our Authentic Ancestral Culture warrants further examination.

The key word in the concept of Authentic Ancestral Culture is ancestral. The word ancestor derives from the Latin and means one who goes before. Long before Latinium existed, however, the ancient Kemites too understood the concept of the ancestors or those who have gone before.

The ancient Kemitic word for ancestor was *tepia*. The word derived from *tepi* meaning first, best leader, chief, captain, and governor. To the Kemites the one who goes before is the leader. The word *tepa* meant the beginning of things and old primeval time. To the ancient Kemite then, the ancestors were not only those who had gone before in time, they were also the best leaders.

In the modern use of the word ancestor we think of them as behind us in the sense of anteriority. But, according to our Authentic Ancestral Culture then, our ancestors, are our vanguard. Ancestors are those who march at the head of the army, those who take the leading position in the movement. They march before us, carrying our shield and sword, our protection and defense, our thought and belief our Authentic Ancestral Culture.

Theodicy

We are a people in search of valiant role models. Our ancestors are our only reliable role models. Their history is already written, their example carved in stone. What they stand for stands for eternity. They cannot betray us or deny us. Their value is enhanced when the present condition of powerlessness of their descendants is considered. The benefit of their example, to us, is knowing our history and of recognizing that our people and their culture formerly attained the highest level of competence, leadership and civilization in the world. Given the circumstances in which we presently find ourselves we are compelled to follow their leadership. To do less would be to reject our legacy as the Light of the World while cursing our seemingly endless sojourn is darkness.

VERIFIABLE AUTHENTICITY AND ANTIQUITY

Let us digress briefly to establish for the record the verifiable authenticity and antiquity of the ancient Kemites.

It can be said, without fear of contradiction, that the Kemites were not only the originators of civilization, but also as a necessary prerequisite, all of the useful arts required for its accomplishment, and also that they were indigenous Black Africans indistinguishable from those who inhabit the Motherland today. These facts have been so richly and repeatedly authenticated that even the most rabid racists, albeit begrudgingly, are forced to concede the point. The concession is a result of three factors:

First, the copious reports of ancient chroniclers who, as eye witnesses, and without rancor, recorded the physical appearance of the most wise, religious, healthiest, cleanest, industrious and cultured people in the world of their time. Who they noted had black skin, wide noses, thick lips and woolly hair.

Second, is the existence of the massive temples, pyramids, tombs and other colossal monuments that have stood for millennia to mock those who find it inconvenient that this great land of wisdom, culture and civilization is located on the African continent a place that has been since time immemorial, the home of the people with burnt faces.

Third, and perhaps most important is the fact that the scholarly world has for more than two centuries been in awe of this African country. So much so that excavation has continued unabated at the cost of millions of dollars for centuries.

These excavations are carried on by so-called Egyptologists from every industrialized country in the world. The centerpiece of many of the world's first class museums is an extensive Egyptian exhibit. Each year hundreds of new titles are published on one facet of Egyptian life and culture or another. A bibliography of the works on the subject, in all languages, would be encyclopedic. It has been estimated that complete excavation of the land our ancestors will require at least another two centuries.

The wealth of information that authenticates the culture of the ancient Kemites is staggering.

As to the antiquity of the culture and civilization of our ancient ancestors suffice it to say that it is conceded to have pre-dated all others. They have dated it most conservatively to 3400 B. C. for the dynastic/historic period. If we choose to believe the word of our ancestors the date becomes 75,000 to 40,000 B.C. By these standards no other civilization, European or African has been so authenticated as to the breadth of its accomplishments or the antiquity of its culture.

Having examined the importance of culture and discovered the identity of our ancestors and their authentic and ancient culture we must now attempt to reconstruct the rudiments of that culture from the detritus and carnage of the centuries-long attempt to misdirect and misappropriate our vital cultural energy. Before we do so, let us review how that cultural energy has been stolen that we may better understand why its value to us is not only inestimable, but also recognized as such by our historic enemies.

Theodicy

CHAPTER SEVEN:

STOLEN CULTURAL ENERGY

It is said that the phrase "knowledge is power" was coined by the 17th century philosopher, Sir Francis Bacon. The phrase, though popular, is both incomplete and inaccurate in ways that Bacon never imagined. The concept upon which it is based is also a great deal older than the 17th century.

In order to transfer sense impressions to the brain they must be transformed into energy impulses that travel along neural pathways to become thought. Knowledge is literally data that are similar to bits in the computer sense. When these bits are transmitted for idea creation they are transformed into electrical impulses. Scientifically speaking, knowledge is so many pulses of energy. Energy and power are virtually synonymous terms.

Whether knowledge is called energy or power it is capable of transmission and conversion like any other form of energy. I may also be diverted and misappropriated. In modern legal parlance unauthorized diversion or misappropriation of energy is a criminal offense known as theft of energy.

If it is conceded that knowledge is energy and that energy may be stolen we may logically expect that in the case of such theft at least two things will happen: (1) the energy level of the entity from which the energy is stolen will decrease; and (2) the energy level of the thief will increase proportionately.

If knowledge is energy it follows that energy can be specific by virtue of its subject matter. Culture, as we have seen, is a body of knowledge whose subject matter is comprised of the technology of survival accumulated by a particular group of people and passed down by them to their lineal descendants. Culture is, therefore, specific energy. It is the energy that provides the ability to do, act or produce according to the standards and dictates of a particular people. It is the energy that expresses and activates the group dynamic of self-determination, and in the political sense, nationalism. It is, most importantly, the reservoir of energy that is the Power of the Will.

This chapter posits that there has been a systematic theft of the cultural energy of the African people that has caused a deep-seated cultural deprivation whose destabilizing effect has prevented us from developing the cultural and political power base necessary to reverse our unfortunate circumstances.

In order to fully appreciate how this theft of cultural energy was carried out we must take a brief look at the history of knowledge in three broad areas: (1) the original source of ancient knowledge; (2) the historical transmission of that knowledge; and (3) the concept of cultural hegemony.

THE SOURCE OF ANCIENT KNOWLEDGE

Before the rise of so-called Western civilization, the world was of one accord regarding the source of the ancient knowledge upon which civilization was based, to wit: the ancient Kemites were the originators of civilization and all of the useful arts necessary for its accomplishment. The universality of this accord was complete. Without exception Pythagoras, Euodoxos, Solon, Thales, Anaximander, Anaxagoras, Plato and Aristole studied in, or were influenced by, the wisdom of Kemit.

Alexander called the Great came to conquer Kemit, but was, in the end, conquered by it. So impressed was he by the culture of the most ancient of people that he adopted their ways and stayed to be buried in the sacred land of our ancestors.

In later times, particularly the 16th through the 18th centuries, the likes of Sir Isaac Newton, Johannes Kepler, Giordano Bruno, Galileo Galilei, Champollion and others, agreed that Kemit was the fountain from which all cultures drank on their long trek to civilization. In short, Kemit was universally recognized as the birthplace of civilization by virtue of her creation of writing, paper, mathematics, stone architecture and sculpture, astronomy, astrology, chemistry, medicine, calendrical systems, time reckoning devices, the division of labor, philosophy and religion. Its people were recognized as the healthiest, cleanliest, most spiritual and cultured people in the world. Their form of government, in successful and tranquil operation for millennia, and so important to the rise of civilization, was admired as the most efficient ever created.

The wisdom of ancient Kemit that set the world on the course of civilization, was the accumulated knowledge and culture of an indigenous African people. This powerful knowledge was the cultural energy of the people of Kemit and the basis of Western civilization.

HISTORICAL TRANSMSSION OF KEMITIC KNOWLEDGE

Let us assume, for the sake of argument, that the popular, time-honored notion that Western civilization is the product of the wisdom of the ancient Greeks is accurate. The assumption does not necessarily mean that the Greeks were the originators of that which they bequeathed to the West in the same way that a truck driver is generally not the creator of the package he delivers.

This section will look at the so-called "Greek Miracle" often advanced to explain the miraculous appearance of a wealth of knowledge in the hands of the ancient Greeks in a remarkably short period of time. The Greek wisdom that accounted for the miracle was essentially, though no exclusively, philosophy and nearly all of their teachers were philosophers. Before we proceed it is necessary to digress momentarily to examine the meaning of the word philosophy.

The popular meaning of the word philosophy seems to be the love of wisdom. The definition is both contrived and modern. In its ancient acceptation the word denotes the search for knowledge and the analysis of the principles underlying conduct, thought, knowledge and the NaTuRe of the universe. It includes the study of the ultimate reality, causes and effects of being and thinking. Philosophy was understood as an expansive term that included the investigation of virtually every branch of knowledge.

It is generally accepted that the Greeks had no true religion or philosophy before the 4th century B.C. It is also said that they began their search for knowledge in the 6th century B.C. by establishing a system of inquiry independent of theology. Of course, if it they did not have a theology before the 4th century it follows that their inquiry had to be independent of a theology that was not their own.

We have stated that the Land of Kemit was the birthplace of the ancient knowledge that gave rise to civilization. It will not be surprising then that the ancient people to whom the word "philosopher" was originally and exclusively applied were the Kemites. When a person professed to be a "philosopher" he was, in ancient times, understood to mean that either he was a Kemite or had received his education in Kemit. Greek "philosophers" were no exception.

It is also important to note that the modern definition of philosophy is limited because it implies a separation between itself and science. It will be remembered that the word science means "to know". In ancient times science did not exist as a separate and distinct discipline. This not because its subject matter was unknown. It is simply because philosophy covered the entire field. Philosophy, the erstwhile Sacred Science of the ancient Kemites, included, but was not limited to, physics (the science of the properties of matter and energy); chemistry (the science of the properties of substances and their conversion) the word chemistry itself derives from the Arabic *Al-Chem* their name for ancient Kemit; and psychology (the science of the mind), from Greek meaning the study of the soul (psyche meaning breath, spirit, soul) and logia (study of). The Greek word *psukhe* is Kemitic in origin.

What has come to be known as Western philosophy is actually a deviation from the teachings of the Sacred Science of the Kemites that were misunderstood and misapplied by the Greeks.

Theodicy

The actual contribution of the Greeks to western thought was an approach that ignored theology and removed spiritual guidance from the search for knowledge. This offering to the god of reason created a discipline that bases theories on empirical evidence alone. Sacred Science recognized that existence and being cannot be unraveled by reliance on empirical evidence alone. Empirical evidence only teaches how little we know and never instructs on that which exists but cannot be perceived by the five senses.

We have digressed to show that the popular notion that the Greeks were the first philosophers is belied by the definition of the word and its history. The Greeks were philosophers only to the extent that they may be said to have studied in or derived their knowledge from the Kemites. It is certain that they were not Kemites themselves. Let us return to the "Greek Miracle" beginning with the so-called epitome of the Greek intellect.

SOLON

Solon was a 6th century Athenian statesman who framed the democratic laws of Greece, was one of the Seven Wise Men of Greece and the epitome of the Greek intellect. He was a contemporary of Pythagoras, Thales and Anaximander. He traveled to Kemit and was instructed by the priests there. Plato reported that Solon was told by the priests that the Greeks were mere infants who possessed not a single belief that was ancient. In "democratic" Greece 90% 6£ the population were slaves.

Apparently, Solon and the other Greeks of his time had no significant knowledge until after they visited Kemit.

Curiously, Solon is best known for having coined the phrase "know thyself". Of course, that phrase was inscribed over the portals of the temples of Kemit and was one of her "First Principles" long before Solon claimed authorship of it.

PYTHAGORAS

The renowned 6th century Greek "philosopher", mathematician and reputed discoverer of the Pythagorean

Theorem (In geometry, the theorem that in a right triangle the hypotenuse squared is equal to the sum of the squares of the other ·sides. In Kemit, the 3,4,5, triangle squared.)

is known to have studied in Kemit for 21 years after which time he returned to Crotona, Italy, where he founded his secret, mystical society.

The doctrine of Pythagoras was one of synthesis, it was a marriage, of sorts, of science and religion. He saw philosophy and science against the backdrop of mystery religions, like Orphism which was itself no more than at retelling of the Legend of Osiris and Isis.*

Among the doctrines that he taught were the transmigration of souls and the belief in numbers as the divine key to the understanding of the universe. The Pythagoreans also followed a strict rule of secrecy and presumably for that reason, wrote nothing down. It is no wonder that the priests of Kemit recognized Pythagoras as the most worthy of the Greeks.

The flowering of the "Greek Miracle" is best exemplified, however, by Socrates, Plato and Aristotle.

SOCRATES

Socrates was an Athenian who like Pythagoras left no records in his own hand. His biographer and most gifted student was Plato. Other than the record provided by Plato and Xenophon (another of Socrates's alleged students) there is no historical record of his existence. The reliability of the account is suspect, among other reasons, because Socrates is virtually the only Greek notable of the time who did not visit Kemit.

The knowledge that formed the body of Socrates's teachings was knowledge that was foreign to Greece. It will be remembered that he was tried and sentenced to death on the charges of not believing in the gods of Athens and

---

*In Kemitic the Legend of *Asar* and <u>Aset</u>

Theodicy

corrupting the minds of the youth of Athens, presumably with his foreign knowledge. It is axiomatic that his teaching could not have been that which was routinely taught in Athens. Were it otherwise his teaching would not have been cause for alarm or criminal prosecution and capital punishment. To determine the content of Socrates' teaching we must turn to his illustrious student Plato.

PLATO

Plato traveled to Kemit. He also studied with the Pythagoreans who carried on the secret society and teachings of Pythagoras after his death. Plato founded a school of "philosophy" in Athens that he called the Academy. He wrote his *Dialogues*, which have been recognized as the most influential body of "philosophy" of the Western world. Among the Dialogues, all of which present the ideas or philosophy of Socrates, is the *Republic*.

In the *Republic*, Plato set forth basic ideas regarding education, justice, law government and the transmigration of souls. That the ideas are placed in the mouth of Socrates, the only Greek not to visit or study in Kemit, does not successfully disguise their origin. An exhaustive analysis of the *Republic* is beyond the scope of this work. Suffice it to say that all of the themes treated in it find their origin in the long established philosophy of ancient Kemit. These include the supreme good, the ideal state, the concept of philosopher king and metempsychosis. That the fundamental philosophical teachings of the Kemites, who at the time were the preeminent educators in the world, and who were universally recognized as such, sprang independently from the mind of Socrates, as reported by Plato, after Plato's visit to Kemit is, in a word, incredible.

ARISTOTLE

The third Greek genius was the incredibly prolific Aristotle. In the relatively brief span of 62 years he is said to have accomplished the remarkable feat of writing 400 books on a wide variety of subjects. If it is considered that he began his studies at Plato's Academy at the age of 17 the amount of time available to author the large number of texts attributed to him is further reduced.

Aristotle remained at the Academy, where he became Plato's most celebrated student, until his mentor's death. If Aristotle began his writing career after the death of Plato, which seems likely since he is said to have disagreed with many of his teacher's doctrines and philosophical interpretations, the span of time available to him to * write 400 books is reduced to 25 years or 16 books per year . At age 49, he opened his own school, the Lyceum, at Athens. It is almost too obvious to state that the claim that he actually wrote 400 books is incredible. This does not, however, exclude the possibility that he may have taken credit for the authorship of that many books or that others may have attributed authorship to after his death.

If it is understood that at the time of Aristotle, and for a considerable period thereafter, the total of Greek scholarship did not include 400 books it is obvious that the texts had to be of other than Greek origin. Modern scholarship indicates that of the 400 books attributed to him only 50 have survived and of those less than half are authentic. For the answer to the apparent anomaly we must look to the relationship between Aristotle and his most famous student.

ARISTOTLE AND ALEXANDER

Four years after the death of Plato, Aristotle became the tutor to Prince Alexander of Macedonia, who would later be referred to as the "Great". Alexander is best known as a world conqueror. His military career is well known and need not detain us here. In 332 B.C. Alexander was wounded at the siege of Gaza and he and his army recuperated in Kemit. While in Kemit the world conqueror was apparently accepted as pharaoh of Kemit without a battle. He was so taken by Kemitic culture and achievement that he adopted their dress and their religion. He then took to calling himself the Son of Amun. So taken was he that he was buried in Kemit in accord with his wishes.

Theodicy

Alexander's "conquest" of Kemit provided him with unhindered access to the wealth of Kemit which, not insignificantly, included the vast store of knowledge contained in her temple libraries. Alexander is credited with having founded great centers of cultural learning in the large cosmopolitan cities of his empire. The greatest of these cultural centers was that at Alexandria in Kemit.

Alexandria is widely noted as the center of Greek culture after the conquest of Alexander. It is curious indeed that Greek culture would flourish after Alexander, in Kemit, rather than, say, in Greece. It is because Alexandria, a city in Kemit, was already the cultural learning center of the civilized world when Alexander arrived. It was also because the greatest library in the world, the famed Royal Library of *Waset*, which contained more than 500,000 volumes comprising the accumulated knowledge of the world, was already there. Of course, the library was renamed It is now known to history as the Library of Alexandria.

Aristotle's Lyceum was said to contain a museum and a *vast library*. The library was "endowed" by his former student Alexander. The generous "endowment" came from Alexander's "acquisitions" made during his conquest of Kemit. It follows that Aristotle had unhindered access to the vast holdings of the Royal Library of *Waset* and acquired from it, by endowment, a vast library that he installed at the Lyceum where he could work, at his leisure, at the arduous task of plagiarizing the wisdom of Kemit.

We must also briefly note Aristotle's reported fascination with Kemitic culture in order to show the depth of his interest in Kemitic wisdom.

While at Plato's academy Aristotle developed his partiality for Kemit under the watchful eye of Eudoxos who himself had been educated in Kemit. Like other Greeks of the time Aristotle believed the Kemites to be the most ancient people and the inventors of geometry, mathematics and astronomy. When these facts a juxtaposed the source of Aristotle's prolific authorship and the "Greek Miracle", of which it is part, becomes less miraculous.

CULTURAL HEGEMONY

The true objective of the theft of cultural energy is cultural hegemony. Hegemony literally means to dominate. The term, in the cultural sense implied here, should be understood as the ability to dominate and control people and the course of events, by control of their specific cultural energy. Put another way, it is the active use of the power or energy of culture to control a group of people whether they be a separate nation or a group within a nation. When cultural energy is stolen it increases power to the thief while decreasing, proportionately, the power of the rightful owner. When viewed in this way it becomes apparent that cultural hegemony is also potent weapon in psychological warfare and whose impact has not been fully appreciated by African Americans.

Cultural domination is easiest to accomplish in the case where the theft of cultural energy is not apparent. That which does not exist cannot be stolen. The successful denial of the existence of our cultural energy·· insures that the cultural domination of the European cannot be challenged. Denial is, therefore, the first phase of concealment of one of history's greatest crimes. The denial alluded to here is, specifically, the denial of the fact that the Kemites, indigenous Black Africans, allegedly incapable of abstract thought or true culture, were the originators of civilization and that they taught the Greeks who, in turn, inspired Western civilization. The importance of this denial must not be underestimated. It is vital to the existence of the cultural and political doctrine of White supremacy that the present and historical cultural inferiority of the African remain forever unchallenged.

In this context denial is a process having clearly distinguishable components. The components are: misinformation, disinformation, indoctrination control and, physical acquisition.

Denial is the act of declaring that something is untrue. It implies repudiation that goes beyond general denial to

Theodicy

encompass the specific denial of the validity or authority of a belief or other set of facts as an *official policy*.

Misinformation is false or misleading information disseminated intentionally and with knowledge of its falsity, for the purpose of misleading another. It is the support of denial.

Disinformation is a variety of misinformation that is distinguished by its source. When misinformation is propagated by government it becomes disinformation. Disinformation is a form of propaganda. When government controls education and disseminates disinformation denial serves the wider purpose of indoctrination.

Indoctrination is a method of teaching people the uncritical acceptance of a specific system of thought. Put another way, indoctrination is a way of instilling the habit (an act repeated so often by an individual that it becomes automatic) of uncritical thinking.

History teaches us that by the late 18th and early 19th centuries the denial of the importance and anteriority of Kemitic culture to the development of civilization had been supported by an elaborate structure of misinformation which recreated the Kemites, out of whole cloth, as an inherently inferior, hopelessly backward people incapable of abstract thought. This patently false information was intentionally disseminated to support the denial of the identity of the people of ancient Kemit. The misinformation was disseminated by flatly and defiantly asserting that the White and therefore genetically superior Greeks could not have learned anything from the Black and therefore genetically inferior Africans even if those Africans were the celebrated Kemites. And to the extent the Kemites were Black Africans the high civilization attributed to them in antiquity was apocryphal.

Such assertions, to be truly effective, were required to be indoctrinated under the guise of education. In societies that develop different levels of caste the educational system serves the unwritten purpose of the maintenance of the *status quo*. In such societies, including the United States, maintenance of stratification is viewed as essential to the ability of the dominant culture to continue its privileged position.

The purpose of education is to train trustworthy and dependable people who will replace those who presently man the engines of society. The replacements are required to accept the culture and philosophy of the society to which they are the grateful heirs. It is vitally important, therefore, to control how and what people think about that culture and their place in it. Education is, by this definition, the process of indoctrination.

The system of thought that is indoctrinated through education includes the doctrines, beliefs and world-view of the dominant culture that must be accepted uncritically. Although the system has proven quite effective it is not foolproof. It is for this reason that the system has incorporated a two-tiered approach.

On the one hand, those who are destined to become the heirs to the wealth and privilege of the society in question must be indoctrinated to believe that they are, in some intrinsic way, superior to those who are destined to become the functional servants of the privileged.

On the other hand, the servant class must be indoctrinated to believe that they are, in some intrinsic way, inferior to those whom they must serve, that they will perpetually and peacefully accept servant status in society.

When it is considered that these viewpoints must be indoctrinated in a compulsory education system that touts the notion that "all men are created equal" we are confronted with a true paradox. The solution is surprisingly simple and can be summed up in one word - *history*.

History is, in one sense, the chronological record of the events in the development of a people, including commentary and analysis of those events. But the root of the word is the Greek *histor* which implies a learned man.

Theodicy

History has a purpose, that is, to create such learned men and women.

If it is conceded that the knowledge of the past is a key component of the collective consciousness of a people, and that the powerful and dominant class will never instruct the subordinate and powerless class how to seize power, the link between history and indoctrination becomes apparent.

The system employed is as simple as it is insidious. Teach the dominant class that they are not only genetically superior, but that their privileged status derives from the historical accomplishments of their ancestors and the superiority of their culture.

At the same time, teach the subordinate class that they are not only genetically inferior, but also that their servant status derives from the lack of historical accomplishment of their ancestors and the non-existence of a unique culture that they may call their own. The result, over time, is that the dominant class comes to believe that they are deserving of, and entitled to, their privileged status while the subordinate class concludes that their status is their own fault. This mentality insures power to the dominant class and obviates the necessity to resort to violence to control the subordinate class.

Control is the power to dominate. The word has a curious and instructive derivation that helps give fuller meaning to the concepts analyzed here.

In the Latin *contrarotula*, from which the word control derives, is formed by the combination of two words: *contra*, meaning against and *rotula* meaning roll, which is also the diminutive of *rota* meaning wheel.

Control implies something that is against the wheel, something that prevents its ability to roll. If the reader will recall our definition of Theodicy as Divine Journey and in that context the Wheel of Time, the meaning of control, as used here, is illuminated.

Control is not only the power to dominate, it is also the force that counters the roll of the Wheel of Time that is part and parcel of Theodicy. But the theft of cultural energy involves more than the control of information. It also involves the control of such energy by physical acquisition of the artifacts that could lead to the re-discovery of the cultural knowledge that has been successfully stolen and denied. We also note that ancestral artifacts are also the repository of the ancestral energy imparted to them by transference through physical contact with our ancient ancestors.

PHYSICAL ACQUISITION

The Ancient Kemites were the first to assemble the components of civilization and taught those components to the Greeks. This fact was universally acknowledged in Ancient times.

Until the rise of the infamous African slave trade there was no necessity to deny the fact of the Kemitic origin of civilization. Denial became expedient, however, to justify the wholesale, government sanctioned, enslavement of Africans. The "justification" was based on the pronouncement, and nothing more, that Africans were sub-human, without culture and incapable of civilization. Of course, the existence of ancient Kemit, the copiously documented historical record of her accomplishments and the high level of her civilization was problematic. The extant record not only recognized Kemit as the land of ancient wisdom, but also that they were Black Africans with broad noses, thick lips and wooly hair. That the country was inconveniently located on the African continent did not help matters.

The rise of the slave trade preceded the rise of European colonialism. This rapid expansion of empire created the necessity for the acquisition of knowledge regarding the language and culture of the people of Africa for the specific purpose of controlling them in the most efficient manner.

During the period of colonial empire, and in spite of the alleged inferiority of Africans, the greatest danger to Europe was recognized as the rise of an African power. *The best way to prevent that possibility was to control that which could make the African powerful -- their cultural energy.*

In time it was concluded that if information about the culture of these people could be commandeered and held in European hands Africans would then be required to learn about their own culture from their colonizers and control would be complete.

Control is both a strategy and a tactic. From the tactical standpoint control involves the physical acquisition and concealment of the bulk of the cultural, ancestral artifacts of the African people in general, and Kemit in particular. It is not coincidental that a wealth of Kemitic artifacts remain, until this day, in the custody and control of European museums and private collections throughout the world . As a direct result most of the published information regarding African and Kemitic culture is written by Europeans in whose hands the stolen source materials are unlawfully held. The United Arab Republic, popularly and incorrectly known as Egypt, is no exception. The current controllers of our ancestral land and cultural artifacts are not descendants of Kemites, nor do they claim to be. They are usurpers and their unlawful control of our cultural heritage is as reprehensible as that of the Europeans whose control they facilitated. By controlling access to the original artifacts, research and scholarship is controlled. The people whose culture the artifacts represent are thereby controlled in their ability to understand their past and to plan, effectively for their future. Of course, the indignity of having to secure permission to use the artifacts of one's ancestors is yet another aspect of the overall power of control.

The knowledge and information represented by these artifacts and ancient documents is stored, tangible cultural energy of the most powerful sort. It may be likened to the energy stored in an battery. The act of removing these batteries of stored cultural energy from their sacred resting place and transporting them to the far-flung corners of the globe, secreting them in museum vaults and private collections, as well as in situ control of Arab usurpers, is theft on an international and unprecedented scale.

Lest we lose heart completely, we must remember that cultural energy is knowledge. Knowledge is a unique form of energy that is not decreased by its use. Knowledge implies knowing. It follows that this form of energy retains its potency while dormant. But it cannot be effectively utilized until it is known and understood. It is for this reason that the effective use of denial and its components insures cultural hegemony.

NaTuRe abhors a vacuum. When cultural energy is stolen it leaves, in its place and stead, a vacuum that is filled by disease that results from prolonged cultural deprivation.

A brief analysis of the cultural deprivation that is a direct and predictable result of the grand theft of cultural energy is required as we journey toward full understanding of our current predicament and how it relates to Theodicy, power and will.

THE EFFECTS OF CULTURAL DEPRIVATION

For nearly five hundred years private and governmental forces in America have conspired to enslave and exploit the labor and land of the African. Whether through chattel or neo-slavery the result has been perpetual servitude and ignoble status for the African American. The calculated, concerted harmony of action undertaken to preserve the functional reality of African enslavement has prevented the descendant of African slaves from developing an effective plan of action. The seemingly inexplicable failure to extricate ourselves from our increasingly perilous , circumstances is the result and effect of cultural deprivation.

It is now well-documented that during the infamous and historically unique period of chattel slavery in the United States slave owners controlled their two-legged property through ignorance. Knowledge being so closely related to power, slaves were denied education by custom and law. Ignorance is, of course, nothing more than the lack of knowledge, and is not indicative of an underlying lack of intelligence.

It is certainly true that the chain, the whip and the gun were important tools of subjugation during that period. But a tool of equal effectiveness and greater subtlety was the manipulation and strict control of knowledge. The effect of such control was profound and unprecedented in history.

The unique strategy began, in earnest, after the ostensible collapse of Southern slavocracy when government approval of slavery was officially abolished. It should be noted here that the Emancipation Proclamation did not abolish slavery. It was the Thirteenth Amendment to the United States Constitution that abolished slavery *except* as punishment for crime. In a sudden, perhaps unanticipated chain of events former slave owners found themselves surrounded by four million freed slaves who represented considerable competitive potential in a free capitalist labor market. Thus neo-slavery was born out of the perceived need to insure that those who were formerly slaves could be controlled in a way that allow them to remain slaves of their former slave masters, and all other white people, in all but name.

It must be understood, from the outset, that the ability of a people to overcome subjugation is directly related to the amount of power they possess. Power, whether political, cultural or economic is directly related to accurate, useful and timely knowledge. But it is cultural knowledge that is most important to people who find themselves surrounded by a strange and hostile culture. Under such circumstances cultural deprivation represented a deadly and ingenious *national plan* that accomplished two related objectives that together prevented African Americans from altering the condition of their powerlessness.

The first objective was to deny the newly freed African access to educational facilities and/or insure that the quality of education received by them was, in all locations, so substandard as to be virtually useless in the quest for power. The United Supreme Court sanctioned policy of "separate but equal" is so well known as to not require repetition here.

The second objective perhaps more pernicious than the first, was to manipulate the content of the information that was taught in substandard schools. To this end the so-called science of race was invented. This doctrine held that Africans were an inferior, sub-specie of humanity whose alleged biological impediments included their inability to engage in abstract thought and to master any but the most menial tasks associated with "fetchin' and totin'

This scientific information was intended to instill in the African the belief that he was genetically inferior. It is axiomatic that a person who believes that he is inferior and incapable of competing, will not compete. Moreover, the denial of access to accurate information prevents him from disproving the so-called scientific basis of the alleged inferiority. Of course, the existence of a high level of civilization and culture among people alleged to be genetically inferior and incapable of abstract thought, if discovered, would significantly undermine the premise upon which scientific racism was based.

We have previously noted that culture is pivotal to understanding ourselves and the world in which we live. Accordingly, cultural deprivation is a way of insuring that we never understand the world around us. It is a system or process that effectively controls thought and thereby action. It is no wonder that African American students do poorly in subjects like history and social studies. It is because history is, in a real sense, the *record of culture*. Our children feel disassociated from history because their only connection to the record of culture depicted in the European-American educational system, is as slaves or savages. When all these factors are combined the outcome of cultural deprivation is predictable.

People who have no perceived stake in society, either because they feel they are incapable of competing or because they feel the system is unfairly structured to prevent their advancement, invariably and predictably, are diverted from legitimate avenues of economic enterprise to criminal and anti-social behavior as a means of livelihood.

Theodicy

The key word is *predictable*. Confronted with such patently predictable outcomes one is confronted with one of two responses. Either correct the system by removing the unfairness and imbalance, or develop a codex of laws and a massive law enforcement apparatus to enforce them. If the desire is for the inclusion of all people the first alternative is the only choice. If, however, one wishes to continue the unfairness he will invariably select the second.

If it is true that every law creates an outlaw, it must also be true that the mere act of creating the law furthers cultural deprivation because the determination of what is criminal is nearly always a political, hence a cultural act.

The criminal justice system, the judicial seal of approval of the law enforcement apparatus, which includes its sanctimonious trappings of courts, judges and prosecutors (the Hebrew word for prosecutor is Satan), surgically removes the subversive threat posed by those who escape the system of indoctrination altogether (admittedly a very small percentage of the overall population) and those who endure it but by critical thinking render themselves immune to its effects.

The observation of human NaTuRe teaches that there will always be a percentage of people who will not respond to indoctrination. These people form a secondary group that must be effectively controlled to prevent their infectious example from undermining the effectiveness of the methods used so efficiently to control others.

The effect of cultural deprivation is the creation of a specifically targeted, seemingly permanent underclass from among the ranks of the "internal enemy" and who become casualties of the War on Drugs and grist for the prison mills.

THE POWER OF FEAR

We have seen that cultural deprivation is a process and system used to control thought and action. All systems require some form of power in order to operate. The power of cultural deprivation is fear.

Thought and the actions that flow from it are susceptible to various forms of disruption. Fear is a paralysis that disrupts biological systems.

Fear has been defined as the anxiety and agitation felt at the presence of danger. The term is synonymous with terror which implies an overwhelming, paralyzing panic. To fully comprehend the concept of fear we will have to call, once again, on the ancient Kemites to provide enlightenment.

The Kemitic word for fear was *senet* which also implies timidity, the timid man, and one who is easily frightened, shows fear or lacks self-confidence. The hieroglyphic determinative for fear was a goose, plucked, trussed, beheaded and of course, dead. It signifies a wealth of cognate meanings that are compelled by the hieroglyph. The trussed goose signifies a paralysis (to paralyze is to make something helpless, ineffective or powerless) or helpless inactivity or of a winged animal to act. The goose is bound, tied up. But the hieroglyph lacks any indication of that which binds the goose. That which has bound it is invisible.

As understood by our ancestors, fear was an invisible paralysis that stopped, impeded or curtailed the ability to fly. After all, the goose is, first and foremost, a bird. Flight is a universal metaphor for the ability to move or flee (to take flight); and to think (flights of fancy). It also implies the ability to ascend above the Earth, above the clouds, where the best survey of the land may be had -- where clear unobstructed vision is possible.

In the modern sense, fear is both psychological and biological paralysis. Fear interferes with the flow of nerve energy and interrupts life forces. This causes disorganization, a loss of direction and cessation of the flow of information in the body. It literally binds the individual in a state of virtual suspended thought and animation.

Fear then, is the inability to move, to ascend, to progress, to think and to flee from danger. Since the paralysis is based on the stoppage or cessation of function it is also akin to the disorganization of the overall operating system of the body.

Theodicy

Fear prevents us from organizing and causes disorganization itself. A disrupted, disorganized system is, at best, less efficient, and at worse, entirely paralyzed.

In this respect we need only cite the example of a deer crossing the road in the dark of night. As soon as it is caught in the glare of the headlights of an oncoming vehicle fear causes paralysis that prevents it from fleeing imminent danger. The result if often death.

In the same way fear is a disorganizer of operations systems such as thought and mobility. It can prevent a person or a group of people, from formulating or implementing plans that may free them from the conditions that inhibit their survival and prosperity. It can even prevent flight from danger.

The *modus operandi* of fear is to disorganize thought and bind action. To disorganize thought is to bind action. Fear can, therefore, stop action by controlling or disorganizing the thought process.

The process is itself simple and straightforward. It consists in the intense, generational application of the instruments of psychological oppression, in order to disrupt the thinking process of the target. The cruel but effective methods of American slave owners provides an instructive case in point.

Slaves who attempted to flee or who dared to indicate the slightest resistance to chattel slavery were immediately and brutally punished in front of the forced assembly of all the slaves, particularly the women and children. The stated purpose of this barbarous display was to instill two separate but interrelated lessons.

The first lesson was to the women. It was to teach them that their men were without power to protect them or their offspring. The effect of this was to eliminate, in their eyes, the most important function of manhood -- to protect the family. The implication was that if the women wished to see their men survive they would be wise to encourage their men not to resist in any way -- even when their children were being sold and their women raped. Hence, the women were unwittingly enlisted in the control of the men.

The second lesson was to show the male children that any attempt at flight, revolt or resistance was futile and costly. If your father, your first god, your symbol of power and strength is helpless against them so will you be. Moreover, the guaranteed consequence was always severe, brutal punishment or death. These combined lessons also taught the greatest fear of all, *the fear of death*.

When we speak of the power of fear, we speak, primarily of the fear of death. People who fear death not only recognize their vulnerability but also a spiritual shortcoming -- their unpreparedness for confrontation with the unknown.

Life, no matter how oppressive or abject is, for most people, preferable to death. As a result virtually all human beings value their own life. When this aspect of human NaTuRe is understood it becomes apparent that fear is a potent method of social control. Conversely, those who do not fear death are the most tenacious and formidable opponents.

Julius Caesar is said to have admired the Celts because of their courage in battle. He canvassed them to find out the reason. He concluded that it was because they believed in reincarnation and as a result did not fear death.

The operation of fear on the human mind is not readily apparent but is, nonetheless, easily explained. Fear works as a restriction on the natural process of thinking. In its most effective application, thought progresses in a straight line from sensory input to problem identification, to dissection of information in constituent parts, and finally to problem resolution. This normal process of thinking generates its solution in the natural flow of the process. If the process is disrupted or paralyzed, as by fear, a secondary and unnatural thinking process supplants the linear one. In the secondary process that disruption appears between sensory perception and problem resolution and causes a sensory loop that function like a magnetic tape, joined end to end, that forms a continuous strip of endless repetition. The loop goes from

Theodicy

sensory input to identification of the problem and then back to sensory input without analysis or problem resolution. The disruption is caused by the introduction of the element of fear into the normal process. The insidious nature of fear is that it is often so unobtrusive as to go unrecognized by its victims.

A case in point is the seemingly inexplicable failure of African Americans to join forces to overcome the circumstances of the oppression that has historically and presently cast us in the role of second-class citizens and condemned our children to a similar fate.

During the entire course of our unfortunate slave experience in America the argument has been prevalent, among slaves and the descendants of slaves, that resistance to oppression is , futile. The argument goes that we are outnumbered, ill-armed and cannot win an armed confrontation with the White majority. Facially, the argument seems logical. It is the argument's underlying rationale, however, that belies its appropriateness. If we are outnumbered and ill-equipped for war, it follows that the result of any such confrontation, either offensively or defensively, will be slaughter and death. But, it is also true that the nature of war is to cause death--it is a predictable and intended objective of war.

Revolution on the other hand, is by definition, the overthrow of a government by forceful means. It is also interesting in the context of Theodicy that a revolution is also a complete cycle of events and a complete or radical change of any kind.

Political revolutions are always violent. And, almost always involve the attempt by an outnumbered, ill-equipped, poorly trained, bunch of rag-tag insurgents who have come to the conclusion that it is better to be dead than live the life of a slave. Their inexperience, insignificant numbers and lack of sophisticated armaments of war are compensated for by their ability to make fast decisions, move quickly, and remain invisible. But their most powerful weapon is their willingness to die for the cause. Of course, these arguments are never considered because the fear of death has disrupted the thinking process. We never consider war because it is synonymous, to our minds, with death. When fear disrupts and disorganizes the normal process of problem resolution the possibility that revolution might succeed is never seriously considered. It cannot be considered because of the concomitant possibility of death.

In order for this disruptive and disorganizing paralysis called fear to be successful one further diversion is necessary. The person, or group, must have some psychological way to solve the problem without solving it, a sort of mental escape route.

In this case the escape route is the unending, ever-winding, Yellow Brick Road of Progress and Individual Achievement. On that fantastic road, strewn with the poppies of timidity and cultural deprivation things are always viewed as better than they were because of the promise that things will get better in the future. It should also be noted here that when Dorothy of Kansas took her journey down Oz's Yellow Brick Road she got there as a result of a concussion.

Unfortunately, the wheels of progress, like the wheels of justice, turn exceedingly slowly. At the present rate of "progress" it will take us more than four hundred years to gain economic parity with Whites in America. It follows that it is not individual progress, but collective progress that important. It seems trite to say it but we are in this together.

Finally, we must not overlook the fact that the power of fear is also operative at the level of the *collective* mind. It is the effect of the power of fear on the group that prevents mental teamwork and causes profound group apathy. Individual fear, therefore, is directly linked to group goals and collective accomplishment.

In this chapter we have seen that cultural energy can be stolen; the methods by which the theft is accomplished; and the effect of the attendant cultural deprivation. We have reviewed the alleged "Greek Miracle" and concluded that it was not so miraculous after all. It was simply the result of the application of the fundamentals of the Sacred Science of the ancient Kemites to a fledgling society attempting to become

Theodicy

a civilization. Though the culturally young and inexperienced Greeks only partially understood the science of Kemit they were able to utilize it as the foundation of their civilization and thereby demonstrated its power, even in diluted form, to transform society into civilization.

Those who are the descendants of the Kemites and who are the rightful heirs of their glorious and dynamic cultural energy must not underestimate its latent power to transform us and our circumstances for the better while improving dramatically the life prospects of our children.

Having understood the importance of our culture and how the why it was stolen, we now return to our task of reconstruction and examination of the components of Sacred Science that is the specific stolen cultural energy referred to in this chapter.

CHAPTER EIGHT:

SACRED SCIENCE -- THE SCIENCE OF TEHUTI

At a time when the mass of humanity remained mired in savagery and ignorance, Kemit, the "Land of the Blacks", and its high civilization, flourished. Nestled on the banks of the great river *Hapy*, in the heart of *Afru-ika*, the indigenous African people, had already developed writing, several interrelated calendrical systems, stone architecture, chemistry, metallurgy, medicine and all the arts useful and necessary to civilized life.

Millennia before Europe was a Germanic dream or China a Mongol inspiration, the Kemites constructed fifty story pyramids that remain the unsurpassed marvel of architectural achievement. They had plotted the stars, discovered heliocentricity, the Precession of the Equinoxes, atomic theory, and erected massive temples whose axes were perfectly oriented to the circumpolar stars. They formulated answers to the fundamental questions regarding the origin of being and the immortality of the soul. They mapped the geographic boundaries of the Netherworld and reduced to formulas the incantations required to navigate its confines.

The basis of their unparalleled achievement was, undeniably, their high, exacting culture. Upon this foundation of the significant contributions of their indigenous African forebears, to whom they gave unstinting recognition, was developed a science of the sacred that has been intentionally mischaracterized by European Egyptologists as mere religion.

Sacred Science was not mere religion. It was the refinement of culture based on the universal laws of NaTuRe now known as physics, biology and chemistry. But Sacred Science was much more than those scientific disciplines.

Sacred Science embraces the relationship of those disciplines to the divine format and the destiny of humanity. In its purest sense it embraces Theodicy as well.

Theodicy

Sacred Science contemplates a purpose for existence and posits a discoverable order in universal and human activities that focuses our attention on a level of individual and collective responsibility that engenders *Maat* (justice) and *Hetep* (peace).

Sacred Science was the bedrock of Kemitic civilization and the impetus of her achievement. Through it humanity divorced itself of brutishness an began the long trek toward the evolution of consciousness. It proved to be the seed from which a harmonious, powerful and cultured civilization was born.

In time organized study and application of Sacred Science became disfavored as a result of the rise of other and foreign cultures which had taken that perfected science, of which the foreigners understood little, and bastardized the teaching into the abnormality of western civilization and thought.

Through unrelenting and vicious persecution of this science and those who advocated it, and under the pretense of stamping out paganism, the world descended, predictably, into the Dark Ages -- a period of one thousand years of intellectual darkness from which the world was only extricated upon the resurrection of the same Kemitic science it had viciously stamped out.

Sacred Science fostered the greatest civilization of the ancient world. This fact alone should be sufficient, when properly understood and earnestly applied, to raise the descendants of the discoverers of this science to a level of achievement in the modern world that is worthy of its demonstrated potential.

Admittedly, the process of retrieval of the principles of Kemitic culture, as embodied in the teachings of Sacred Science, will not be easy. It will, however, reward the energies of those who so succeed far beyond their wildest imaginings.

Sacred Science then, is the corpus of knowledge and information distilled from the millennia long observation, by our ancestors, of NaTuRe in her myriad aspects, human NaTuRe in its frailty, and the vital correspondence between the two.

Sacred Science is the science of organization from fetal becoming to transference of seed as well as the concept of organization as applied to all aspects of life. It is the soul of art and the beauty of divine proportion. It is music at the level of divine vibration and literature that focuses spirit and forges will. It is a compilation of the universal and unalterable laws of harmony, number and NaTuRal order.

Sacred Science is also the divine formula by which the descendants of the Kemites can attract and focus the active power that is God to energize our individual lives and construct the power base from which to launch the cultural revolution that betokens the Age of *Hapy*

Finally, a word on the connection between knowledge and Sacred Science. It should be noted that the Kemitic word for mankind* means *the knowers*. The word science means *to know*, while something that is sacred is unpolluted and set aside or devoted to an exclusive purpose. The term Sacred Science implies, therefore, a body of unpolluted or pure knowledge that is set aside for an exclusive purpose. The purpose for which it is set aside is the attainment and maintenance of civilization in perpetuity. The Kemites apparently recognized the relationship between knowledge, survival and prosperity.

When it is further considered that the teaching of Sacred Science had both an overt and a covert purpose that focused on the control of NaTuRal forces, it will be understood that the notion of knowledge as power is ancient indeed.

In order to apply this scientific knowledge of the sacred to our lives and circumstances we must reconstruct its

---

*The Kemitic word for mankind and people is *rekhiu*. It refers to both males and females as both are depicted in the hieroglyphic spelling of the word.

fundamentals from the debris of our ancestral past. We must begin then, at the beginning.

THE SCIENCE OF TEHUTI

It has been said that the fundamentals of Sacred Science were developed by the ancient sage Tehuti in 18,000 B.C. Legend holds that he compiled 39,000 books containing the accumulated knowledge of mankind as well as the intelligence and knowledge that is properly called divine.

Tehuti was an ancient and revered Kemite who by virtue of his laudable accomplishments was deified as the *NeTeR* of divine intelligence. He was the personification of intelligence and the husband of *Maat* the Goddess of righteousness, justice and unerring accuracy. He was known by many titles, each of which memorialized a facet of his multi-faceted character. He was called the "Lord of Writing", "Master of Papyrus" "Maker of the Palette and Ink Jar" in recognition of him as inventor of the *medu NeTeR* or words of the god and writing, arts, astronomy, mathematics and the sciences in general.

Through the agency of his voice he persuaded the people of Kemit to accept the teachings of Sacred Science and was thereafter known as the "Mighty Speaker" and the "Sweet Tongued". Because he introduced the precepts that enabled the people to live together in harmony and forge alliances that advanced the common interests of the whole people he was proclaimed the *Lord of Law*, the *Begetter of Law* and the *Maker of Law*. He was also the Chief Judge of the Kemitic Supreme Court.

Tehuti was also recognized as being responsible for the bringing back, each morning, the light of the sun that had been extinguished the night before. By so doing he became the *Reckoner of Time* and the *Righteous Judge of the Cycles of the NeTeR*. He kept count of the days and insured that all cycles were carried out according to their time. His connection to cycles, the Wheel of Time and by extension, Theodicy, is obvious.

During the interminable contests between Heru and his uncle Set (see Appendix, The Night of the Teardrop.) one of Heru's eyes was violently dismembered. The impairment of his vision jeopardized his ability to see clearly and to gain victory. Tehuti reconstructed the eye and returned to Heru. This act of returning the *Oudjat* or sound eye to Heru marked the turning point in the battle and permitted positive forces, represented by Heru, to overcome, for a time, the negative forces represented by Set. For this reason Tehuti is often depicted as presenting the *Oudjat* eye to symbolize his function as the deliverer of Oudja or clarity of vision. It is for this reason that Tehuti was known as the one who caused the "brothers to go home in peace".

It was also Tehuti who, as *NeTeR* of Divine Intelligence, first distilled the fundamentals of the science of the sacred that was utilized to establish the high and incomparable civilization of the ancient Kemites. It is for this reason that Sacred Science was first known as the *Science of Tehuti*.

Modern Egyptologists scoff at the legend and its claimed antiquity. They cannot, however, deny the historical fact of the high civilization and political organization of Kemit. Nor can they deny the repeated references to an ancient and valuable collection of knowledge possessed by her and referred to in the ancient writings of the Greeks, Arabs, Hebrews and others. Moreover, the existence of the Great Pyramid of Khufu remains yet another irrefutable testimonial to the advanced level of their knowledge. That this great architectural feat remains a mystery that cannot be duplicated today, despite several millenia of so-called technological advancement, confirms that modern knowledge is, at best, incomplete.

We are able to infer from these facts that (1) the Kemites attained a high level of civilization and culture; (2) that they apparently possessed a corpus of knowledge of ancient origin; (3) that they attributed their high civilization to that corpus of knowledge; (4) the existence of that corpus of knowledge was known to others and attested in ancient

Theodicy

records; (5) that the knowledge was called the Science of Tehuti and eventually Sacred Science.

History informs us that the system of government employed by the Kemites was widely extolled as the most efficient, just and admirable by virtually all ancient observers. It is also important to note that this unique form of government continued in unbroken succession, without revolution, for longer than any political structure in the history of the world. This evidently superior form of government was true theocracy and was based on the spiritual, intellectual and philosophical observations derived from the Science of Tehuti.

The repository and dispenser of this Sacred Science was the Temple. This is as might be expected since the Temple was equipped with astronomical observatories, vast libraries and a coterie of Servants of the *NeTeR* who were specially selected and trained in the Sacred Science. Both science and government were sacerdotally administered.

We also know that this science included the Ritual of the Divine Cult and that the ritual was modified periodically in accord with the Precession of the Equinoxes. In order to fulfill this aspect of the function of the Temple employed observation of the stars (astronomy) and the interpretation of the effect of the positions of the stars (astrology) as well as the sciences derived from the observation of the Earth and its relation to numbers and measurement (geometry).

Sacred Science consists of two equally important and inseparable purposes, one was overt and the other covert. What has been described above is the overt purpose in that it deals with the maintenance of universal balance through the performance of Ritual of the Divine Cult and the orderly functioning of society through superimposition of the order and harmony of the universe as the model of individual achievement and as the model of political governance.

The covert purpose of Sacred Science, again promulgated under the auspices of the Temple, was the selection and training of individuals in the aspects of the science that dealt with the knowledge of the *Neters*. This aspect of Sacred Science is to be understood as the knowledge that the *NeTeRs* possess. It is characterized as the ability to control the active power that produces or creates things in regular recurrence and that bestows new life upon them or gives them back their youthful vigor.

The intent of this aspect of Sacred Science was to establish a corps of enlightened persons, male and female, who would, without fanfare, fear or favor, protect, maintain and transmit the sacred knowledge that formed the golden thread that guaranteed the order and balance of society, without which high civilization is impossible, in perpetuity. These enlightened ones, called the Sahu, after rigorous testing to insure their selflessness, and thereby their worthiness, were granted the keys to the full knowledge of Sacred Science in the name of and exclusively for the benefit of the larger society.

The justification for this rather clandestine aspect of the purpose of Sacred Science is based on the fact that the knowledge was considered so dynamic and potentially dangerous that it was transmitted only from mouth to ear, never written down, and then only to selected, tested and trained persons in the mystery schools of the Per Ankh or House of Life.

The knowledge imparted in the House of Life was considered potentially dangerous because it was the science of the fundamentals of power in all of its myriad manifestations. Its proper, controlled application builds strong, vibrant civilizations populated by responsible persons whose goal in life is harmony and the blessings of *hetep*. *Hetep*, or *hotep*, is the Kemitic word translated as "peace". The word actually implies the order that is manifested as the result of the attainment of perfection.

Its misapplication results in the release of destructive, decadent energy like the radioactive energy of nuclear waste. The awesome NaTuRe of knowledge contained in Sacred Science explains why it was kept from the uninitiated. Yet, to the Kemite it was not secret. It was simply difficult to

Theodicy

acquire. But all who were willing to subject themselves to the rigorous testing, preparation and selfless sacrifice demanded were admitted and transformed. The foregoing information leads us, inexorably, to further conclude that Sacred Science or the Science of Tehuti was (1) a body of knowledge distilled from the accumulated knowledge of the world; (2) that it was maintained in and promulgated under the auspices of the Temple; (3) that its purpose was simultaneously overt and covert; (4) that it served two purposes: a)the maintenance of balance and order in the universe and the collective activities of humanity; and (b) to select and train a corps of enlightened persons to maintain and transmit the sacred knowledge to insure balance and in order in society.

When the existence of this science and the fact that it was taught to selected persons in the mystery schools of the Temple and the high level of civilization born of it are juxtaposed, it becomes evident that the Science of Tehuti is a formidable corpus of knowledge worthy of investigation. When it is further considered that it represents the exclusive knowledge of our ancestors and is the embodiment of their unique culture, the necessity for serious and urgent investigation, is compelled. The fact that this corpus of knowledge was the foundation upon which the Kemites, an indigenous Black African people and our ancient ancestors, became the world's first "superpower", is viewed through the lens of our present state of powerlessness the investigation and application of this Sacred Science is absolutely mandatory if we truly seek to insure the survival and prosperity of our people and to improve the life prospects of our children and our children's children.

If the reader will permit, even if only for the sake of argument, that a Sacred Science does exist, that it can be discovered and that it offers at least the possibility of generating the power, plan and leadership we so desperately need to change our collective circumstances for the better and improve the life prospects of our children, further analysis of this science and the culture from which it derived is clearly warranted.

In times of turmoil or foreign domination our people have invariably returned to the Temple and its spiritual leadership to inspire, protect and defend them. The importance of this fact consists in the understanding that the foundation of dignity, integrity and the Power of the Will is, and can only be, derived from the steadfast adherence by a people to their Authentic Ancestral Culture. With that admonition in mind, us begin with the First Principles taught by our ancestors through their and now our, Sacred Science.

FIRST PRINCIPLES

The term First Principles is, admittedly, redundant since the word principle also means first. Nevertheless, first principles are basic, predetermined laws or assumptions regarding fundamental circumst11nces of life and the action to be taken when such circumstances arise. The most important of these may be broadly categorized as *laws of survival* and their application the *technology of survival*.

Let us clear up an unfortunate discrepancy at the outset. It is said that "self-preservation is the first law of NaTuRe". Although the statement is appealing, it superficial and misleading. It is certainly accurate to state that the survival of individuals is required for the survival of the specie. This is not the same, however, as saying that the survival of the individual is the first law of NaTuRe. Since it is axiomatic that procreation, by which survival of the specie is accomplished, is a fundamental requirement for all living things to exist, self preservation cannot be a first law.

Self-preservation cannot be a first law because if followed to its logical conclusion it would insure that the specie not survive since it is clear that the individual cannot procreate alone. It is also a dangerous proposition because an individual who sees his survival as the first and therefore most important goal necessarily places himself and his preservation before anyone else.

It is posited here and acknowledged by Sacred Science that survival of the group, whether the group be family, tribe, clan or nation, not self-preservation, is the first law of

Theodicy

NaTuRe. It is important to note this at the outset of our discussion of First Principles to focus attention on the insidious NaTuRe of current internalization by our people of the European/American preoccupation with individualism. Clearly, a people who are oppressed en masse will never find the answer to their collective problems in a strategy that requires them to advance their individual interests over those of the group. We should also consider, in this regard, that our ancestors abhorred competition and we will search, in vain for eternity and not find a single example of individualism among their ancient records.

We should not be surprised to find, as a result, that the First Principles of our ancestors focus on survival of the group. They observed that the key to survival was useful, timely and efficiently applied knowledge. The focused on three areas specifically. These were self, heritage (culture) and destructive forces (enemies).

PRINCIPLE NUMBER ONE: MAN KNOW THYSELF

Civilization is not possible, unless and until, humans are raised, by enlightenment, from their naturally selfish and counter-productive ways. The advanced state of collective cultural, material, political and social complexity, as well as progress in the arts and sciences, that is the hallmark of civilization is only obtainable by those who have been so enlightened. Thus, advancement toward civilization must begin by raising individual persons from their instinctive, animalistic tendencies. Hence, the necessity for each individual to know herself in order to control herself and thereby control society.

The Kemites believed and taught that knowledge of self was of primary importance because the self is the first thing over which we can and must exercise the power of control. Such knowledge permits us to observe that we have power to control ourselves and compels the following conclusions: (1) we are innately powerful, that is power in the form of Sacred Essence, resides in each of us; (2) therefore, power itself may be controlled; (3) knowledge is superior because it is by knowledge that power in controlled; (4) self-knowledge is, therefore, the foundation of all knowledge and the means by which all power may be controlled.

Self-knowledge begins with the realization of our innate animalistic tendencies and the need to control them in order to advance toward civilized life for individuals and civilization for the people collectively. As a result the mastery of passions is of primary importance. It was further believed that when passions were controlled the energy normally expended its pursuit could be converted to unlimited power to be used for other and more productive purposes to that end emphasis was placed on the Ten Virtues that released the self from the Ten Fetters. The first and second of the Ten Virtues were the *control of thought* and the *control of action*, respectively.

CONTROL OF THOUGHT

Control is itself a power. It is the power to direct or regulate. The power of self-control is discipline. By the control of thought is sought the discipline of the mind. The mind is like a garden whose flowers are matured thoughts. As one would cultivate a garden the mind too must be cultivated. Thought may also be likened to a seed that once planted in the garden germinates to bear fruit of its kind. Each seed-thought planted in the garden of the mind will also bear fruit of its kind. Uncultured seed-thoughts are like weeds that grow rapidly and, if left unattended, suffocate the cultivated seed-thoughts in the garden of the mind. Cultivated seed-thought will not grow if it is sown among weeds.

At this level the control of thought is the exclusive power of the individual. It is an internal process that is self contained and operates without the assistance or intervention of others. It is, therefore, individual and exclusive and its impact is internal. When the power of thought is transformed into action it becomes dispersed and effects the actions of others.

Theodicy

CONTROL OF ACTION

The control of action is the second level of control implicated by the First Principle "know thyself". Its importance lies in its potential effect on society. Though it is often said that people act without thinking the fact remains that human action is always preceded by thought. Thought is the impetus of action.

The most destructive ideas are only potentially so. It is when they are acted on that the effect transcends the individual and has societal consequences. It is for this reason that control of action was the second of the Ten Virtues.

The Ten Virtues were part of the initiatory program of the Kemitic Temple. The remaining eight Virtues are: (3) a demonstrated and firm purpose; (4) evidence of spirituality; (5) evidence of a spiritual calling; (6) evidence of a life's mission; (7) absence of resentment when persecuted; (8) confidence in the power of the teacher; (9) confidence in your own power to learn; (10) evidence of readiness for initiation.

Society precedes civilization and is impossible unless people can be enjoined to refrain from activities that impede order and efficiency. Many of our natural inclinations, based as they are on instinctive and animalistic passions, would be destructive of society and prevent entirely the attainment of civilization if acted upon. The person who thinks of committing murder or mayhem threatens society only potentially. If he permits his thought to be manifested in action it is then that society becomes tragically involved.

In a very real sense then, the control of action is the manifestation of the individual's recognition of his or her responsibility to others and to societal order and advancement. In the absence of such control society remains, hopelessly, at level of the uncivilized.

PRINCIPLE NUMBER TWO: MAN KNOW THY HERITAGE

Heritage is the combination of birthright and tradition. It is that which belongs to a person by right of birth. But, it is more than material inheritance. As tradition it is a mode of thought and behavior passed down to a people by their forebears and followed by them from generation to generation. It is, therefore, closely linked to culture.

Knowledge of one's heritage is of tremendous importance to survival for several reasons. To be complete, knowledge of self must include knowledge of one's origins. Not merely in the sense of creation (a question that is, in any event, unanswerable) but of kinship. Heritage is the intimate knowledge of familial relationship magnified through the lens of antiquity. Heritage is, at one and the same time, personal history and the umbilical connectedness that creates belonging and desire for inclusion.

Heritage is also the placement of beings in time and the expression of their obligations and responsibilities in life and society. It is the beacon of pride, nobility and dignity. It is the spark of achievement and the fire of collective ambition. It is the burden of the past that is simultaneously the hope of the future. Heritage is the anchor of life and its fixity. Inspiration, goal-orientation and motivation are its perpetual partners.

In the vast universe that imposes the recognition of our comparative smallness, heritage counters that we are great and powerful precisely because of its magical influence. Heritage is our connectedness to a line of ancestors whose origins are so ancient as to be obscured in the mists of antiquity. It ennobles and strengthens our determination and resolve. We survive because of the inestimable value of their ancient yet timely traditions.

Heritage teaches that it our obligation to continue those traditions, for whatever the level of their nobility they are ours. We cannot help but add our contributions to them that the chain of existence will remain unbroken and be strengthened by our having forged new links and joined them to the old.

Heritage and tradition form the chain of culture whose links in time are the individuals of each new generation. To the extent that these individuals are aware of the existence of the chain and their place in it, the chain will continue as the anchor of our stability. Heritage is, therefore, that from which we cannot be separated without adverse and debilitating consequences.

In importance of and reliance upon heritage and tradition is evidenced in a people by their use of myth and the practice of so-called ancestor worship. The Kemites were no exception. It should be noted here that the Greek word *mythos* derives from the Kemitic *mdt,* meaning the content of words. The essential meaning of the word, however, is *that which is given from mouth to ear.*

MYTH

Societies with strong oral traditions, such a those of the African continent, have always expressed the fundamental realities of life through what has come to be called myth. Because current usage defines myth as fiction or half-truth the word is misleading as it detracts from the significance of the concept as it was understood by the people who used it.

To the peoples of the world who developed and transmitted the myth over time considered it to be the true and unquestionable history of their origins. When myth is seen as fact it is deserving of equality of status with history as a statement of fact.

Myth views reality as a totality. It is more than fact, it is the symbolic expression of the perception of a people based on their unique view of the reality of the world.

The purpose of the myth is to refer a group of homogeneous and interdependent people back to their ancient beginnings. By doing so myth connects people to the reservoir of knowledge from which their current society has evolved and to which they can refer in times of crisis and uncertainty. It is a golden thread of immeasurable strength that binds the people together.

Myth are most often stories about individuals who have lived lives that are, in some specific way, exemplary and worthy of remembrance. Myth, therefore, strengthens tradition by documentation of the ancient reality upon which tradition and heritage are based.

Myth is also the story of symbols. As such it is a form of thinking. The symbolic story relates to a set of ideas about people and events combined to form a symbol system that demonstrates not only history but also a hidden and valuable truth.

The myth, therefore, expressed the First Principles of the society by example of the activities of their ancestors. The preeminent example of mythology (the science of myth) is the Kemitic legend of *Asar* and *Aset*, called in the Greek Osiris and Isis.

The legend is of extremely ancient origin. It is attested in all periods of Kemitic history as a true account of the lives of historical beings. *Asar*, known as the "Good King" and his wife *Aset*, known as the "Divine Mother" were revered as the original ancestors of all Kemites.

The legend tells of the life and times of the man who civilized Kemit and the world, and of his lovely and compassionate wife. It is the story of the eternal battle between positive and negative forces and provides encouragement that in the end balance and harmony will always prevail.

The Legend of *Asar* and *Aset* clearly fulfills the criteria of the myth. It is a true, historical account of a real person(s) whose life was, in some specific way, exemplary and worth of continued remembrance. Through the legend the people re strengthened in their traditions and apprised of the noble heritage in which they all share.

The Legend of *Asar* and *Aset* also relates the basis of a set of ideas through symbols that become part of a symbol system that gives meaning to the things of the past and explains their present value and application. Suffice it to say that this legend is the Kemitic myth which served to present First Principles as they relate to heritage.

PRINCIPLE NUMBER THREE: MAN KNOW THY ENEMY

First Principles are basic, pre-determined laws regarding the fundamental circumstances of life and the action to be taken when such circumstances arise. *The underlying concept upon which all First Principles and life itself are predicated is, in a word, survival.*

If one is diligent in pursuit of self knowledge and heritage the chances of survival are dramatically increased, it not guaranteed. *Survival requires security.* Security implies safety, protection and defense. Safety is freedom from danger; protection is that which shields from danger; and defense is the power to guard against danger. Interestingly, the word danger derives from and is closely related to the concept of absolute power. The root of the word danger means master and was originally understood as the power of harm.

Survival requires, therefore, self-determination or will (as the terms are defined in this work) and security against the power of harm.

THE POWER OF HARM

The power of harm can decimate or render extinct. It may be of either human or non-human origin. The non-human category of harm includes, but is not limited to, disease, natural disasters and animal predators. The human category is obvious. Both these categories of harm are forces that are destructive of survival and require eternal vigilance. Each is so prevalent as to have required First Principles regarding them. To this end principles were developed regarding animals (their behavior, dangerousness, territory, etc.) as well as natural disaster such as periodic floods. The development of the art of medicine was also an outgrowth of this category of principles. (The subject of medicine in ancient Kemit is beyond the scope of this work. Suffice it to say that the Kemites are widely recognized as having developed the art of medicine and the Greeks and other learned it from them).

The human category was less amenable to codification because, unlike the others, it was characterized by hostility. In each case, however, the impact of destructive forces could be controlled by some form of adaptation aided by accurate knowledge. Human hostility was, however, far more problematic because of its unpredictable NaTuRe and because of the element of deceit it involved.

THE ORIGIN OF DECEIT

There are two principal forms of deceit: utilitarian and malicious. Utilitarian deceit is practiced by some animals to gain advantage in the acquisition of food or reproduction and seems to be instinctive. Malicious deceit is characteristic of human beings alone.

Whether in animals or human beings, deceit is a behavior pattern. In humans such behavior may have originated from something as simple as a smile. Facial expressions are the long distance communicators of intention. By the simple flexing of the muscles of the face we communicate that our intentions are friendly, ferocious, hostile or even indifferent. Each of these facial expressions sends a message that is interpreted by another person who then responds accordingly.

The smile is inherently disarming. Perhaps it was the first person who discovered that another person could be caused to drop her guard and could be more easily taken advantage of by flashing a big smile, who was the originator of the human variety of deceit. Following a sufficient number of encounters in which persons were deceived to their material, or mortal disadvantage, two conclusions would have been virtually compelled: (10 that a smiling person may have altogether unfriendly intentions; and (2) that to judge another's intentions by the presence or absence of a smile was to court danger by uncertainty. The overall conclusion would be that, at best, reliance on facial expressions as an accurate indicator of another's intentions was an exercise in futility. Because of the difficulty of determining, with any degree of certainty, whether a stranger was hostile or not, the concept of the enemy was, in time, arrived at.

Theodicy

The connection between hostility and enemies is not only apparent, it is also linguistic and historical. It is more than coincidence that the words are cognates. Enemy implies one who is unfriendly or hostile to another. In ancient times the word enemy literally meant hostile. The word hostile, on the other hand, means unfriendly, warlike, and characteristic of an enemy. Not surprisingly, the word hostile derives from the Latin *hostilis* meaning enemy.

When the concepts of enemy and hostility are understood and combined, danger is clearly implied. This danger, which is the power of harm, mandated the First Principle to know your enemy.

KNOWLEDGE OF THE ENEMY

Knowledge of the enemy is subdivided into two facets: (1) identity; and (2) overall characteristics. The first of these is the simplest because it is categorical. *Anyone not a member of the ancestral clan was, by that fact alone, an enemy.* The method was simple and efficient. If the person was not a member of the clan, smile notwithstanding, defensive measures were immediately taken. The second facet required reconnaissance. Information regarding the enemy's number, location, weapons, habits, strength and even courage had to be observed, recorded and transmitted.

This information became the basis of the concept of military preparedness that is implicit in the ideas of safety, protection and defense. Defense is the science of protection aimed at the prevention of attack by enemies and which is comprised of strategy and tactics. Knowledge about one's enemy is, therefore, prerequisite to the development of military strategy. Though essentially defensive, such thinking must include offensive strategies as well. Only a fool, or a traitor, would sit idle while his enemy marshals resources and strength to be used against him. An enemy who grows in strength represents *imminent danger*. By this reasoning pre-emptive attack becomes a necessity that is strategically defensive and, at the same time, tactically offensive. Survival and security, its counterpart, provide the justification for such attack. Together these components define the constant armed conflict between enemies.

Theodicy

CHAPTER NINE:

THE NEW CULTURAL IMPERATIVE

The New Cultural Imperative teaches that a people without culture will never rise above the level of abject survival and foreign domination for the reasons that:

(1) culture is both the mooring and foundation of collective achievement;

(2) the cohesive, binding energy that is prerequisite to achievement and prosperity of a group of people is virtually impossible without a cultural foundation; and

(3) culture is unique, specific and developed by progenitors to teach the tools and technology of survival, prosperity and longevity to their progeny.

A people without knowledge of their own Authentic Ancestral Culture are forced to use their collective energy to perpetuate and advance the culture of others.

An imperative is simply a command that one is obligated to obey. In this case the imperative is the command of our ancient ancestors that we adhere to the teachings developed over thousands of years and richly preserved in Temples, monuments and hieroglyphs throughout our ancient homeland. In these living Books of Life and Culture they have painstakingly recorded what we must know and do and how we must think and act, not merely to survive, but the attain and maintain the greatness of spirit, accomplishment and civilization that derives from the steadfast application of their teachings and the *Power of the African Mind*.

We must always be mindful that this life-giving, empire-building legacy has been bequeathed to us because their blood courses through our veins. We are their immortality. Through us, their children, they continue to live and we and our children continue to live more abundantly.

Since an imperative is a command it carries a sanction for failure to obey. The sanction, in this case, is historically self-evident. It is slavery, segregation, disintegration, genocide and extinction. The sanction is self-imposed, and self-perpetuating. The longer the imperative is ignored the worse becomes the plight. We are truly prisoners who hold the keys to our cells.

The New Cultural Imperative impresses upon those who have attained *Oudja* or clarity of vision, and who are, with few exceptions, the only ones who recognize the command, the necessity for presently effected, radical change in order to avert the planned genocide of our people.

The New Cultural Imperative also dictates that a master plan by which the planned genocide will be averted and how our cultural rebirth and political resuscitation will become reality, is necessary and itself, imperative.

In order to act on the *New Cultural Imperative* we must accurately understand the necessity that compels it. We must understand the elements of genocide in order see them when they appear.

THE COMPELLED NECESSITY

African Americans believe that things are getting better. Some of us believe that we stand head over heels above the condition of our ancestors. Michael Jordan, Oprah Winfrey, Bill Cosby (Editor's Note: since this writing Mr. Cosby has fallen from grace and is now considered *persona non grata* among those whose culture he helped to emulate) and others of their mean accomplishment may find solace in that misleading notion but for the overwhelming majority of our people the notion is as misleading as it is untrue.

It may be simply stated, without fear of contradiction, that we are virtually as powerless today as we were during the days of chattel slavery. In fact, it may be persuasively argued that we are worse off when it is considered that at least slavery provided full employment.

A brief analysis of the primary indicators of economic stability and advancement show that we still have the highest unemployment rate; lowest per capita income; the highest incarceration rate; highest infant mortality; the

Theodicy

lowest educational achievement; the lowest percentage of savings, stocks, bonds and land holdings per capita; lowest number of professionals, doctors, lawyers, ph.d's; the highest rate of AIDS infection, drug addiction, tuberculosis, diabetes and hypertension; the highest homicide rate and the lowest life expectancy. In short, we are no better off than some so-called Third World countries in spite of the fact that we reside in the wealthiest and most powerful nation on the planet. Those who conclude that this sorry state of affairs is somehow indicate of progress are more than misguided, they are *traitors*. For the record, a traitor is simply one who betrays. Betrayal is the act of handing over to the enemy by deceit.

Equally treacherous and disloyal are those who parrot the argument that our economic and political position of dependence is somehow the result of lack of initiative or inability to put the past behind us. They assume, having been taught to do so, that the forces of private, governmental and institutional White supremacy have played no part in this centuries-old psychodrama. The depth of their misunderstanding is the benchmark of their inability to see clearly. It is this myopia that obscures the nature of our problem and, in turn, causes us to fail to recognize the *Compelled Necessity*.

These unfortunate impediments aside, compulsion, by definition, may not be ignored. To be compelled is to be forced to act. The compulsion is to do that which is necessary for our collective survival and to insure that our children survive and prosper.

The Compelled Necessity operates as an enforced flash-point. It is best understood as the critical moment when the collective awareness of impending disaster occurs. Without this compulsion the possibility that African Americans will awaken from their potentially fatal lethargy is virtually non-existent.

The Compelled Necessity is a defense mechanism that forces effective and timely response to the threat of annihilation. This defense mechanism is activated by the occurrence of any combination of the following events: (1) the enactment of laws that have disparate impact on the African American community and result in the mass incarceration of African Americans disproportionate to their numbers in the population and to the numbers of persons involved in the particular targeted activity;

(2) the imposition of Draconian penalties as punishment for conduct that is non-violent and victimless and which is applied most severely to African Americans;

(3) active retrenchment in the area of civil rights, voting rights, and public assistance;

(4) increased, racially disproportionate, use of capital punishment;

(5) decreased funding for educational opportunity;

(6) nationwide appointment of "conservative" judges and prosecutors;

(7) appointment of conservative federal judges, including justices to the United States Supreme Court, who are advocates of a "law and order" agenda;

(8) passage of laws that impede access to the courts or limit the amount of damages a jury may award;

(9) judicial resort to unpublished opinions and one word affirmances;

(10) restriction or elimination of bail pending trial;

(11) increased expenditures on law enforcement combined with the deployment of law enforcement agents in ever increasing numbers in the African American community, ostensibly to protect us from ourselves;

12) increase in the number of hate-mongering white supremacist organizations, lynchings, draggings and other racially motivated hate-crimes, including the bombing of African American houses of worship;

(13) increased sterilization, abortion and birth control efforts targeted at the African American community;

(14) increased foster care assignments of African American children resulting from state interventions for alleged drug abuse or alcohol use or addiction;

(15) increased incarceration of juveniles for extended periods creating increased numbers of "state babies";

(16) lowering of the age at which juveniles may be treated as adults in the criminal justice system;

(17) increase in the number of African American woman being incarcerated for non-violent, victimless crimes;

(18) government declared wars intended to be fought on domestic soil and against its own citizens, i.e., the War on Drugs;

When any combination of these events exist the necessity for defensive maneuvers is compelled. To sit idle while all of these events take place is suicidal, and cannot be justified by any claim that things are getting better. There can be no question, at this late date, as to the existence of all these factors. The war against the African American family and community of families is apparent and undeniable. Whether it is recognized to be the result of mere happenstance or the result of a planned, concerted effort on the part of our enemies is immaterial. Under the foregoing circumstances the necessity for immediate action on the part longstanding circumstances of those of us who breathe the fire and are concerned for the future of our children is compelling indeed.

THE ELEMENTS OF GENOCIDE

Genocide is the use of deliberate, systematic measures such as killing, bodily or mental injury, unlivable conditions and prevention of births, calculated to bring about the extermination of a racial, political or cultural group or to destroy the language, religion or culture of a group. Genocide must be planned. It cannot and does not occur randomly or by chance. In its most virulent form it includes the extermination of culture as well as people. Genocide may be accomplished over long periods of time or in one generation.

Racial genocide is the most well-known, not necessarily the most prevalent, because of the prominent historical examples are of this sort. In this category the attempted extermination of Native Americans and the actual extermination of the Tasmanians immediately come to mind. It is significant that each was carried out by Europeans or Caucasians against non-white peoples.

In the case of the Native Americans the attempted extermination occurred on the North American continent at the hands of the United States Government, under the auspices of the United States Constitution and as official policy. It represents perhaps the most appropriate example in the context of our present analysis.

From the standpoint of the European the extermination of the Native American was necessary to acquire his land and to fulfill something called "manifest destiny'. The existence of the Native American as the lawful inhabitant of the North American continent presented problems for the European -- they were useless and in the way. There were many ways to maintain peaceful co-existence with the Native Americans but these seem to never have been considered. The allure of millions of acres of undeveloped, fertile, virgin land seemed to rule out all but the most drastic measures.

It should also be remembered that the extermination of the Native American was part of a two-pronged strategy. The second and equally necessary prong was the enslavement of the African. It would not be enough to merely acquire the millions of acres of land. Some means of cultivating it had to be found or it would be worthless. The backbreaking, unrelenting task of clearing, planting, harvesting, building and maintenance require manpower. This arduous task fell to the lot of the African. That they were kidnapped, at gun point, and brought to these shores in chains was apparently of little moment to the good European Christians who enslaved them.

Theodicy

Because the land was so vast, the task so tremendous, millions of slaves were required. That perhaps 100 million Africans were killed in the infamous triangular slave trade, again, was of no concern to the Christian benefactors who boasted of having saved their sub-human charges from a barbarous and savage existence far worse than that of the "Benevolent enslavement" in America.

As the European interloper's enterprises prospered in America and the number of European immigrants increased, additional African slaves were required to labor in served of the White man's destiny that was made manifest by virtue of the existence of the land and his greedy desire for it.

Predictably, and in short order, African slaves outnumbered the free White population is some areas and were dangerously numerous in nearly all the others. It seems axiomatic that one can rest easy around those who he has brutalized, raped and enslaved. This simple and predictable fact gave rise to the concept of the African as the "internal enemy", a threat that became more real and more dangerous with the birth or importation of each new slave.

Thomas Jefferson, himself a slaveholder, despite his lofty pronouncements about the equality of man and the inalienability of certain rights, remained troubled· that Divine Justice might someday actually prevail. Jefferson also noted that Africans and Europeans could never live together as equals in the United States because the European would always fear that if the African ever became powerful he would do the European what he had done to them. The author of the Declaration of Independence also noted that Africans would never forget what had been done to them by the European which memory would prevent the African from ever trusting them.

The European's fear of retaliation by the African explains why it has been the longstanding policy of the United States, its people and its government, sometimes written sometimes not, to find and utilize every conceivable means to keep the African American in an unarmed, subservient and powerless position under the direct observation and control of the European power structure.

Objectivity and reasonableness are the first casualties of fear. It was the fear of the overwhelming numbers of Africans in the South that explains, more than anything else, the vicious, brutal, unrelenting policies, both private and government al, to prevent, at all costs, the accumulation of economic and political power in the hands of African Americans who . rapidly became the "internal enemy" of Jefferson's nightmares.

Fear of the "internal enemy" was, for a time, tempered by the necessity for his labor. The result was a policy that permitted him to work but denied him anything that would enable him to change his position of abject poverty and servitude. In short, the threat of the "internal enemy" was softened and made more tolerable because of his utility.

It seems apparent that the measure of value of a thing, (African slaves were legally things) is at least partially, its usefulness for a particular purpose. Conversely, when a thing is useless for its intended purpose it becomes, more or less valueless and even burdensome if care and maintenance is required once its usefulness has ceased.

Aristotle is credited with having said that when the shuttle works by itself the slave will not be necessary. His words were an admonition *against* improvement of the shuttle.

In the twenty-first century the descendants of African slaves are no longer useful to the American economy. *We have outlived our usefulness.* The problem is that we still represent the threat of the "internal enemy". The threat looms large, is more foreboding and dangerous now because our numbers are significantly greater. More ominous, however, is the fact that the present generation of "internal enemy" are increasingly more violent, disillusioned and disdainful of any authority they do not respect. The "internal enemy" is now an African American male between the ages of 14 and 30 who is less fearful than his forebears because of his greater historical distance from the atrocities of slavery,

Theodicy

blatant Jim Crowism, lynchings and the activities of the Ku Klux Klan. He is young, unafraid and increasingly strident and threatening.

The government's options for dealing with this growing problem are few in number. It can accept the African American as a full-fledged citizen of this republic with all the rights, privileges and emoluments that go along with it, including but not limited to, reparations for the centuries of labor and wrongful deaths of generations of our children, or he can simply *eliminate* the problem.

History teaches us that genocide has been repeatedly recognized by the European as a viable option when he feels threatened by real or imagined enemies and the when the enemy in question is *unorganized* and *unarmed*.

When it is further understood that the endemic European view, born of centuries of underserved privilege on the one hand, and inflated, distorted racial pride on the other, that the improvement of the African's economic or social position will necessarily and inevitably supplant or significantly undermine their position, the recent events occurring in the United States take on the contours of an ominous plan, the reality of which African Americans ignore at their peril.

The European has maintained the dual posture of preventing the rise of a national African power as a foreign policy objective and the rise of a Black Messiah, domestically. Of course, a Black Messiah linked to a national African power is to be prevented at all costs.

We must recognize, at long last and based on historical precedent, that the European, whether of the continent or American variety, will never accept the African or the African American as an equal. Nor will he repay the multi-trillion dollar debt owed to the African and African American which has accumulated, with interest, for past atrocities of slave trade and unfair treatment since. His only viable option is to *eliminate* the source of the threat both domestically and abroad. It follows that the only possible option is genocide. When the elements of genocide are known and understood they signal the apparent implementation of the final settlement of the Negro problem and the call to arms for a people who have no reason to believe in the good will, trustworthiness or honesty of the European.

THE FINAL SETTLEMENT

The final settlement of the Negro problem and genocide must be understood as virtually synonymous concepts. Genocide is the genus while final settlement is the specie.

The final settlement, like genocide, includes three components that are being used quite effectively at present. The first is the prevention of births. This component includes high infant mortality rates among the targeted group as a result of non-existent or sub-standard pre-natal care; free abortions; paid sterilization; inexplicable high rates of prostate cancer; and mass incarceration which is actually a forced separation of the sexes.

The second component is drug related. It includes the impairment of mental faculties of the members of the targeted group as in their planned addiction as a result of government orchestrated or condoned importation and distribution of heroin and cocaine in African American communities throughout the United States. Another dimension of the second component involves the mass incarceration of the targeted group by selective prosecution for drug offenses as well as the simple expedient of making drug amounts necessary for trafficking offenses so minute as to turn all drug users into drug traffickers effectively making the local user an *El Chapo*.

The third component entails the subjection of the targeted group to conditions of life that are intended to cause physical destruction of the group. The conditions of life in America's ghettos and impoverished rural areas is the result of centuries of government planned and orchestrated criminal neglect.

The fourth component is a form of biological warfare that includes, but is not limited to, Acquired Immune Deficiency

Syndrome (AIDS), and perhaps prostate cancer. It should be remembered that the AIDS pandemic, curiously, affects and infects mainly Africans whether indigenous or of the Diaspora.

The Final Settlement of the Negro Problem implicates a government conspiracy of mammoth proportions. Whether the conspiracy can be proven is unimportant. The statistical possibility of the components of the final settlement being present at one time is all but impossible. In any event, no one can logically argue the non-existence of the components.

DIGRESSION OF CONSPIRACY THEORY

It will surely be argued that this section, if not the entire book, is reminiscent of yet another "conspiracy theory" that blames our problems on a group of unidentified co-conspirators lurking behind every one of our myriad social problems. The author makes no such assertion. This fact notwithstanding, the possibility of the claim being raised by my anticipated detractors requires a brief statement regarding conspiracy theories generally.

To conspire means to *breathe together*. By this definition alone it is clear that the United States Government and its agents have historically breathed together the design and implement political and social systems whose primary goal was to enslave and then segregate African Americans to insure white supremacy and perpetual second-class citizenship of former slaves and their descendants.

It must be understood at the outset that a conspiracy against African Americans does and has always existed. But, *the conspiracy is not one of individuals but of the system of laws by which this country is governed*. It is the law itself, from the high spirited, lofty and hypocritical pronouncements of the United States Constitution to local ordinances in every far-flung corner of the country, that conspire against the African American in his every attempt to gain economic, social and political parity with the European majority. It is found hidden in the laws that govern every operation of government from the Supreme Court of the United States to the cop on the Harlem beat. Enlightened African Americans know and have always known it. It is only the European majority enshrined in their ivory towers of privilege that deny it. Their indignant denials are, however, most disingenuous. The proof is found in the law of conspiracy itself.

Observers who denigrate "conspiracy theory", particularly when it is advanced to explain the plight of African Americans, invariably ask for the substantive proof, the "smoking gun" of the conspiracy. Their arguments lack merit and are, therefore, unavailing. The law of conspiracy amply illustrates the point.

If the alleged conspiracy against African Americans were federal indictments, the proof necessary for conviction beyond a reasonable doubt, under the laws of the United States or the several states, would not only be sufficient to sustain conviction but would be considered overwhelming.

Conspiracy is known to the law as the "prosecutor's darling" precisely because it requires so little by way of proof. This is particularly true if it is a drug conspiracy that is to be proven beyond a reasonable doubt.

In order to prove a drug conspiracy the government must prove (1) an agreement between two or more persons to engage in conduct that violates a federal drug law; and (2) the defendant's willful joinder in that agreement. Nothing more need be proven. The key is what is considered sufficient proof of the two elements. Not surprisingly, since the vast majority of drug conspiracy offenses are prosecuted against African Americans, circumstantial evidence is all that is necessary for conviction. Circumstantial evidence is defined as testimony not based on actual personal knowledge or observation of the facts in controversy, but of other facts from which deductions are drawn, showing indirectly the facts sought to be proved. Circumstantial evidence is no evidence at all. It is a bunch of inferences that may or may not be accurate.

Theodicy

In drug conspiracy cases the connection between a defendant and the alleged conspiracy need only be slight.

The members of the conspiracy do not have to know each other or even know of each other. Moreover, direct evidence of the agreement, or meeting or collective planning is not required. The point is that conspiracy, as a matter of law, requires little by way of proof to indict or convict.

It follows that any requirement that "conspiracy theory" be proved by a standard more demanding than that required to send a young African American to prison for the rest of his or her productive and reproductive life is no more than intellectual dishonesty and legal obscenity.

African Americans do not need proof of the existence of a conspiracy. The very circumstances of our everyday lives prove it. The time has passed when we will deterred by the specious requirement that we provide proof. We submit the same level of circumstantial evidence that would be sufficient to send us to prison for life for conspiracy.

SECTION THREE:
VISION

CHAPTER TEN:
THE TRIAD OF VISIONARY POWER

The Triad of Visionary Power is comprised of three interrelated and equally important components. These are *Oudja* or clarity of vision, *Critical Thinking* and the *Intelligence-Of-The-Heart*.

The overall concept of vision examined in this section is based upon the understanding and application of these concepts to the quest for empowerment implicated by Theodicy and the Wheel of Time. Each of the components assists the other in creating the mental framework prerequisite to formulation of the plan that will extricate us from the precariousness of our present dilemma. *Oudja* allows us to clearly perceive the information with which our minds are constantly bombarded. Critical Thinking permits us to analyze the information. *Intelligence-of-the-Heart* enables us to see the entire picture by supplying the only direct, unimpaired information at our disposal. Together these components amount to visionary power, without which the people will surely perish.

OUDJA - CLARITY OF VISION

The future is, at best, a possibility. The contours, dimensions and realities of tomorrow's landscape are malleable, susceptible to alteration and change. The certainty that tomorrow will arrive does not assure what it will be like when it does. All we know is that when it arrives it will be the present and that as a result, the time is always now.

The future is, in a very fundamental sense, based upon circumstances and conditions that preceded and perhaps precipitated it. In one respect then, the future can be seen as an if/then equation that is variable depending or pre-existing conditions. If the present condition of a people is one of power and supremacy, then it may be logically predicted that their privileged condition will continue in the immediate future. But the past is not always an accurate predictor of the future precisely because the future is a *possibility*.

A person who is alive today could be logically predicted to be alive tomorrow and forever because he has never been dead in the past. The person's entire life is that of one who has only experienced life. But uncertainty is a fundamental element of possibility. Possibility, or that which can be, is based on probability, or that which is likely to be.

The Principle of Conditional Probability holds that each time a coin is tossed there will only be two possibilities (heads and tails) but only one outcome (heads or tails), regardless of how many times either heads or tails has appeared in the past.

The theory of probability is also concerned, however, with equally likely possibilities and how they relate to a desired outcome. In order to determine the likelihood of a particular outcome the number of outcomes must be envisioned.

Vision is, in the sense used in this work, the ability to accurately envision the numerous possible outcomes of the human condition. If it is true that the future is a possibility, it must also be true that awareness of the number of possibilities will enable us to reach some conclusions as to the probability of a particular, desired outcome.

The future is not engraved in stone. It can be changed or altered in accord with its possibilities. People have been known to have precognitive abilities as uncanny as they are unexplained. Apparently, the future is concrete enough to be perceived and changeable enough to be susceptible to alteration. It follows that the future may be altered if (1) its possibilities may be accurately determined and (2) the collective will of the people is powerful and focused enough to change it. The first step toward changing the future is, therefore, to cultivate the ability to see its possibilities clearly.

It has been said that without vision a people are doomed to perish. The statement, taken as accurate, is incomplete. It neglects to define the vision that is so necessary to the survival of the people. It also fails to instruct about how best to attain it.

Theodicy

Vision is the ability, hence the power, to see the possibilities and potential of times, places and people. It is the talent for seeing the reality that is contained in the seed that is unapparent on its face yet resident in the seed nonetheless. It is more than the eyes behold. It is the combination of life experience, human NaTuRe and the gift of intuition. It is that which finds release in the stirring of the energy in motion that i born of suffering, pain and humiliation.

Vision is the receipt of a permanent spiritual communication that is the lifeline, the vital force of human advancement. Though perpetual and ever present it appears intermittently because its revelation always awaits those persons who have cultivated the ability to tune into a frequency that yet defies scientific evaluation of acceptance.

It is however, apparent that a civilization bereft of the beneficial quality of vision is doomed to failure when it attempts to direct the course of human affairs on the basis of scientific knowledge alone. Western civilization has shunned the guidance of such vision and has, as a result, created the tools of its own destruction. Those who have by choice or compelled necessity adopted its spiritless approach to life will likewise suffer its spiritless fate.

At a time when the fortunes of Africans, in America and abroad, seem to diminish in inverse proportion to the effort we put forth, it becomes critical that we seek to understand how to cultivate vision as an important tool in our arsenal of weapons assembled to insure that we, nor our children, shall cease to exist on this Earth.

Vision, whether in the mundane or spiritual sense, is always dependent on clarity. To the ancient Kemites the concept of clear vision was known as *Oudja*.

Oudja is a complex concept, but it's essential meaning is derived from the Eye of Heru, also known as the *Oudjat* or Sound Eye. The hieroglyphic determinative of the word reproduces the distinctive markings of the peregrine falcon, a bird of prey sacred to *Heru*. The Kemites believed that bird to be the perfect symbol of clarity of vision for two reasons:

First, the falcon was believed to be the only animal capable of staring directly into the blazing sun without being blinded by it and thereby evidencing a direct, piercing vision that cannot be distracted or impaired. Second, they utilized the dissected Eye of *Heru* to represent the six fractions of the whole, implying the ability to accurately reduce things to their constituent parts which ability is a vital aspect of discernment and perception.

As the Sound Eye, *Oudja* relates to the Legend of *Asar* and *Aset* in which Heru, the avenging son of the Good King *Asar*, suffered the loss of an eye at the hand of his uncle *Set* during one of their interminable combats. *Heru* would have lost the battle were it not for the intervention of *Tehuti* who healed the eye and made it sound. This divine act of the restoration of clear vision proved to be the turning point in the battle. When *Heru* was able to see clearly he was able to defeat *Set*, avenge his father's death and restore peace and prosperity to the Land of Kemit.

Oudja is the attainment of a level of understanding and clear vision that is marked by direct, undistracted, unimpaired perception, at which the individual perceives accurately the purpose of life and her destiny in it. It is precisely at that point that the individual is raised from a dead level of confusion and misunderstanding to the living perpendicular of *Maat*.

Oudja is the method by which we control our thought and ultimately our actions. The ultimate goal of *Oudja*, however, is the attainment of collective clarity of vision.

Oudja necessarily implies two levels of vision: (1) the faculty of sight in the mundane sense known as perception; and (2) in the spiritual sense of divine intuition. An individual or group that attains *Oudja* is rewarded with the rare ability to see the world clearly and is thereby enabled to make intelligent life choices for themselves and those whose life and fortunes they are responsible.

Theodicy

In the specific case of African Americans, the attainment of *Oudja* is equivalent to the healing and restoration of the Eye of *Heru* -- the turning point in the battle.

Oudja is, therefore, comprised of two interrelated, though distinct functions: these are *perception* and *intuition*.

The relative value of knowledge is determined by its accuracy. Accurate, timely knowledge, put to efficient use is powerful. Accurate knowledge frees the mind, inaccurate knowledge enslaves it. The accuracy of our knowledge is dependent on the accuracy of our perception. *Perception is, therefore, the doorkeeper of knowledge.*

The influence of our environment is constant and cannot be overemphasized. It is by virtue of the stimulation of our environment that we can conclude that we are living, sentient beings. But it is also true that we never directly experience our environment. It is through our senses that we are informed of the NaTuRe and reality of the world around us.

We are essentially energetic beings imprisoned or contained in material bodies. We reside in material shells fashioned with openings that permit information to enter but we never get to experience that information first hand. We spend the course of our entire lives acting upon information that we receive, at best, second hand.

It is generally assumed that the information relayed to us via the senses is direct and unaltered. That is, we believe that the world is actually as we perceive it. The reality, however, is that the information we receive and subsequently act upon is indirect and manipulated. It is, in the truest sense of the word, inaccurate because inexact and imprecise.

Our senses are susceptible to trickery. Ask the masters of prestidigitation. Their conclusion that the hand is quicker than the eye is more than a term of art, sight is, in fact, the least reliable of the senses because it is so easily deceived. Yet we frequently hear understanding referred to as seeing. Sight is only partially dependent on the eyes. Dreaming is a perfect example of the fact.

In the dream state there are actually no images or light from the outside world. What we .see is actually being seen by the mind. The dream is visual, but what we see does not exist in the outside world. Our eyes certainly assist us in seeing but they are not absolutely necessary for us to see. What the senses do then is to serve the process of selection.

Perception, the doorkeeper of knowledge, is a process of selection and discrimination. It is a breaking down of information received through the senses is indirect and inherently unreliable. The process is controlled by what we have learned in life through formal education and experience, that is by our world-view.

Experience is the product of what our senses have told us over time. Formal education is an elaborate form of indoctrination, the content of which is dictated by culture. *Education is, therefore, indoctrination in a particular culture. The mechanism that controls our perception is, in large part, manipulated by cultural conditioning.*

It follows that our perception determines our view of reality, while our view of reality determines our actions in response to a given situation. As a result, our action toward mates, offspring, our race and our enemies are perception oriented as well.

When the culture that provides the foundational information of the educational system in question is a culture of White supremacy and is replete with references to African Americans as criminal-minded, lazy, or inferior, the importance of accurate perception becomes apparent. *Oudja*, in its mundane aspect refers to the ability of individuals and groups to perceive the world and all things in it accurately. But accurate perception alone is not *Oudja*.

Intuition is properly understood as the faculty by which we receive information without the use of rational processes. It is immediate and direct cognition. Since this faculty involves the receipt of information by the human mind it may be referred to as a sense. It is, in fact, the sixth sense. It is as vital to our overall perception as are senses of sight, hearing, touch, taste and smell. Intuition literally rounds out our perception and functions as the only truly direct sense. It turns the sum of the parts into the whole.

It is interesting to note that the number six was considered by the Kemites as the number of material existence. It was seen by them as absolutely necessary for a thing to come into existence, that is, to have material substance. Nothing can exist unless and until it has six sides or faces. It follows that full perception, that is, the power to see the entire picture is not possible without the sixth sense.

Unfortunately, the ability to intuit has, for several reasons, fallen into disuse. This is primarily because it is intangible and difficult to quantify. Modern (Western) science frowns on anything it cannot verify, which is not to say that that it accepts everything it can verify. Since intuition is both internal and specific to individuals it is doubly suspect.

A second reason concerns the number of dishonest persons who have professed the ability to see the future, communicate with the dead or read minds. These are all based, theoretically on the sense of intuition. These often well paid charlatans, confidence men and women have bilked the public of not only their money but also the ability to affirm something they have experienced first as true.

Rare is the person who has never experienced the feeling that something was about to happen only to have it occur just as they expected, to dream of something that later occurs. These experiences are recorded all over the world among people of every race and culture. Many people who have had such experiences refer to themselves as psychic, seers, channelers and fortune tellers. They are, if they have any genuine ability, simply persons who are practiced in the use of their innate sixth sense, a sense with which we are all endowed.

The fact that intuition has been given a bad name does not mean that it does not exist. It, like an organ of the body, is subject to atrophy through disuse. With training and practice this indispensable component of human perception can be utilized. As a component of perception and that which rounds it out, it is absolutely essential to the second level of *Oudja*.

Perhaps the most important goal of *Oudja* is the development of the group of individuals who will comprise the minimum number of persons necessary to cause the cultural/political chain reaction that will serve the dual purpose of resuscitation of our Authentic Ancestral Culture and inaugurate the Age of *Hapy*.

The cultural/political revolution predicted by Theodicy is an explosion in the way we think, an upheaval in level of our consciousness. It is the collective attainment of Oudja that will enable us to perceive the past, the present and the future potential and possibilities of times, places and our people.

The apparent disintegration of our people and our communities is a sign of our inability to analyze and understand the origin of our societal malaise. Until we recognize that we are governed by a culture and a world-view that is not our own and one that is inimical to our interests, we will continue on our present course because of our inability to form appropriate and successful strategies to effect affect desperately needed change.

Oudja enables us to recognize that we have invested our lives and our children's future in the culture, vision and government of those who have proclaimed and demonstrated, unabashedly, for centuries, at every conceivable level of enterprise and existence, that they intend that we shall be their servants, lackeys, nannies and slaves -- forever.

We have adopted a social doctrine of submission to the will of others by the simple and illogical expedient of calling it our own. We have, in effect, abdicated our responsibility to our ancestors, our children and our national identity by doing so.

Theodicy teaches that this unenviable state of affairs cannot continue always. The movement of the Wheel of Time

Theodicy

elevates and it casts down. This predictable movement is Divine Justice in action. With each precessional change the central focus of the energy of the universe is altered and a new cosmic age is created. Each cosmic age has its own color, vibration and note. Its distinctive light permeates all that exists within it and transforms or differentiates all with which it comes in contact.

By virtue of its unique vibration the age intones a distinctive cosmic note that harmonizes with the music of the universe. It is the color, vibration and note that creates the cosmic ambiance -- an atmosphere of harmonious counterpoint that raises consciousness and evokes the characteristic will of the Age. This divine combination is the soil and the nutrient that nourishes the people, animals and plants of the age. Just as in the case of the human will, the will of plants and animals s carried out instinctively and without deviation. In the case of humanity, however, the will must be discovered, demonstrated, activated and controlled. For the human will is the force, the power that changes the course of human events and carries out the details of the cosmic change dictated by Theodicy and the new age. But, the details must be seen, envisioned before they can be carried out. That is the power of *Qudja*. Without it power cannot be understood and cannot be seized. Without it the plan cannot be developed and the leadership cannot be trained.

CRITICAL THINKING

We have defined *Oudja* as clarity of vision. *Oudja* is the attainment of level of understanding that is marked by direct, undistracted, unimpaired perception, at which the individual accurately perceives the purpose of life and his destiny in it. The ultimate goal of *Oudja*, however, is the attainment of *collective* clarity of vision.

Critical Thinking is related to *Oudja* in the same way that perception is related to analysis. Critical Thinking is a technology of reasoning by which we analyze or think about what we see through the clarity of perception and vision that is *Oudja*.

Critical Thinking is based on the Kemitic understanding that since there always exists at least two truths, no single truth can be accepted without structured, in-depth analysis. Neither belief, faith nor passion is a substitute for analysis.

Critical Thinking is a systematic, analytical approach to the discovery of reality. It is not, as some have assumed, thinking that finds fault. It is certainly true, however, that critical thinking will uncover and expose fallacy if it is found. Its fundamental purpose, however, is to apply careful analysis and sound judgment to popular as well as unpopular assertions in order to arrive at an accurate assessment of reality. It is premised on the notion that illusion is the inaccurate perception of reality and that it may have its origin internally and externally. The perception of reality is, therefore, a function of the raw data that the senses gather and the analysis to which that raw data is subjected. The end result is what we call reality. The accuracy of our observation and analysis determines the accuracy of our view of reality. It is, of course, our view of reality that determines the plans, strategies, and tactics that we employ in our quest for collective survival and prosperity.

To think critically is to indulge the mind in *radicalism.* Radicalism is the conscious effort and will to uproot or reform, if possible, that which is established and detrimental to our present and future collective interest. It is to go to the root, source or foundation of something.

Critical Thinking is the mechanism of the radical mind. The radical mind pursues that which is fundamental and basic. The radical mind deals with origins and the time before complexity obscured and hid the simplicity of our own cultural and original way of thinking.

A person is not required to actually be a radical in order to engage in critical thinking. Critical thinking does not require that a person adopt radical ideas. It does require that a person analyze all ideas and information *radically.*

Critical thinking is also the opposite of indoctrination and its antidote. As we have seen indoctrination involves the teaching of the uncritical acceptance of a specific system of thought. The key word is uncritical. To be uncritical is to lack discrimination or evaluation. It is to fail to use procedures or standards of evaluation that permit one to accurately judge and discern.

It follows that people who have suffered the centuries-long effects of indoctrination must employ critical thinking as the only effective antidote. Even after the passage of centuries as small dose of critical thinking can go a long way.

Like *Oudja* critical thinking has an ultimate objective. The objective is the attainment of an accurate, collective assessment of reality that will permit us to make informed decisions and life choices on behalf of ourselves and those for whose care and protection we are responsible. Together *Oudja* and Critical Thinking form two of the components of the *Triad of Visionary Power*. The *Intelligence-of-The Heart* rounds out the trio and makes it whole.

THE INTELLIGENCE-OF-THE-HEART

Intelligence-of-the-Heart is the third component of the Triad of Visionary Power. It is both a concept central to the understanding of the thinking and culture of our ancient ancestors and fundamental to the emergence of the new level of consciousness that will usher in the Age of *Hapy*.

The Intelligence-of-the-Heart is an elusive concept that resists explanation because it defies conventional wisdom. Since it does not derive from the five senses its perception and explanation by them is, in a word, difficult.

It is perhaps easier to begin by stating what it is not. Intelligence-of-the-Heart is not something that one can learn, it is not knowledge in the sense of learnable information. It is not perception that derives from the five senses. It is not arrived at, or deduced from anything. It is not located in any place or at any time.

The Intelligence-of-the-Heart is a Kemitic concept was symbolized by the heart-lung complex called *hati*. In ancient Kemit, as in many civilizations that followed it, the heart was considered the seat of all intelligence. The heart was considered a complex that included the lungs. Even at the beginning of our civilization our ancestors understood the inseparable connection between heart and lungs.

The heart is the pump that drives the blood, the carrier of the vitality of life, to all parts of the body. The heart is in continuous operation from conception to death. Its two cavities pump blood throughout the rest of the body. But the heart and lungs operate together and the understanding of the function of the heart is incomplete without an examination of the corresponding function of the lungs.

The lungs are dual. The left lung has two lobes and the right three. Together they effect respiration, the single most import and essential aspect of existence. Respiration is the process by which oxygen is absorbed by body cells and by which carbon dioxide and water are expelled. The combined action of inspiration and expiration occurs 18 times per minute.

During this process oxygen combines with cell constituents thus creating energy. The immediate source of the energy is believed to be the splitting of high-energy chemical bonds. It is, therefore, a process similar to fission and indicates that the life force and its power are contained in the air. The heart-lung complex, or *hati*, is the place where, functionally, the life of humans is maintained.

The heart-lung complex is also the place where the synthesis that is life takes place. It is there that energy is distilled from oxygen and de-vitalized air is expelled. The entire life of the body, both air (the breath of life) and blood (the carrier of the life force) are commingled in time and place in the heart-lung complex. The heart is the place where the beat and rhythm of life is counted and maintained. But it is also a place and function that is not controlled by us consciously. Its mechanism is fine-tuned and kept functioning, repetitively, exactly, for the entire course of our lives without our having to do anything. This vital function, without which life is impossible, is maintained though we never called upon to act in any way with regard to it. This wondrous

Theodicy

timekeeper of life is both the symbol and the fact of the *Intelligence-of-the-Heart* that operates and commands it. If either heart beat or respiration stops for any length of time death inevitably results. Clearly, something controls the breathing and heart beat and apparently controls it well.

The *Intelligence-of-the-Heart* is the transforming, transcendent force behind all initiative, innovation, creativity, inspiration and will. It is the direct uninhibited, undiluted voice of the *Neter Neteru* that communicates through and by the heart and that was universally recognized by the ancients as the seat of all direct human cognition.

In the so-called lower animals the equivalent of the *Intelligence-of-the-Heart* is referred to as instinct. Although the term instinct does not seem to have a universally accepted definition it does lend itself to a number of points of agreement with the concept of the *Intelligence-of-the-Heart*.

Instinct is considered innate and peculiar to each species. It seems to drive certain activities that are characteristic of the specie but are not the result of past experience of the individual. Instinct points to a way of knowing that is totally divorced from experience and learning but that is also indispensable to life and survival. There are many examples in NaTuRe.

The caterpillar who erupts from the cocoon as a butterfly takes wing immediately and thereafter reproduces without hesitation having never done or experienced either before. Clearly, it is acting on instinct. Among mammals suckling of young and the ability to suckle also seem to be instinctive. These "instincts" are accomplished by a way of knowing that simply exists in spite of our inability to explain it.

In humans the equivalent way of knowing is often referred to as intuition. To our ancestors it was the *Intelligence-of-the-Heart*. We have previously defined intuition as the faculty by which we receive information (knowledge) without the use of rational processes, that is, immediate and direct cognition.

But it should also be understood as specific, direct knowledge in the case of the *Intelligence-of-the-Heart*.

In this respect the *Intelligence-of-the-Heart* may be seen as a connective fabric of understanding that links the individual to the NeTeRs, to her inner self, to humanity and all living things and to the universe and cosmos beyond. The universe is one song while the cosmos is what exists when that song is played in harmony. This specific, direct knowledge is only glimpsed by intuition, it is experienced full-blown by and through the *Intelligence-of-the-Heart*. The *Intelligence-of-the-Heart* is, therefore, the knowledge that comes directly from a reservoir of collection of knowledge that forms the collective consciousness that is humanity's greatest NaTuRal resource and the source of its greatest and unlimited power.

The *Intelligence-of-the-Heart* is referred to as intelligence because, strictly speaking, intelligence is the ability to employ comprehension of current situations that have been acquired by past experience. There are, however, two types of intelligence. The definition stated above refers to cerebral intelligence, brain power, intellect, reasoning. It is based on, observation, experience and rote learning. It is directly dependent on the five senses. As such it is as reliable or unreliable as the senses upon which it relies. This empirical intelligence is two dimensional, and as such it lacks depth.

The second type of intelligence can be described as non-empirical or *a priori*. It is innate. It does not require experience because it is an unmistakable and perhaps indescribable phenomenon that can only be understood as a way of knowing. It is not what we have learned, but what we know. It is the overwhelming feeling of certitude that comes directly and immediately without preparation or contemplation. This second type of intelligence is derived from the same source as that which controls breathing and heart beat.

Intelligence is a function. Reason is a power. it is the power of the mind by which knowledge is obtained. It is through the power of reason that we attain knowledge. It is through pure reason that we know. The *Intelligence-of-the-Heart* is a way of knowing that is derived from pure reason.

Consciousness is implied by the concepts of knowing and reason. It is itself an elusive term. There seems to be no universally accepted definition of it. Our ancestors, however, had definite thoughts about consciousness and located it and the seat of pure reason in, or just above, the heart.

Since consciousness is literally knowing, the *Intelligence-of-the-Heart*, attained only through the faculty of pure reason, is the purest form of consciousness. It is the consciousness of the Neter Neteru.

We often hear people talk about the stream of consciousness. it is tmore properly descrived asthe Ancestral Stream of Consciousness. it is the unending flow, pure and undiluted, taht comes directly from a reservoir of collective consciousness that is best understood as the *Mind of the Neter Neteru* or if you prefer the *Mind of God*.

This way of knowing that is literally consciousness (or should we say that knowing is consciousness) exists. Since it is apparently a flow or stream it must include a point of origin and a point of return. At first blush and by uncritical thinking, one might conclude that the obvious location of this stream is in the brain. But the consciousness that is pure reason, that which fuels the *Intelligence-of-the-Heart*, cannot reside in the brain. By definition this source of unlimited power flows from a reservoir of universal, collective consciousness that is, and must be, external to the brain, if not otherwordly.

Consciousness is not a function of the brain. It is more accurately described as a function of the mind. Interestingly, the word mind derives from the Greek *menos* meaning spirit and s synonymous with soul. In a real sense then, consciousness is a function of spirit.

In our ancient ancestral tongue the concepts of both mind and consciousness were described by two words. The first is *ab* a word whose primary meaning is heart, but which also has the secondary meanings of wisdom, understanding, intelligence, desire and will. It should also be noted the Kemitic word *ab* when transposed is *ba*, meaning soul.

The second word is *hati* which, as we have seen has a primary meaning of heart and which has a secondary meaning of mind and will.

We should also mention that in ancient Greece, where we have seen philosophical and metaphysical ideas were by and 1arge derived from Kemitic teachings, the another word for mind was *noos* or *nous*. The word literally means to see. Curiously, the *noos* was located not in the eyes, but in the chest along with the heart. You see through or with the heart.

Another Greek word may be mentioned here. The word *psyche* from which the words psychology (the study of the mind) and psychiatry (the study of disorders of the mind) derive means to breathe. Again, we have the recurring connection, in ancient times of the heart-lung complex to mind or spirit.

The *hati* is the heart-lung complex. It is the place where consciousness enters the body. It is the seat of the soul. But the consciousness that is pure reason and the *Intelligence-of-the-Heart* are received in the *hati* much as a radio or television receiver picks up broadcast signals but is not the originator or place of origin of the signal itself. We must look for the location of the universal, collective consciousness outside of the brain, the physical body and outside of time. We must look to the ancient Kemitic concept of *Maat*.

Maat has been defined in many ways. In its exoteric sense it refers to the feminine *NeTeR* of law, order, rule, truth, right, justice, straightness, integrity, uprightness, and the highest possible conception of physical and moral law known. She was also the wife of *Tehuti* and the daughter of *Ra* the visible manifestation of the Life Force.

Maat is esoterically described as the NaTuRal order of things, the right, exact order as in the perfect universe. *Maat* includes all consciousness and all evolution. It begins with

Theodicy

the perfectly balanced scale, a device that necessarily implies comparison. To the extent we are conscious it is the result of the act of comparison.

Our ancestors believed, and so taught, that act creation was accomplished by the *NeTeR NeTeRu* looking at itself. It is said to have looked upon itself, saw its reflection and by so doing created, simultaneously, the existence of the other. In a very real sense then, it was the *NeTeR NeTeRu's* realization of comparison that brought all else besides itself into existence.

On the earthly plane it is also comparison that is the core of consciousness. it is indisputable our ability to weigh, judge and balance things, and through that faculty alone, that we determine the reality of things.

Consciousness exists at many levels. There is the consciousness characteristic of the animal, vegetable and mineral kingdoms. These cover organic consciousness as well as human consciousness. Each represents a level of *Maat*. Because each acts according to the NaTuRal order, each is an expression of the consciousness that is *Maat*. Each level of *Maat* includes itself and the level below it. Therefore, each level is imminent in the succeeding level.

The highest level of *Maat* consciousness resides, potentially, in human beings whose consciousness alone includes all the prior levels. But even human consciousness can be developed further by a comparison that too is *Maat*. That level of comparison leads to the development of Universal *Maat*, the consciousness that is the *NeTeR NeTeRu* and the Divine Ra whose daughter is *Maat*.

Maat was so important to our ancient ancestors, so pervasive, that she was depicted as performing three significant and indispensible functions at the *Weighing of the Soul*.

THE WEIGHING OF THE SOUL

The Weighing of the Soul, or *psychostasia* was the ceremony at which the deceased was called upon to account for his life on Earth in the Judgment Hall of *Asar* where his soul was weighed against *Maat's* "feather of perfection". At the ceremony it is *Maat* who delivers the soul of the deceased to the place of weighing known as the Hall of the Two Truths or the Double *Maat*. She is also the *NeTeR* who greets the soul when it arrives there. In that capacity she holds the scepter of authority. Finally, the soul is weighed against the "feather of perfection" which is the symbol of *Maat*. Apparently, we are all judged, weighed; if you will, by our consciousness, that is, our compliance with divine order and exacting justice. We are delivered to that judgment by the level of consciousness we have attained in life, that is, the level at which we have live according to *Maat*. When we arrive at judgment we are greeted by *Maat* who now has authority to weigh our actions and deeds, non-judgmentally, against here exacting requirements to which we have adhered or not during the course of our lives.

If it is understood that *Maat* is unerring justice, it follows that it would be unjust and against her own unalterable laws for our souls to be held responsible for acts taken in disregard of information, rules or principles unknown to us. This is why the *Intelligence of the Heart* is inborn, direct and uncontaminated. It comes to us pure and direct from the reservoir of pure reason that is Universal Consciousness of *Maat*.

We may conclude from this that the *Intelligence-of-the-Heart*, the third component of the *Triad of Visionary Power*, is the consciousness and pure reason of *Maat*. It is the sixth sense whose collective attainment represents the quantum leap of consciousness that will characterize the Age of *Hapy*. It is to this level of consciousness that we must aspire and to which all will be transformed upon the attainment of the requisite Critical Mass that will cause the predicted and anticipated chain reaction that represents the movement of the Wheel of Time that is Theodicy.

We have alluded to the Stream of Consciousness. This phenomenon is actually an Ancestral Stream. To complete our understanding of the concept of the *Intelligence-of-the-*

Theodicy

Heart we must take a closer look at the concept of the Ancestral Stream.

THE ANCESTRAL STREAM

The Ancestral Stream is a flowing or movement of energy and consciousness that carries a people toward their ultimate destiny. It is a forceful movement that has been set in motion by the collective consciousness and combined energy of our ancestors, which travels within and emanates from the cosmic ocean called the *Nun* by our ancestors.

The Ancestral Stream is a cosmic stream that has been variously called the River of Heaven, the Celestial Stream and the Celestial River by the ancient Kemites.

The Ancestral Stream is not unlike ocean, air and electrical currents, and my be usefully analogized to them. A current is a continuous flow of water that moves in a specific direction and travels within a larger body of water. The world's oceans contain numerous currents that although recognized and predictable, still represent a poorly understood phenomenon. Perhaps the best known of these is *El Nino*, the one held responsible for the devastating *El Nino Effect* on global weather.

Air currents operate in the same way as ocean currents and have the additional property of invisibility. Both ocean and air currents represent a separate and distinct movement within a larger movement. Both form the center of the larger movement, move in one direction, and are self-propelled.

The movement of electrons through a conductor is also referred to as a current whose movement is called electricity. The word electricity derives from amber (a fossil resin that is quickly electrified by friction) because it was first produced by rubbing amber to produce static electricity.

BRIEF DIGRESSION ON
THALES OF MILETUS AND ELECTRICITY

The discovery of electricity is credited to Thales of Miletus, another Greek "philosopher" who studied in Kemit. It should be noted here that Thales was one of the Seven Wise Men of

Greece. He is recognized as the first Western philosopher. He wrote nothing, but is credited with having brought geometry to Greece (nearly all the ancients agreed that geometry was invented by the ancient Kemites). He was also reputed to be an accomplished astronomer. Not surprisingly, most, if not all of the data attributed to him was of Kemitic origin. Finally, the feat for which he was most famous (the accurate prediction of a total solar eclipse) was unquestionably beyond his capacity since the Greeks did not have sufficient knowledge to calculate it. He was also unable to explain how he did it. Thales "discovery" of static electricity is also an indication that the Kemites knew of the properties of amber and, by inference, of the existence of electricity. That being said let us get back to electricity.

Electricity, while itself poorly understood, is responsible for the wealth of conveniences upon which the modern world relies for its progress and so-called modernity.

The basic structure of matter is electrical. We need only to look at atoms to verify the point. Atoms are the basic building blocks of matter and are comprised of electrically charged particles. The particles of matter may be negatively charged as in the case of electrons, or positively charged as in the case of protons. Neutrons are electrically neutral.

The Ancestral Stream is best understood as a combination of the characteristics of ocean, air and electrical currents. Like the ocean and air currents it is a continuous flow that travels in one direction, faster than the larger body in which it is contained. It is independently propelled and although invisible represents a predictable movement within a movement. It is perpetual, always moving and always existing.

Like electrical currents, the Ancestral Stream is a dynamic flow of energy. It is an electromotive force. It is created by the movement of energy and its strength is directly proportionate to the strength of that movement.

Also like electricity, the energy that is the Ancestral Stream requires a conductor and insulation in order that its

Theodicy

unlimited energy may be properly contained, channeled and utilized.

A conductor is a material that readily allows an electrical charge to pass from one place to another as in the case of some metals. An insulator, on the other hand, is material that does not readily pass on an electrical charge such as rubber and other non-metals.

Once the electrical flow is conducted through a properly insulated channel its movement creates a magnetic field. It is the current that generates the field. The magnetic field is the ambiance of the force produced by the electrons in motion. It should be remembered that the electrons are negatively charged particles.

The magnetic field is a result of the movement of negative energy. Though invisible the field is both physical and measurable. The presence of a magnetic field causes materials that come in contact with it to become magnetized. Magnetism is a power. It is the power of attraction. It is simultaneously the power of repulsion. A curious and unexplained phenomenon is the fact that a magnet has constant negative and positive poles. If a magnetized bar is cut in half, each half will then have another set of negative and positive poles in each of the severed halves. Clearly, positive and negative must always exist, side by side. It follows that although electricity is negative, it is only nominally so, because the negative and positive are co-eternal and inseparable. Again, the Two Truths of ancient Kemit are eloquently manifested.

Finally, materials that are capable of being magnetized may be magnetized by contact with a magnet or by placing them within a *magnetic field*. The magnetic field is to electricity as the *group field* is to the Ancestral Stream. The flow of the Ancestral Stream, when properly conducted and insulated, enables us to create energized persons who themselves become attractive forces that may be seen as magnets who have become such because of their exposure to persons who have been energized or to the group field.

A person may be energized by being in contact with an energized person. The process by which this phenomenon occurs is known as *induction*. The possibility that the phenomenon will occur is dependent on several factors. First, it is dependent on the receptivity of the person to be energized. Receptivity consists of willingness and innate susceptibility to energetic charge. Those who are willing to be energized are, obviously, easiest to energize. Unfortunately, those are easily energized are often those who retain the charge only as long as they are surrounded by the energy of the group field. Other persons are hard to energize initially, but once they have been successfully energized they retain the charge whether surrounded by the energy filed or not. These persons are like steel. The o hers are like iron. Of course, steel is merely soft iron that has been transformed by the intense heat of the blast furnace.

The innate susceptibility of the individual to be energized, like the properties of ferromagnetic metals (those strongly attracted by the force of a magnet) and paramagnetic metals (those less attracted to the force of a magnet) are part of the internal composition of the individual. Iron is metal that is ferromagnetic. Aluminum, for example, is paramagnetic. To the extent that an individual is ferro or paramagnetic her suitability to be energized may be accurately gauged.

The second factor to be considered in understanding the process of induction as it relates to the Ancestral Stream is the group field itself. The group field is, as we have seen, analogous to a magnetic field. A magnetic field is created as a result of the movement of electrons. When electric current passes through a wire it forms a magnetic field around it. The wire serves to conduct the electricity which is an energy or power. By the conduction of electricity the electrons become focused and directed.

In the same way the Ancestral Stream, in order to generate its greatest power, must be focused and directed by a process similar to induction. We shall call this process of focusing and directing the power of the Ancestral Stream the invocation of the *NeTeRs*.

Theodicy

To invoke something is to call upon it. But the word invoke derives from the Latin *vocare*, meaning voice and which implies both to remember and to affirm. By invoking the *NeTeRs* we cause a specific idea that has been previously perceived, known, felt or intuited, to enter the and occupy the mind. Once in mind this specific idea is stated positively and confidently, as fact.

To invoke the *NeTeRs* then, is to energize our thought, which, in turn, amplifies the power that is thought and forges an invisible link with the Ancestral Stream of Consciousness and its unlimited power. By collectively invoking the NeTeRs we create and *energized thought pattern*, a fabric of thought, that draws upon our Ancestral Stream and simultaneously creates the group field that is the direct result of the movement or flow of specific energy and whose movement or flow causes the group field.

Once created, the group field takes on a life of its own. It becomes a source of potent energy that, in effect, energizes that which it comes in contact with while simultaneously drawing to itself those who are predisposed to its magnetic attraction. It follows that *the creation of the group field insures and facilitates its growth.* The method of invocation is Sacred Science.

When the group field operates at maximum capacity and efficiency it generates the energetic impulse that begins the process of cellular construction that building upon itself procreates what we shall call a *New Body Politic*.

CHAPTER ELEVEN:

THE VISION OF THE NEW BODY POLITIC

The vision that this section examines is a power. In order to be utilized this visionary power must envision something real and concrete that will be its purpose to achieve. In the case of African Americans that which is envisioned and sought to be achieved is the birth of a New Body Politic that will be able to spearhead the cultural revolution that will usher in the Age of *Hapy*.

A body politic is a group of people organized politically and culturally in a system and structure that so mirrors that of the human body, in its key functions and composition, as to be identical to a living organism. The form of a body politic is an organization. Because it is comprised of human beings it is a living organism as well. Like any living organism it must be born. All living things are born of seed.

The seed of the organization is an idea. It is, therefore, a seed/ idea that must precede the birth of each new body politic. A seed/idea whose time has finally come will take root and an organization will grow from it and will prosper. If the seed/idea is untimely or ill-conceived the organization will be stillborn or hopelessly deformed and ineffective for the purpose for which it was conceived.

A timely well-conceived seed/idea consists of formal, detailed procedures for the recruitment, training and coordination of the political and cultural activities of a group of people specifically formulated for the purpose of carrying out their collective and predetermined will.

Like the human body the body politic is also comprised of individual cells. Cells are literally the building blocks of life. The vital characteristic of the cell is its ability to grow. Growth in cells is a process of division or fission. Cells grow individually and when they reach the limit of their growth they divide.

This innate propensity to divide is the reproductive system of the cell. All cells of the human body, except those of the brain, reproduce by the process of division. Growth is marked, therefore, by the increase in the number of cells. *That which is not actively growing is actively dying.*

Each cell contains a power generating plant by which it creates the energy by which it sustains its life. When cells are combined it is their cumulative energy that powers the entire organism through a network of energy transmitters. Each cell is an energy source with its own surrounding energy field. When energy fields combine the energy of the whole organism is increased exponentially creating, thereby, a group field. It is this combined energy that serves as the strength and energetic force of the body politic.

The body politic functions as a body. Its energy alone is insufficient to transform it from a mere organism into an organization. The amoeba is a living energetic organism. It is not, in any sense of the word, an organization. It follows that in order for the body politic to mirror the human body it must be comprised of those elements that distinguish the human being. Among those important to our present analysis are mind, and spirit.

THE MIND OF THE BODY POLITIC

The mind may be described as a self-preserving, physical process by which symbols are manipulated and communicated. The operative components of manipulation are novelty and initiative.

Novelty is the power of the mind to make new combinations of information previously stored in the brain's databases. By combining old information with new the mind literally creates ideas that have not previously existed in that particular brain. This process becomes the operation best described as creativity. Put another way, the power of the mind is its ability to grow through the creation of new seed/ideas. If the mind is growing, expanding and reproducing it must be creating new seed/ ideas by recombination.

In genetics recombination is the formation of new combinations of linked genes resulting in new heritable characters or new combination of such characters. In nuclear physics it is the union of a positive and a negative ion to form a neutral atom or molecule. As used here recombination is the innate and unexplained ability of the human mind to take new knowledge and join it with previously stored knowledge to create knowledge that is new and distinct from that which previously existed. Novelty then is the function that results in the creativity of the body politic. But novelty also causes a by-product of recombination. It creates not only new ideas, but also entirely new patterns of thought. In this way new patterns of thought emerge that generate an entirely new way of seeing things.

Initiative is the act of implementing the new ideas and new thought patterns in a way that creates new strategies, tactics and goals to be pursued by the body politic. Initiative is the power to change old methods that have proven ineffective or outmoded. Initiative is, therefore, the bridge between thought and action. It is the vehicle by which the seed/idea goes from drawing board to production. This may seem an insignificant step but it is extremely important. Its importance is best illustrated by the "million dollar idea" we have all had but failed to *initiate*. The seed/idea is the product of the mind bit it is useless unless acted upon. Initiative is the power that both originates and initiates action. When it is recalled that the will is, at least partially, a product of the mind we can see that the body politic must have a mind in order to produce its will and release its power.

When thought, which is literally the mind energy of the individual cells of the body politic, is combined it becomes a collective mind, or more precisely, the mind of the body politic.

Just as combined energy increases its output exponentially, so does mind energy. The potential energy of the collective mind is so immense as to be virtually unlimited. Its potential is greatest, however, when the collective mind is conductive or open.

Theodicy

THE OPEN MIND

An open mind is one that is able to conduct mind energy effortlessly and without internal resistance. Because of its high grade conductivity it is receptive to bombardment by accurate, nonbiased information. When in regular contact with other open minds it applies creativity and initiative to the information it receives and continues to grow and reproduce.

An open collective mind is the ideal mind of the body politic and is capable of developing ideas unavailable to the individual because the level of creative energy necessary to evolve such ideas is beyond the capacity of individual minds acting alone. The open collective mind creates a reservoir of information that is most effectively utilized, and perhaps only capable of being utilized, by other open minds acting in tandem.

A closed mind, on the other hand, is incapable of tapping the creativity that is the product of open and unhindered access to group information. The whole is greater than the sum of its parts. The collective closed mind is the embodiment of the negative resistance that prevents creativity and initiative.

It follows that since mind is a physical process of communication that necessarily depends on physical facilities to function, its power cannot be tapped unless and until a body politic exists. The body politic cannot exist, unless and until it has been envisioned by the *Critical Mass*.

The Critical Mass is essential because it is a given that the mental processes here described are beyond the ability or access of individuals not conjoined in a pre-existing nucleus. When a group of individuals combine the power of their minds to form a collective mind their stored records, their past information forms the contours of culture that may extend over several generations for they are as ancient and accurate as our collective and living memory. This is because the collective mind is a cultural form. It consists in the collective mind and spirit of the body politic.

THE SPIRIT OF THE BODY POLITIC

As a living organism the body politic contains the equivalent of a spirit. The spirit of the body politic is composed of the rules and regulations by which it operates. These rules are the fundamental teachings of the Authentic Ancestral Culture. The importance of this is that the spirit of a living thing is literally that which animates it.

To our ancient ancestors everything that lives was considered to be driven by a portion of the Sacred Essence. In this sense, and to the extent that the body politic is truly alive, it too must partake of that essence.

The Sacred Essence or spirit of the body politic is manifested in the group field that is the energy field that is brought into being by the joining of the energetic impulse of all the cells that comprise it.

The New Body Politic begins with vision. The vision is the seed/idea from which it will grow. In order to become reality the vision must be shared by the minimum number of persons sufficient to establish Critical Mass (CM). The joining of these persons of like mind and spirit creates the visionary power that conceives the New Body Politic.

The New Body Politic is the equivalent, in energy and potential for independent movement and growth, to a human infant. But unlike the human infant it is born with the combined, matured intellect of the individual cells from which is born. This New Body Politic is a living organism, embodied in an organization, that is driven by a mind, spirit and will of its own. It is by the vision of the New Body Politic that we, as a people, existing within a group field, become capable of giving birth to this new political being whose will cannot be thwarted and whose vision will become the reality of the New Age.

Theodicy

CHAPTER TWELVE:
CRITICAL MASS AND
THE BIRTH OF THE POLITICAL BEING

Critical Mass (CM) is here defined as the minimum number of enriched persons necessary to sustain a cultural/political chain reaction.

The principle underlying CM is best understood by analogy to its use in nuclear physics. In the science of nuclear physics critical mass is the minimum amount of fissionable material necessary to sustain a nuclear chain reaction. Specifically, it is the minimum amount of uranium or other nuclear fuel, such as plutonium, needed to create the controlled release of energy in a nuclear power plant or an uncontrolled release of energy in a nuclear bomb.

The science of nuclear physics is based on atomic theory or atomism. The theory of atomism was first developed in ancient Kemit and was introduced to the Western world by Democritus, a Greek "philosopher" who studied in Kemit. According to the Kemitic theory atoms are the basic components of the universe.

The atom is, by this theory, considered to be the smallest unit of an element consisting of a dense, central, positively charged nucleus surrounded by a system of negatively charged electrons. *The nucleus is held together by the strong force. The energy released in an atomic explosion is the strong force contained in the atom. That which binds the atom together is what gives it it's power.*

Critical Mass is a necessary prerequisite to the release of the energy of the atom. Only after critical mass has been attained can the tremendous energy contained in the nucleus of the atom be released. The method of release is known as nuclear fission.

Fission is a method by which the atom is split to release its tremendous energy. In this process the nucleus of the atom is split into two or more fragments. Interestingly, the term fission is taken from the biological process by which one celled organisms divide into two smaller organisms of equal size. Fission is, therefore, similar to the process of growth discussed in the previous chapter.

In the case of nuclear fission, however, neutrons (particles with no electrical charge) are freed by the splitting of the atom and in turn split other atoms releasing additional neutrons. If the fissionable material use is sufficiently great (has reached Critical Mass) the result is a chain reaction. A chain re action is best defined as any sequence of events each of which results in, or has an effect on the following events. The domino theory and the domino effect in which the toppling of one domino will in a row of dominos will cause the other to fall, is a chain reaction.

The amount of energy released by each individual atom in a nuclear chain reaction is miniscule. It is the combined energy of released by millions of atoms that accounts for the tremendous explosion. As the chain reaction gathers momentum it produces greater and greater amounts of energy.

There is a second process by which the energy contained in the nucleus of the atom can be released. In nuclear fusion the nuclei of two atoms join together to form a new and large nucleus. When the electrons (positively charged particles) surrounding the nucleus of the atom are shared by

Theodicy

other atoms a chain reaction occurs. When a nucleus collides with another nucleus, all the particles involved are said to reorganize themselves and a nuclear chain reaction is the result.

In reorganization the nucleus may simply absorb the new particle or it may absorb one type of particle while rejecting another. When nuclei join some of the mass is converted into energy. This form of energy is referred to as binding energy. It is the energy that binds the new nucleus together and it is equal to the total amount of mass (matter) that is transformed into energy. The amount of energy created by fusion is considerably less than that created by fission. Simply put the nuclear chain reaction is the process by which mass (matter) is transformed into energy. *The mass to energy transformation cannot occur until Critical Mass is achieved. Critical Mass is more than a number or an amount. It is further dependent on type, concentration and structure.*

Type refers to the type of fissionable material used. Critical Mass for uranium is considered to be 11 pounds, while that for plutonium is only 4.5 pounds. Critical Mass is, therefore, dictated by the specific of fissionable material employed.

The second factor on which Critical Mass is dependent is the concentration of the fissionable material. Uranium 235 must be separated from its twin Uranium 238 by a process called enrichment in order to be used in nuclear power plants or atomic bombs. Most uranium is only enriched to about three percent. the lower the concentration of enriched uranium the higher amount to achieve Critical Mass.

Finally, Critical Mass depends on the physical structure in which the fissionable material is contained. In most cases the Critical Mass is surrounded by a reflector that prevents neutrons from escaping and reflects them back into the Critical Mass. The physical structure, therefore, increases the likelihood that neutrons will strike an atom and create the desired chain reaction. As a result, the Critical Mass required is lower. An amount of fissionable material greater than that necessary for a chain reaction is always a critical mass.

In the context of our overall premise of Theodicy, Critical Mass is defined as the minimum number of enriched persons required to initiate a cultural/political chain of events that will lead to the release of a controlled explosive force. In order to fully understand the concept of Critical Mass as applied here we must also look at its relationship to *power*, *Theodicy* and the *New Body Politic*.

CRITICAL MASS AND POWER

Energy and power are virtually synonymous terms. Energy is related to mass. Under certain conditions mass can be transformed into energy. The rate at which the transformation takes place is fixed. The fixed exchange rate of mass to energy is represented in Einstein's now famous equation $E=Mc^2$. The equation implies that the exchange rate of mass to energy is a universal law. It also indicates that a small amount of mass transforms into a tremendous amount of energy or power. As we have seen Critical Mass is a condition precedent to the release of energy. Power, therefore, follows Critical Mass at a fixed and predictable rate. When Critical Mass is attained, and the necessary preconditions of . concentration and physical structure are

Theodicy

in place, a chain reaction is set in motion that culminates in the explosive release of energy according to the mass-energy exchange rate embodied in Einstein's equation.

When Critical Mass is understood as the minimum number of enriched persons necessary to sustain a cultural/political chain reaction the result and its potential impact on the course of future human events is explosive and revolutionary. The attainment of Critical Mass is, therefore, the single most important objective of any organization whose sincere goal is the empowerment of African Americans. It follows that the release of energy that will precipitate the radical the revolutionary cultural/political chain reaction awaits the accumulation of Critical Mass. But, Critical Mass is more than mere numbers. It requires the proper type, concentration and physical structure.

The type of people needed for Critical Mass are those who have been enriched. Enrichment is the process of enlightenment by which people of ordinary intelligence, capability and determination are transformed into persons of extraordinary intellect, selfless leadership potential and transcendent will by the attainment of *Oudja*.

The number of people required for Critical Mass is directly related to the type of people (enriched or non-enriched) who will be the mass. The number of enriched persons in the core Critical Mass determines its concentration. A high concentration of enriched persons has two advantageous effects:
(1) smaller numbers are required to attain Critical Mass; and (2) the amount of energy or power released increases in direct proportion to the percentage of the core that is

enriched. Therefore, the energy level or explosive potential of the cultural/political chain reaction is directly related to its concentration.

The third vital condition is the pre-existence of an appropriate physical structure within which the chain reaction can created, contained and controlled. Without a way to the contain the massive force of the energy released by the chain reaction the result would be catastrophic as in the case of an atomic bomb. In order to put the energy to constructive rather than destructive use it must be contained and controlled. By way of example: The potential energy contained in the world supply of deuterium would last 6,400 million years. But because of the tremendous temperatures generated by the process of fusion of deuterium any material used to contain it would be vaporized --its energy cannot, therefore, be contained. The Critical Mass must, therefore, be surrounded by a physical structure sufficient to both facilitate the desired chain reaction and to contain and control the energy produced.

Nuclear physicists have determined that although the shape of the physical structure surrounding the Critical Mass may be any geometric form, the sphere is the most efficient. The sphere, called a reflector or tamer in nuclear physics, serves a two-fold purpose: (1) it prevents neutrons from escaping and reflects them back into the Critical Mass thereby increasing the probability that of the chain reaction; and (2) it lowers the amount of fissionable material needed to attain Critical Mass.

In the case of the cultural/political chain reaction the sphere is the symbolic circle. It is a circle consisting of three concentric circles decreasing in circumference down to an inner circle that contains the nucleus. This symbolic circle is

Theodicy

the place where the bombardment will take place. In nuclear physics bombardment is the process by which neutrons are fired at the Critical Mass to spark the chain reaction.

In our cultural/political chain reaction knowledge and information form the equivalent of neutrons in the nuclear process. Like its counterpart in nuclear physics this knowledge in neutral. As used here neutral means accurate and non-biased.

The symbolic circle is the symbolic physical structure in which specially selected persons will form the Critical Mass, are knowingly, intelligently and voluntarily exposed to accurate, nonbiased information that reverberates from the structure itself, and who will as result, become enlightened, enriched and empowered. Once the sufficient number of persons are enriched, and the Critical Mass is thereby attained, the energy released may be used to either create an explosion or to generate energy to accomplish collective goals or both.

CRITICAL MASS AND THEODICY

Theodicy portends a great and imminent cultural/political chain reaction. As cataclysm it denotes earthquake and war. These terms necessarily implicate a violent, loud, bursting forth that is usually due to pressure from within as in an explosion. In this sense the cultural/political chain reaction will have, at least initially, wide-reaching, explosive impact. Whether it be earthquake or war remains to be seen.

As a generator of energy or power that will fuel the accomplishment of collective goals, Critical Mass generates the power of Theodicy on the political level and may be usefully likened to a nuclear power plant.

A power plant is a physical structure erected to house Critical Mass in order to generate power that serves useful, productive ends. In a nuclear power plant the critical mass and its container are housed in a physical structure from which the generated power is converted to useful form and radiated to end users. In the cultural/political setting the power plant is the Temple and its network of power radiating facilitc.ies. (See Section Four, Chapter Fourteen for explanation of the Temple as Power Generator).

CRITICAL MASS AND THE NEW BODY POLITIC

Critical Mass is vital to the establishment of the collective, living human organism that is the New Body Politic. Like any organism it must be born. Birth requires ovum and sperm. In the New Body Politic the ovum is represented by the existing population of African Americans. The sperm is represented by the enriched Critical Mass. Those persons who comprise the enriched Critical Mass carry the idea that is the seed/idea that will inseminate or fertilize the population to become the New Body Politic.

When fertilization takes place the sperm fuses with the nucleus of the ovum and an entirely new nucleus is formed. Thereafter, the process of cell division of fission begins and birth takes place, predictably, 280 days later. Suffice it to say that when Critical Mass is viewed as the sperm that impregnates the existing population of African Americans with the seed/idea of Theodicy another form of fission associated with Critical Mass is also demonstrated. The form is known as the Golden Section, or the Divine Proportion.

The Divine Proportion

Critical Mass refers to an amount or number as threshold at which chain reaction is possible. In the case of nuclear fission the amount is 11 pounds of uranium 235 and 4.5 pounds of plutonium.

Theodicy

In the cultural/political context Critical Mass refers to the number of persons necessary for the chain reaction to begin. The formula for determining the number is based on the Divine Proportion.

The Divine Proportion is a geometric proportion. It was discovered by the ancient Kemites and has also been referred to as the Golden Section and the Golden Mean. It has been the object of fascination and veneration by sages, mystics and artists since ancient times.

The Greek mathematician Euclid, who studied in Kemit and later taught at the school at Alexandria, referred to it in his Elements. The Divine Proportion gave Plato his idea for the foundations of knowledge; Aristotle his ethical analogies; and it was embraced as a sacred part of the philosophy of the Pythagorean school. Even Johannes Kepler is said to have posited, in 1611, that the Divine Proportion was an idea used by the Creator to generate the similar from the similar.

The Divine Proportion has been recognized in anatomy and other forms and patterns of NaTuRe. As to form it is the proportion for the construction of the regular polygon of ten sides. It is recognized in the properties of regular solids such as the dodecahedron and in the diagonals of a regular pentagon. Its importance is now recognized in architecture and art as fundamental to the creation of harmonious proportions.

In NaTuRe the Divine Proportion is said to appear in the spiral arrangement of leaves around the stem of a plant, the scales of a pine cone, and the florQts in composite flowers.

In anatomy it manifests itself as the proportion by which the human body increases in size from birth to full maturity. The Divine Proportion is referred to as divine because it seems to underlie all aspects of growth. It is the living proportion according to which all living things increase in dimension over the course of their existence. The divine aspect of the proportion is its connection with the process of creation itself.

The 'Kemites taught that number was the key to knowledge. Creation was understood by them to occur between the numbers one and two. In this respect the Divine Proportion was recognized as the formula creative division or Divine Fission. After initial division into two parts the Divine Proportion governs the further stages of growth. At birth the body of a human being is divided into two equal sections by the umbilicus. Thereafter, growth obeys the Divine Proportion. This proportion is intimately involved, from the inception, in both creation and growth of that which has come into being.

To recapitulate, the Divine Proportion is a transcendental ratio that is evident in all living things. It represents the point at which Divine Fission occurs in the organic explosion that is the life of the organism and the organization alike. As the numerical value at which creation occurs Divine Proportion is the number of creation.

The Divine Proportion was the sacred, and secret ratio employed by the ancient Kemites in erecting their temples and other colossal works in stone including the Great Pyramid of Khufu. It is, therefore, also the soul of geometry.

The Di vine Proportion is the formula by which the exact number of Critical Mass is to be discovered. The equation for Crtical Mass in the cultural/political sense, may be stated as: $CM = PHI (AAP)$, where CM is the Critical Mass, PHI is the ration of 1:1.618, and AAP is the African American Population.

The Divine Proportion indicates that less than two percent of our people, having been properly enriched, whose combined energy is contained in an appropriate physical structure can

Theodicy

affect the explosive impact, radical change and radiant growth that will be the result of the cultural/political chain reaction.

SECTION FOUR:

POWER

Theodicy

CHAPTER THIRTEEN:
POWER AS SUBSTANCE AND IDEA

Power as Substance

Theodicy is a teleological concept whose forward movement is purposeful, directed and dependent on the presence of power in an amount sufficient to propel the theoretical Wheel of Time. The events attendant upon Theodicy, whether quiescent or cataclysmic, require abundant power to effect its purposes.

Theodicy is then, power-in-action. It is the movement of Natural forces that propel time and circumstance. To the extent that the actions of human beings are to be complicit in the foreward movement of the Wheel of Time, as it simultaneously elevates and degrades, we must understand power and its myriad manifestations and applications.

Power is a word that is used repeatedly by people who have little first-hand knowledge of it. We speak of power with a familiarity that seems to indicate an intimate, pre-existing relationship with it. Yet, our inability to effect meaningful change in our life circumstances and those of the people to whom we owe the duty of protection and care, belies the existence of such a relationship.

Power is such that even in the absence of an intimate relationship with it we instinctively respond to its presence. When someone with power speaks we are immediately attentive. The mere vocalization of the word raises our expectations and manifests the sensory experience of what it must actually be like to possess it.

Power is both a physical substance and an idea. It is energy and thought, process and principle, reality and potential.

As physical substance power is defined by the law of physics. Physics is the science of the properties of matter and energy.

It defines power as a physical substance because power is both energy and matter. It can be defined, therefore, by the law of quantum, atomic and nuclear physics as well.

Power as idea, theory or concept is revealed by the science of politics. Though it has been said that political science is the science of government or political institutions the definition is far too restrictive. The science of politics, as the term is used here, is more accurately defined as the science of the acquisition, distribution, utilization and control of power in the governance of human affairs. The science of politics is, therefore, the science of power.

Power is neutral and expansive. Because of its neutrality it will serve any master. Because of its inherently expansive NaTuRe it will reward the master whom it serves with ever increasing portions of it and will do so without remorse or compassion. In order to acquire and utilize power its elements, both substantial and theoretical must be identified and understood.

In the mathematical sense power is the result obtained when a quantity is multiplied by itself a specified number of times. The product of self-multiplication is always exponential. As a result power may also be accurately defined as an exponential increase in a base quantity that is determined by the number of times the quantity is multiplied by itself. If the quantity is energy then the formula $AP = p^n$, where AP is Active Power, where p is a power unit, and n is the number of times the power unit is multiplied by itself, is suggested. Put another way, when "power units" are multiplied by themselves the actual increase in their combined energy level is always exponential.

Each human being is an energetic, self-contained power unit. When power units, having a common goal and objective, join together they multiply themselves and their combined

Theodicy

power will exceed the total of the individual power units by a measurable, predictable and exponential rate of increase. The whole is greater than the sum of its parts.

Each of us is a self-contained power unit but we cannot, at least mathematically, multiply ourselves. One times one will always be one. One to the first power is always one. But as soon as we join with other power units multiplication is possible. Two power units are the energetic or power equivalent of two to the second power ($2^2 = 4$); three power units combined represent ($3^3=27$) twenty-seven units of power.

In physics power is the rate of doing work, or the ability to get work done. Work is the transference of energy (power) by application of sustained physical or mental effort that overcomes obstacles to achieve and objective or result. The equation P= w/t, where "P" stands for power, "w" for work and "t" for time. By this equation *power equals work divided by time.*

Power is also defined, in physics, as the rate of producing or expending energy because the units of energy and work are the same. In equation form, P = E/ t, where "P" is power, "E" is Energy produced or expended, and "t" is time. Power, therefore, also equals energy divided by time.

Apparently, power may be defined in many ways. In order to fully understand power and powerlessness we must also examine it with regard to the different ways it may be manifested.

Power may be broadly characterized as *force, energy* and *strength* depending on the way it functions at any given time. Power and energy are interchangeable and are the key to all activity on Earth. Force and strength are applied and stored power respectively.

Force is simply any kind of push or pull. It is the *application* of power. There are four distinct forces recognized by modern physics. These are: *gravity, electromagnetism*, the "strong" force and "weak" force.

Gravity is the force of attraction between massive objects. It is also the weakest of the forces. It is so weak as to be virtually undetectable and has no apparent affect between bodies as small as human beings. But it is also pervasive. It serves to hold all other stellar bodies in orbit and thereby give cohesiveness to universal order.

Electromagnetism is the force that is responsible for the basic building blocks of the universe. It is the force that holds the electron in its orbit around the nucleus of the atom. It holds atoms together and thereby forms molecules. Matter cannot exist without this force. It also operates at the bacterial level giving living cells the ability to move and take collective action in their quest for growth and reproduction. Because magnetism is produced by an electric current our brain cells function with the assistance of the electromagnetic force.

The "strong" force is perhaps the strongest force in the universe. It is estimated to be 137 times stronger than the electromagnetic force. It affects the particles of the nucleus of the atom and operates only at very short distances.

The "weak" force opposes the "strong" force. Where the "strong" force holds the nucleus of the atom together the "weak" force serves to push it apart. When the nuclei of atoms become unstable the weak force pushes them out of the nucleus· causing radioactive decay. It is the force that is responsible for the decay of matter. It is the death of matter. Since all material things are subject to it weakness is, in a very real sense, indicative of the of decay that is death.

Theodicy

Energy is recognized as the basis of life because it is the core that links all living things in the universe. All matter is comprised of energy. All things, animate as well as inanimate are expressions of energy. Two types of energy are recognized: Kinetic and potential. Kinetic energy is the energy of a body generated by its motion. Potential energy is energy that is stored, and available for use. Heat and light and motion are also forms of energy.

Strength is simply the innate capacity of a thing to resist or endure. *It is the power of opposition.* Power is, therefore, a composite of force, energy and strength. It is force when it is exerted; energy when it is creative or in motion; strength when it causes things to resist or endure. Physicists are now on the brink of proving (admitting would be more accurate) that the four forces are actually one great force that undergirds the universe and is responsible for all life and matter in it.

POWER AS IDEA

Power is also a principle. It is a fundamental, universal law from which many others derive. Simply stated the Power Principle provides that those who have power shall prosper, those who do not shall serve. Given the implications of the Power Principle it is inescapable that knowledge of the substance of power is insufficient to assure that we acquire and utilize power proportionate to our numbers. We must also analyze the idea and theory of power.

The Power Principle is best observed through the science of politics, which is, more concisely, the science of the acquisition, utilization, distribution and control of power in the governance of human affairs. It is in the political arena that power is most profitably observed.

In politics we can see, through the long lens of history, the importance of power to the development and maintenance of cultural identity. For it is the relative amount of power held by the one country vis-a-vis others that determines it relative position in the world of nations. Even on the intranational scale the situation is not dissimilar. Groups within a given nation will be influential and prosperous according to the amount of power they control relative to other groups within the society. Indeed, every aspect of governance from law and morality to poverty and affluence is informed by the wishes and world-view of the dominant culture. The dominant culture is such, of course, precisely because of its control of power and the power-driven technology known as government.

POLITICAL POWER

In the political sense power is the ability to take unilateral action in the face of the existence of actual or potential resistant force and to succeed in doing so. Political power is the triumph of the will of one people over that of others. It is the force that overcomes resistance. It is, at the same time, the strength of opposition and the audacity of confrontation. Political power is manifested in the acceptance by others of your right to take action, that is, to use power in ways that you deem legitimate. Authority cannot exist without power. Power becomes institutionalized or accepted by cloaking it in the guise of authority.

In order to have maximum effectiveness political power must be codified in laws and regulations that are themselves based upon the traditions and norms, that is the culture, of the group that comprises the society. Here we have the marriage of politics and culture we have referred to as political culture and which gives rise to political organization.

Political organization is a relationship. It is that which exists when power units combine for a stated purpose and

Theodicy

objective. It is the order of collective human affairs. Since the order is imposed it is a regulation consisting of rules promulgated by those whose superior power permits them to make the rules in the first place.

Political power is generated by collective action. It comes into existence when and only when the group decides to act as one. Collective goals born of collective vision become collective mandates. Because politics also involves conflict and confrontation over the control of power, those who act collectively and decisively are most successful in obtaining their goals.

Political power may be enhanced or undermined if the general culture sends mixed messages to some or all of its citizens. If the general culture is one that is founded on suspicion of all people, the people who adhere to will see others as generally dishonest and untrustworthy. As a result, their ability to act collectively will be undermined. General culture can, therefore, undermine or destroy the development of national political culture and simultaneously prevent the acquisition of political power.

Political power is also undermined when the general culture teaches that positive change can be effected through collective action but the reality experienced by a particular group within the society is that of political impotence. *In such a case the group tends to see politics as inconsequential or concludes that their failure at the science of power is in some way a result of their own actions.*

By contrast, a general culture that respects and incorporates national political culture tends to produce individuals who view themselves as politically savvy, capable of political conquest and entitled to political power at least proportionate to their numbers.

In the case of African Americans it is apparent that we have succumbed to the belief that we are dishonest and untrustworthy and the reality that we are politically impotent. The combination has all but removed our ability to see ourselves as a politically powerful people capable of taking unilateral action to change our collective circumstances for the better. Without the ability to see ourselves in this way we have effectively handed our fair share of political power over to enemies who have used it against us.

THE POWER PROCESS

Power is also an observable process. When it flows it is like electrical current, either direct or alternating. When its flow is regular it appears as structure. When it moves quickly and takes an irregular course it is more characteristic of what is generally understood as a process.

Power's ability to alternate is an apparently fixed reality. Like electricity, power may be static, appearing randomly causing dormant power to be released wherever friction occurs. This may explain the collective feeling of power experienced by rioters whose random action, like static electricity causes the release of power, albeit destructively.

The flow or current of power may also be generated purposefully and from a specific location. Whether it moves slowly or rapidly it is constant and multiplicitous in its origins. it is also inevitable. Power, like electricity, always exists somewhere.

The power process is contributed to by all people. Most are unaware of their contribution and are, therefore, more or less inactive participants in its use. Others, always a minority, are more or less active and in control of greater power not because they are inherently more powerful, but because they have gained control of the power of inactive

Theodicy

participants. The inactive participants are actually the *majority* because they contribute the bulk of the power. *It is an unalterable and universal law that power always resides with the inactive majority and can never reside elsewhere.* It is also they who unwittingly dictate the course of action a leader will take. If the leader discerns that the group will accept crumbs in lieu of real positive accomplishments, he will lead them to the crumbs that will mark his success. If, however, the group seeks and the entire loaf, the leader's success is measured by that standard. In short, they dictate what course the leader will take by what they will accept.

Power is greatest when combined. This is why the *group field* is also the location of the *power base*. The power base, in turn, resides within the New Body Politic. It cannot exist without it. The power base is not, however, the people themselves. It is the power that is generated by their relationship. It is virtually unlimited power hidden in each individual that is only energized when the individuals combine in purposeful, harmonious relationship.

In this respect the power is said to be hidden or *cheta,* to use a Kemitic term, that is, apparent but only accessible with extreme difficulty. It is for this reason that power must be made to appear centered in one person who seems to control it and who can bring it to bear on any obstacle. It is *focused* power that gains attention and is respected.

It is this hidden, unfocused and diffuse power that leadership successfully channels for the benefit of the New Body Politic and which the unscrupulous, self-anointed leader uses for his benefit alone. The leader who has not been carefully selected and trained to implement and articulate the plan that has preceded her, will always tend toward conspicuous consumption and the abuse of power. This is because she never learned that power is generated at high voltage and transmitted at even higher voltage. Like electricity at high voltage does not light the bulb, it burns it out. At high voltage power will electrocute rather than illuminate. The leader is the conductor of the power, not the power itself. He or she is the person who assists in the acquisition and transmission of the power for the benefit of the true owner - the New Body Politic.

The understanding of the power process is central to the understanding of Theodicy, because it is power that drives all other forces. The accomplishment of any objective, even the movement of the Wheel of Time, virtually impossible without power as its motive force.

We require power to protect and defend our families and our heritage. We require power to survive and prosper. We need power to secure our possessions. Without it we cannot effectively or assuredly do either. That is why power also creates or destroys self-respect. Powerless people tend to have low-esteem and limited horizons. They also tend to violence. It follows that powerlessness impedes meaningful cooperation and nation-building.

The power process also embodies and demonstrates power's confrontation with resistance and opposition. To the extent that egalitarian society, as distinct from democracy, is possible it is only so when power is diffuse and proportionate.

Politics, the science of power, is also said to be the art of compromise. But compromise is only possible when the power held by opposing factions is comparatively equal. Truly, compromise only exists when neither faction can defeat the other, except Pyrrhic sense. The illusion of compromise notwithstanding, any attempt to overcome resistance and/or opposition is a struggle between at least to powers -- a lesser and a greater. The greater power is only

Theodicy

greater because it has accumulated the power of others and focused that power for its own use. Necessarily, someone has convinced the actual possessors of the power, the inactive participant majority, that it has some authority to exercise their power for them. The lesser power is only so because it has not recognized that power resides with it and can be exercised by any collectivity this focused, organized and purposefully directed.

So long as power is in the hands of those who seek to further their own agenda of self-aggrandizement, they will, of necessity, manipulate and deceive in order to prevent the true possessors of power from removing it from their undeserved control.

When those of lesser power recognize that organization and collectivity creates power and that the more focused the organization, the larger the membership, the stronger the power base and the greater its ability to overcome resistance and opposition, a conflict of epic proportions is engendered. It is the outcome of the conflict which is, at base, a struggle for power, that is the soul of the revolutionary idea and the recurring nightmare of those in power. The reason is simple. *Those who control power and use it to further their own personal agenda will never voluntarily give that power, nor will they teach others how to take it from them.*

Substantial improvement in the lot of the powerless is directly and causally related to their control of power. It follows that the only way for them to extricate themselves from their centuries-old condition of powerlessness is through conflict and struggle that overcomes resistance and defeats opposition - *by any means necessary.*

The power process also encompasses the utilization of power. It begs a question. How is power acquired and most effectively and efficiently used? To answer the begged question two broad categories may be outlined to illustrate the potential uses of power. Both are important and each may be used separately or in tandem to achieve the specific goals and objectives of the New Body Politic. The two categories are *inducement* and *compulsion*. *Inducement* is accomplished by an appeal to reason and functions as a *technology of inspiration*. It induces the desired activity or response by intellectual means. Some may interpret this approach as "non-violence" but it should be remembered that words can be as violent as a well placed blow from a blunt object.

Compulsion is the power that wields the club of inducement. It is accomplished by an appeal to force and functions as the *technology of fear*. It compels the desired activity or response by violent means.

Inducement includes the use of models and information. Compulsion includes bluff, threat and violent, physical force.

Once a power base is developed the mere use of its power both increases its numbers and multiplies its power exponentially. This is because of the operation of the law of power units and the fact that power is neutral and expansive. This too is part of the power process.

When properly understood and observed over longer periods of time the power process crystallizes as structure. That structure is most profitably observed in organizations. An organization is, itself, a potential generator of power. This is, of course, the law of power units in action. Organization is a structure that imposes order, cooperation and division of labor upon itself. By so doing it literally forces persons with special and unique abilities and talents into areas where they are most needed. The organization facilitates the power process by giving it structural identity and definition.

Theodicy

One of the primary functions of the organization is its superior ability to galvanize individual power units and to focus and concentrate their combined power and thereby overcome the inertial effect of powerlessness that otherwise impedes the activity of its members.

If it is true that power must be focused and directed it is also true that some device must be utilized to focus and direct the power generated. To our ancient ancestors the power generator, par excellence was the Kemitic Temple.

CHAPTER FOURTEEN:
THE TEMPLE AS POWER GENERATOR

The Kemitic Temple is a complex, living phenomenon. The understanding of its multiple, coordinated function to the schematic of Theodicy is essential is order to appreciate the overall theme of this work.

The Kemitic Temple was the repository and dispenser of cultural and spiritual energy. It generated the power that fueled and animated the most efficient, prosperous and long lived civilization is history. The reason for this unprecedented phenomenon is that the Temple was the place where several important and interrelated functions were performed. It was, at once, the physical structure that both contained, or more properly focused the active power that is the *NeTeR NeTeRu* and trained the servants of the *NeTeR* who were the guardians of the unlimited power the Temple housed.

The Temple was also the location of vast libraries containing the accumulated cultural knowledge of the nation. It was also an astronomical observatory that made reckoning of time possible. It held a superior educational center for scholars, artisans and philosophers where professionals needed for the orderly and efficient functioning of society were trained and deployed. Together these functions represented the cultural energy of the Body Politic that was ancient Kemit.

The combination of cultural and spiritual energy focused and magnified in a central location, generated unlimited power. When it is understood that accurate, useful knowledge, timely and efficiently applied is powerful, and that knowledge is a form of specific energy, the notion that the temples of ancient Kemit were literally power generators becomes an accurate and instructive description of their function and importance.

Theodicy

A Brief History of the Ancient Kemitic Temple

The records of our ancient ancestors indicate that at an undeterminable and remote time in the past, the Earth was submerged in the primordial ocean called Nun. As the life giving waters subsided the first mound of Earth emerged. The primordial mound brought forth a sprout that grew up and upon which a hawk thereafter alighted. It is said that the hawk, later called Heru, held a mysterious piece of wood in its beak. The hawk departed but left the piece of wood behind. The mound was thereafter referred to as the place of the "First Appearance" of the *NeTeR* -- the first manifestation of the power and presence of God. The "First Appearance" was said to have taken place in the area of the foothills of the Mountains of the Moon. Thereafter the Ancient Ones constructed a bamboo enclosure, open to the sky, around the mound and the piece of wood left behind by *Heru*. The shelter became the first temple and the piece of wood it contained the first sacred object.

The "First Appearance" of the *NeTeR* marked the beginning of time. The sacred mound represented the place where earthly existence began. The bamboo enclosure became the first place dedicated to the service of the *NeTeR*. It was variously called Per Ankh and Per *NeTeR*, the House of Life and the House of the God. It was literally the place where the *NeTeR* dwelt and the dwelling place of the animating force --the energy or power of growth and reproduction. It was considered more than just the place where this mysterious power was situated. The structure itself was considered to be alive by virtue of its association with the vital life force it contained. The life force animated anything it touched, including the Temple itself.

In time the bamboo enclosure received first a thatched roof to shelter the sacred object, and was later entirely enclosed in stone. This innovation marked the appearance of the first stone temples. It was from this living center, this energetic focal point, that the first cities grew. It is more than coincidence that in older civilizations whenever a city plan is excavated there are always a number of structures gathered around a larger more extravagant building which invariably houses the shrine or temple of the local deity. Curiously, these are always built on a sacred "mound" where a temple or shrine has existed from the earliest times. The structures always contained some "sacred object", usually made of wood, that was believed to have sacred power to protect the people by whom it was maintained and to guarantee their survival and prosperity.

As a living and breathing structure the Temple literally grew within its own enclosure and also generated the growth of civilization as it brought the people together, instructed them in the Sacred Science and all the useful arts necessary to the attainment of civilization. First the Temple, then the city, then the nation. The starting point of civilization was, therefore, and indisputably, the Temple.

This information is part and parcel of the Authentic Ancestral Culture of our ancestors, the people of Kemit. It is confirmed by the etymology of the Latin words *templum* and tempus from which the English word temple is derived. To understand the magnitude of the Science of *Tehuti* and its importance to the Temple, the culture and civilization it created we must briefly review the origins of those Latin words.

The word *templum* has several seemingly unconnected meanings. As we shall see all are intimately related and become perfectly coherent when the history .of the Temple in Kemit is used as the key to interpretation.

Theodicy

In the Latin the word *templum* originally meant, a space for observation marked out by an augur. The augur was a priest and the highest official diviner of ancient Rome who duty it was to predict the future by interpreting signs and omens. When it is recalled that Kemitic temples were astronomical observatories, administered by priests, who predicted the future by signs and omens indicated by the stars, we begin to understand why the word temple derived from *templum*.

The word temple has an additional meaning, previously unexplained, of *a small piece of wood or timber*. Only when the legend of the "First Appearance" is known does the connection become clear. The temple was literally an enclosure that contained a small piece of wood.

The word *templum* is a cognate of the word *tempus*, meaning *a period of time*. The relationship between time and ancient Kemitic temples is instructive. One of the functions of the temple, because of its connection with the observation of the stars, was the reckoning of time. The centrality of this function to the overall purpose of the Temple and its influence on civilization must not be overlooked.

In Kemit the predominant factor that confronted the population was the annual overflow of the river *Hapy*. The discovery of the annual rising of Sirius as the harbinger of the annual flood was the result of temple observation of stellar activity. From this process was developed the concept of the year and led to the development of the first calendar and the division of the year into days, weeks and months. It should not be surprising that the first calendar, in operation in 4241 B.C. and the first clock were of Kemit invention.

Another curious meaning of temple, again from *templum,* is as a device for keeping the cloth in a loom stretched to its correct width during weaving. It is also interesting to note that the device known as temple in weaving was originally *a small piece of wood*. It is in this context that the temple was considered as the place where the *fabric of thought* and the *fabric of life* were woven. When it is also considered that weaving, like thinking, is a process by which things are brought together and interrelated so as to form a coherent whole that the connection between temple, thought and weaving is revealed.

In Kemit the Temple was the nucleus from which civilization was born and grew. The construction of a temple was, therefore, occasioned by an elaborate and ancient ritual called the "Stretching of the Cord". Present at the ritual were the King, himself the First Servant of the *NeTeR* and embodiment of the people; *Seshat*, the *NeTeR* of divine books; *Tehuti*, *NeTeR* of divine intelligence and creator of writing; and *Net* the *NeTeR* of divine weaving, reasoning and perception and counselor to *Tehuti*. The symbolism is profound. We have here assembled, at the foundation of the Temple, the King, divine books, intelligence, writing, weaving, reasoning and perception. The presence of each of these *NeTeRs* seems self-explanatory with the exception of *Net*, the *NeTeR* of weaving. A brief elaboration will demonstrate why weaving is important to the Temple.

Net was represented hieroglyphically by two symbols: the shuttle (a device used in weaving to carry the woof thread back and forth between the warp threads) and two crossed arrows. Ancient tradition also refers to *Net* as *NeTeR* of reasoning and perception. As we have noted perception is the doorkeeper of knowledge. Interestingly, *sia*, the Kemitic word for ideas and understanding is represented hieroglyphically as a piece of woven fabric. Through *Net* ideas, thought and understanding are associated with the ancient process of weaving and the foundation of temples.

Theodicy

Weaving consists in the interlacing of threads at right angles to produce fabric. The threads used in weaving are themselves lengths of fiber that have been twisted together or spun to make yarn.

Fabric, the product of weaving, is itself a structure or anything made of parts put together. This explains the shuttle by which *Net, NeTeR* of weaving and thought, was represented.

Net was also represented by two crossed arrows that immediately imply two related concepts: the combination of different things or *hybridization* and *opposition*. The process of thought is both the mixing of varieties and the opposing of one idea against another. When we think the process in operation is a delicate balance of comparison and negation.

Comparison involves taking one idea and comparing it with another. In doing so, dissimilarities become more or less apparent. The result of this placing of one thing beside another dictates the answer or solution which is in the form of a thought. Often, if not always, the comparison is between new information and previously acquired and stored information that is recalled during the process of analysis.

Negation, on the other hand, is the simple ability to human beings to say no to a given reality or set of facts. Information that is presented to us by our senses can be accepted or rejected. The ability to say yes or no is a fundamental distinguishing characteristic of humans that is unavailable to the so-called lower animals. In fact, the name *homo sapien* means to discern. Discernment is the, ability to mentally separate one thing from another or to perceive and recognize what is different. It is, in the truest sense, the knowledge of the "other". The animal lacks this ability because it cannot, as far as is known, say no to information presented or to the instinct that dictates its response.

These two concepts, hybridization and negation were known to the Kemites. The crossed arrows of *Net* symbolize how thought operates and complements perfectly the concept of weaving which symbolizes the product of that operation. It can be seen from this way *Net* was the *NeTeR* of thought, reasoning and perception. It also explains why *Tehuti,* the *NeTeR* of divine intelligence has her as his counselor.

The last and most compelling proof of the Temple as a power generator is the design of the Temple itself. Each Kemitic Temple contained what has been called a Holy of Holies. It was the place within the Temple that contained the sacred object. This was referred to by the Greeks as the *naos*.

Most, if not all, ancient religions have made use of temples in one form or another. The Hebrews (*Khabiru*), Greeks and Romans all erected temples to their Gods. All were built on the Kemitic model all contained a *naos* or its equivalent.

The Hebrews, more properly the *Khabiru*, claim to have erected a magnificent temple at Jerusalem. Although there are no verified remains of that building, it is said to have been flanked by pylons and to have housed a Holy of Holies or *naos* that contained the Ark of the Covenant. The connections to ancient Kemit are so obvious that it seems unnecessary to state them.

First, assuming for the sake of argument that the *Khabiru* resided in Kemit for 400 years they can be properly called Kemites themselves. Second, the Temple of Solomon was constructed not by the *Khabiru* (they did not possess the technology to do it) but by the Phoenicians under the direction of Hiram Abif the fabled widow's son. The Phoenicians were descendants of Kemites who founded Phoenicia as a Kemite trading colony whose most famous city-state was Carthage. Third, the Ark of the Covenant was a wooden chest stored in the *naos* that is said to have

Theodicy

contained two stone tablets allegedly inscribed with the Ten Commandments. Here we have a sacred enclosure that contained sacred objects.

Greek temples also contained a *naos* and were originally constructed of sun-dried bricks and wood. Temples constructed of stone on a defined floor plan were not erected in Greece until after their contact with Kemit. Greek temples were also considered the dwelling place of their Gods. Roman Temples were based on the Greek style, housed the statute of the deity and also contained a *naos*.

The word *naos* is said to derive from the Greek and means an ancient temple or enclosed part of such a temple. The word from which it derives is *nes*, meaning to unite, to be protected. A satisfactory explanation for why the name of the most sacred part of the temple is derived from the root to unite and protect has yet to be advanced.

In ancient Kemit, the place where the temple originated, the enclosed part of it contained the altar for the King's offering. It was called the *nes*. It should be noted here that the Kemite's deleted vowels in writing, therefore, ns with the addition of vowels easily becomes *nes* or *naos*. In ancient times the only person officially permitted to enter the *nes* was the King. Even the High Priest acted in the name of the King. The *nes* was, therefore, the most sacred part of the temple. It contained not only the altar but also the sacred object and the Divine Presence. The animating force of the living structure that was the temple was, therefore, contained in and radiated from the *Nes*. Although the Divine Presence was symbolized by a statue, it was not a physical being. It was a spiritual, active and energetic power. This active power was understood to undergird the universe and to control, by its presence or absence, all living things.

It must also be understood that Kemitic letters were ideographs, that is each letter represented an idea. We must look to the individual letters of the word *Ns* in order to glean a fuller understanding of the idea underlying the word.

Let us begin with the letter "n". European Egyptologists have often been led astray in the interpretation of Kemitic concepts by their inability to divorce themselves from a restrictive European mentality when attempting to understand or explain African spiritual concepts. In the case of the letter "n" they have concluded that it is the symbol for water. The conclusion is patently erroneous. The letter "n" represents energy and power. Although it is true that the letter "n" is often associated with water and aquatic concepts it does not itself represent water. The source of the misunderstanding is easily discovered.

The Kemite word for water is *mw* which, curiously, does not contain the letter "n". To determine the meaning of the letter we are required to look to the words in which it is used. For the purposes of this analysis two examples will suffice. We will examine the Kemitic word *NeTeR* and *Nu*.

The word *NeTeR* is translated as God but actually means the active power or energy which produces and creates things in regular recurrence. The connection between *NeTeR* and energy seems self-evident. Moreover, the Kemitic word for energy is *ner*, spelled with the symbols for energy and speech. One of the Kemitic explanations of the creation of the world states the *NeTeR NeTeRu* created by the spoken word.

The symbol for power and energy also appears in the word *Nu*. This word refers to the primeval watery mass from which all the *NeTeRs* evolved. It was also the place upon which the "Bark of Millions of Years" carrying the sun floats. Clearly, the "primeval watery mass" on which the sun floats cannot

Theodicy

be the ocean or anything else consisting of H_2O. The "watery mass" is the pool or ocean of cosmic energy from which the *NeTeRs*, themselves energetic pulses, evolved.

These two examples (many more could be cited) are sufficient to demonstrate that in the *Medu-NeTeR* (sacred words or writing) of the Kemites the letter "n" denotes energy, not water. It symbolizes the cosmic energy which is the alternating current of life. The ocean of energy and power is potential power. It is the available supply that is drawn upon in the ct of creation and which continues to sustain life after creation.

The second letter is the word *Ns* is found in the following words: *skhm*, meaning power; *st*, meaning ability (also a power); *sh*, meaning to transform into spirit; *shm*, meaning to control; *shr*, meaning to counsel or plan. When these appearances of the letter "s" are interlaced they weave a fabric of meaning that expresses the idea embodied in the letter s. The letter represents, therefore, the transforming power that controls, plans and directs. In the sense of setting by operation of pre-existing and universal laws, the parameters within which a thing will act. The letter " s" is the perfect complement of the letter "n" where "n" represents potential energy, "s" represents the transformation of that energy into kinetic or active power. When combined these definitions set forth the meaning of *Ns* as the place where the energy of the *NeTeR NeTeRu* is transformed in the active power that controls, counsels, and plans.

From the Temple, which itself grew from the *Ns*, the power that fuels civilization was radiated. It was this energetic, focal point that caused the people to unite around its powerful epicenter for the protection that enabled them to survive and prosper.

The *Ns* was the symbol of cohesion because through it and by it the people, individually and by clan, tribe and nome, joined together to form a new and stronger social and cultural unit for the common and inseparable causes of protection and prosperity.

The *Ns* also contained the altar of the King's Offering to the Divine *NeTeR* of the Cult. But the word *ns* also referred to the Royal Ancestors and ultimately all ancestors. It will not be surprising then that the Kemitic word for king was originally *nesu* for the one who makes the offering.

Finally, the *Ns* contained, as we have seen, the Divine Presence, also called the sacred essence. This sacred essence was literally the soul of the living temple that was, in turn, the soul of the nation.

In Kemit the soul was understood as the animating force in humans that included the power of speech, thought and action. When it is further considered that the word *ns* had the triple meanings of tongue, summon and director, the use of the word to describe the enclosed part of the temple is understandable since speech, thought and control are clearly implied by those words.

The *Ns* was also then, the place within the Temple that contained the power or ability to speak, think, plan, control and direct, the activities of the people and the nation.

The characteristics of the soul also describe the functions of the mind. It is no wonder that originally soul and mind were synonymous terms. This fact leads us to an additional clue that will assist us in reaching a full understanding of the word *ns*.

In ancient Greece, the place alleged to have been the birthplace of the concept of mind, the word for mind was *nous*. The word meant the intelligent, purposeful principle controlling the world of matter. Ancient Greek

Theodicy

"philosophers" expressed the following ideas regarding the mind:

To Anaxagoras *nous* was the *prime mover*, the cause of all motion and the *supreme power* underlying all things in the universe.

Plato saw *nous* as an *insubstantial principle, teleological in NaTuRe and involving intuition and direct insight.*

Aristotle, Plato's celebrated student, saw it as *reason, either perceptual or active and creative.*

The Neoplatonists, who originated in Kemit, saw *nous* as the divine reason that was the first creation of God.

That all of the above mentioned persons gained their fundamental ideas, directly or indirectly, from Kemit cannot, at this late date, be seriously denied. The mind of Greece was apparently the soul of Kemit. When the meanings of the two terms are compare the connection is transparent. We may also note here that the word *nous* is now recognized to be of Kemitic origin.

The Ns was the part of the Temple that contained the mind and/or soul of the living structure. It was to this place that the sacred essence was summoned and from it that its power was utilized to plan, direct and control human affairs and from which the unspoken voice of the *NeTeR* could be heard. Whether this "belief" was ever considered by the priests to be literally true is doubtful. It is true that a two-fold philosophy was employed in Kemit by which vehicle the people were left to their own beliefs while Sacred Science was practiced by those who had been selected and trained. In any event, the people were never involved in the inner workings of the Temple and were not, therefore, instructed in its philosophy and science.

This chapter deals with the concept and reality of the ancient Kemitic Temple as a power generator. We have seen, as a threshold matter, that the Temple is an ancient living structure that housed the sacred objects relating to the origins of the nation and the sacred essence that was the power and energy of the *NeTeR NeTeRu*. It was also the place that maintained their mythology, history and culture. In this sense the Temple was also a cultural *entrepot*.

The Kemitic Temple was also the place where the national thought was structured. It was the place where the very fabric of civilization, its pattern of ideas about the supernatural, life, growth, reproduction, death and the afterlife were woven on the loom of divine intelligence.

We have seen also that the Temple functioned as the national timepiece. It served the dual purposes of calendar and clock and regulated the rhythm of the Body Politic in strict accord with the celestial rhythm of the universe. In this way it was also the heartbeat of the nation.

When these concepts are combined we see that the Temple was the focal point of the power and energy of the Body Politic. Its function was similar to that of an optical system in which rays of light (also a form of energy) are caused to converge and diverge. In the Temple setting the energy is of two kinds. First, it is cosmic energy derived from the presence of the sacred essence *in situ*. The second, is the energy or power of the knowledge accumulated through observation, philosophy and culture. The Temple is the focal point in that it is the place where the two kinds of energy meet and intersect. From that point the combined energies branch out and are radiated throughout the Body Politic.

The Temple as Powerhouse

The Kemitic Temple may be accurately and usefully described as a powerhouse because of its ability to generate power. A generator is a device that converts potential energy into kinetic energy. By this definition the Temple attracts or

Theodicy

more accurately, summons energy that is random and unfocused, concentrates it in time and location, and thereby changes it into active power that generates not only life, but civilization, prosperity and political power.

The temples of our ancient ancestors were powerhouses, par excellence. They were the living entities that gave birth (to generate means birth and to produce) to civilization and were themselves animated, hence alive, by virtue of the active power that they attracted, focused, contained and transmitted.

It is unfortunate that as African Americans and aside from our disregard for the general importance of traditions of our ancestors and our loss of Authentic Ancestral Culture through the theft of our cultural energy, we have also failed to erect and maintain powerhouses. This failure has resulted in a lack of illumination, and loss of memory and consciousness. We suffer from a failure to generate our own and. unique brand of power. It is more than coincidence that a power failure is referred to as a *blackout*.

History is replete with examples of blackouts of one form or another. Most people recall the "Blackout of 1965" that crippled the City of New York on November 9th of that year. Most will remember the looting and crime, fear and anguish that held the entire city in its grip for 13 hours. Few know what caused the blackout. It resulted from the failure of a backup relay on one of the transmission lines from a generating station in Canada. The failure created an overload that caused the entire system to blackout. Within minutes parts of Canada, New York and New England were in total darkness. Millions of people in an area more than 80,000 miles square were affected.

Africans and by extension African Americans, have suffered a cultural power failure, literally a cultural blackout that began in 391 A.D. when the Roman Emperor Theodius the Great issued a series of edicts that prohibited pagan, that is Kemitic worship. The edicts ordered the closing of our temples, authorized the confiscation of temple property and the destruction of our libraries. These acts signaled open season on priests and adherents to our Authentic Ancestral Culture. By 394 A.D. the Kemitic culture and religion had been successfully silenced. The same year marked the establishment of Christianity as the official religion of the Roman Empire.

Two interesting facts should be added here. Theodius received his title "The Great" not as a result of military prowess, statesmanship or sagacity. He was awarded the title for his victory over the power of Kemitic culture and religion. In his ignorance of the value of our ancient teachings and his need to utterly wipe out any vestiges of the culture and religion that by its very existence undermined the claims of Christianity to authenticity or priority he brought the power of the Roman Empire to bear on everything Kemitic. By doing so he also extinguished the light of the world that was the culture of ancient Kemit and thrust the world into a period of one thousand years of ignorance now referred to as the "Dark Ages".

Our power houses have been closed, blacked out, for more than sixteen hundred years and with them our ability to raise ourselves from our present lamentable circumstances to the pinnacle of prosperity, success and world-class power that is our legacy and our birthright.

We have suffered the adverse effects of a cultural power failure for more than a millennium and a half. This thick, suffocating darkness has caused us to act in savage ways out of fear of darkness. In a blackout pandemonium reigns. Fear becomes common fare. All because of the failure of our

Theodicy

power houses to function, to produce spiritual and cultural power and light.

A perfect light bulb is a useless without electricity. Illumination absolutely requires *power*. The generation of power absolutely requires a *power house*. Our people cannot see without light. There can be no light with a power source. The Temple is the beacon of light that, when fully operational, will illumine our path to glory and will inspire and magnify the collective power of the African will.

The preeminent source of our power is derived from our Authentic Ancestral Culture and service to the traditional living African *NeTers* of our ancestors. But the voices of our ancestors have been brutally silenced. Their power to uplift and energize us has lain dormant since 394 A.D. Until such time as we resuscitate the religion of, and service to, our ancient ancestral *NeTeRs*, until we reconstruct a national powerhouse and perform the rituals that once made us great, we are doomed to second-class citizenship and the life prospects of our children will diminish with each passing day.

The Temple is a living, breathing, exuberant entity that creates the abundance of life and all it implies. As the Temple thrives and generates power so shall we become powerful.

We must also remember that the Temple, by its ability to direct, regulate and instruct in the fundamentals of leadership, is functionally, a *social control center* that creates cohesiveness among the members of the Body Politic. It directs, regulates and controls social intercourse by its adherence to, and promulgation of, Authentic Ancestral Culture. It does so by making that which is culturally acceptable easy and that which is culturally unacceptable difficult. But it does so not by prohibition but by social discouragement and acceptability.

A National Temple operates as a central powerhouse that generates spiritual and cultural power. It does so by attracting and focusing the active and unlimited power of the *NeTeR NeTeRu* at a fixed, central location and then radiates that power throughout the Body Politic.

Radiation, as used here, implies the process by which the power of the *NeTeR NeTeRu* is transmitted to the cells of the New Body Politic for their individual use. The physical transmission is accomplished through the use of a *power network*.

A power network is a interconnected system of electrical transmission lines and power substations that distribute generated electricity over a large area. The power network serves several functions. It enables power to be quickly and efficiently transmitted over great distances. Transmission requires, however, that the power be transformed to voltages far too high for normal consumer use. As a result it is necessary to have power distribution centers that receive power at high voltage and reduce it to voltage levels that permit distribution to end users.

In the Temple context, the power network is one that permits transmission (radiation) of the power of the *Neter Neteru*, attracted and focused at a national power house to be transmitted to the entire Body Politic. This is accomplished through local, subordinate temples (power substations) whose function it is to receive the power transmitted from the national power house, reduce its voltage to usable levels and make it available to the cells of the New Body Politic. it must be remembered that the power transformed and transmitted is both *spiritual* and *cultural*. The subordinate temples are, therefore, the places where the power radiates whether individual cells are there to partake of it or not.

Theodicy

The Temple also provides power as the heart, pulse and animator of the New Body Politic. As such it is the rhythm of the body and that which cleans, purifies and rejuvenates, along with the lungs, the blood that is the carrier of the vital force that is life itself. It is through this national, central powerhouse and its network of power substations that the heart beat of the New Body Politic is established.

When it is understood that it is our failure to generate spiritual and cultural power that affirmatively assists our enemies in their ability to undermine our quest for our rightful share of the world's wealth and· resources, and ·payment for our past labor, we see that we have no alternative than to build powerhouses, connect them to a national power network, bring them on line, generating power, immediately and before it is too late.

The concept of the Temple as a powerhouse presupposes a power that it will generate. The reader may logically inquire, at this point, what kind of power the Temple will generate. The power that the temple will focus and direct is the power of the *NeTeR NeTeRu*, in popular parlance, the power of God.

God is Power

Theodicy is a concept that clearly requires power to effect its purposes. That power can only be divine. To discover what that power is and is not we must look at the connection between God and power. We must immediately conclude that the very concept of God is meaningless if not aligned with the concept of power. Even God cannot fulfill its universally recognized roles as Creator and Sustainer of the universe unless it is, at very least, powerful. In short, no power --no God. Whether we refer to God as Jehovah, Allah, Vishnu, Odom or Amun, all agree that it is powerful. God is full of power and without power God is, well--not God. No one, no group of people has ever paid homage to a weak God. No one worships a God that is believed to be powerless. No one boasts of their allegiance to a God that can do nothing. All Gods must, at least, have enough power to protect and defend its worshippers form the hostile forces of the world whether they by human or diabolical.

Religion too is dependent on power since it is defined as the belief in a supernatural power and since it functions as the format for communion with that power. To the extent that religion serves to bring humanity closer to the realization of God it simultaneously serves to bring humanity to the realization of power. To the extent that religion is the act of worship, the acts that we perform, our pious genuflections, devoted prayers and mysterious rituals are no more than elaborate attempts to seek favor with power by flattery.

We have isolated, distilled if you will, a truly provocative, even revolutionary idea here. In the final analysis we must conclude that no matter what we call it *God is Power*. Before we explore the full implications of this revolutionary idea we must digress momentarily to examine what may be the most misleading and detrimental notion of God extant today.

There is a popular and historical recent notion that God is love. Much of the popularity and acceptance of this notion stems from its association with Christianity. That fact notwithstanding, its accuracy is still open to question.

If love is understood as intense affection and devotion it seem illogical to apply the term to God. Is it possible that God is affection and devotion? Affection is a feeling, a mental or emotional state. Devotion, on the other hand, is a vow or a religious practice. Neither of these seem to encompass an omnipotent, omnipresent and omniscient Supreme Being. Love may be intense affection, but intense affection is not God.

Theodicy

Love may also be defined as attraction. But even by this definition we find no support for the supposition that God is love. As attraction love is directed toward one person by another person. Even if it is assumed, for the sake of argument, that God is a person, love is the attraction itself not the person to whom it is directed. The person is the object of the attraction. God cannot logically be both love and that which is loved. If it is conceded that God is not a person then it follows that God cannot even be loved.

Biologists have a curious definition of love. They dispense with the theological and define love simply as sex. They make no pretense that the attractive force, that others call love, is anything other than the biological need to reproduce effectuated by the natural and instinctive male/female attraction. Not surprisingly we find a similar concept in ancient Kemit. Again, we must return to our Authentic Ancestral Culture to discern the NaTuRe of concepts that we frequently use but infrequently understand.

In Kemit the word for love was *mer*. *Mer* was one of the Seven Sacred Powers that are manifested on Earth. It was understood as the power of affinity (affinity is used here as it is defined in physics, i.e., the force that causes atoms of certain elements to be combined and stay combined). According to our ancestors love was only one of the sacred powers of the *NeTeR NeTeRu*. It was one of seven powers that existed as a result of the division of the divine unity. It is one of the powers created by the necessity to rejoin that which was divided and is itself the NaTuRal effect or reaction to the division. *Mer* was also recognized as a feminine impulse that was the first to exist in the world of time and substance. The reader should not overlook the profound implication here that if God is love it would then have to be female, a concept that would, needless to say, throw

Christianity, Judaism and Islam into a tailspin from which they would not likely recover.

It follows from this that love or *mer* was understood as the power of attraction but was only one of the powers of God. The concept that God is love only makes sense when understood in this way. No matter how you look at it God is still power.

It will not be surprising therefore, to find that the oldest extant word for that which we now refer to as God is *NeTeR*, an ancient Kemtic word. The word is mentioned in all ancient texts and predates European and Asiatic concepts. It is so ancient that the time when it began to be used cannot be determined. The word always appears in association with life forces that are referred to, in the plural, as *Neteru*.

The word *NeTer* has been universally translated by Egyptologists as god. It has been variously defined, however, as the *active power* in the world. According to Wallace Budge, the word refers to the active power that produces and creates things in regular recurrence, that gives life and restores youthful vigor.

From this we conclude that at the first appearance of a recorded conception of God in human history it was conceived as the *active power that produces and creates regularly*. The implications of this are indeed profound when applied in the context of the present analysis. It implies that to define power is to know God.

If it is true that God is power we would expect to find the components of power to be embraced by the concept of God. Power, as we have seen, is a composite of force, energy and strength. Power is force when it is exerted. Power is energy when it is in motion and when it is creative. Power is strength when it causes things to resist, act or endure. When

Theodicy

the constituent aspects of power are applied to the ascribed attributes of God the fit is, in a word, divine.

God is strong. God is mighty. God is the possessor and dispenser of all strength. If God were not believed to have such power prayer would be an exercise in futility. We pray to God because we believe that it is the strongest of the strong, the mightiest of the mighty. Clearly, in every aspect of power we see an attribute of God and vice versa.

God is, according to all religions, alive and active in the world of human affairs. The proof of this fact is found in the fact that God's primary characteristic is recognized as its creative power. Without the ability to create animate as well as inanimate things God would be powerless, ineffectual and unworthy of reverence. It is God's ability to animate things that gives rise to the laws of motion. God is, therefore, the force or power behind creation and movement. The key indicator of life is, after all, independent movement.

God is not only power, it is kinetic or active power. It is the power that is dynamic and which tends constant change. But we must be aware of the implications of this revolutionary idea. If God is active power, power must be actively present for one to have formal evidence of the presence of God. To the extent that the presence of God is manifested by the presence of active power, we the descendants of the most powerful, creative, innovative and energetic people in the history of the world, are Godless, because we are powerless.

The Temple is our powerhouse. The power that it generates and distributes is the power that is God. *Those who seek God, seek power. Those who have no power have no God.*

SECTION FIVE:

THE PLAN

CHAPTER FIFTEEN:

DEVELOPING A PLAN OF ACTION

The concept of Theodicy posits that Divine Justice, as evidenced in the movement of the Wheel of Time, will at regular intervals, alter the balance of power in the world by replacing those who are on top with those who now occupy the lower rungs of power. But Theodicy also informs us that this inevitable change will only reward those who have diligently prepared to take advantage of the predicted cosmic reorganization. Planning is, therefore, absolutely essential if African Americans are to benefit from the cosmic influence of the Age of *Hapy*.

This seemingly simple requirement presents a fundamental problem for us. As a people, at least in this the land of our captivity, we have been unable to engage in the level of effective planning required to secure collective prosperity and power proportionate to our numbers. It is axiomatic that by failing to plan we have unwittingly planned to fail. The problem is that we have never learned to plan or never recognized the importance of it. Without planning we are, at best, disorganized and ineffective. The result is that we are left at to the caprice of enemies who have historically styled themselves our benefactors.

We are, indisputably, the victims of a planned assault that can only be described as an undeclared war. The fact that the war is undeclared does not lessen the impact of its devastating effects on lives and fortunes.

In order to meet and defeat this aggressively launched, relentlessly pursued, undeclared war we must learn to plan both defensively and offensively. Our enemies, the centuries-long aggressors in this war have never failed to plan strategies for our continued subjugation. To persist in the failure to plan is tantamount to standing idle while our enemies rape and imprison our men, women and children.

We must develop a simple and effective plan of action that will embolden those who breathe the fire and inspire those who time and failure has rendered complacent. This section is a modest and admittedly imperfect contribution to that desperately needed effort. Once again, we begin with the wisdom of our ancient ancestors.

In ancient Kemit the word *skhr* or *shr* denoted a plan. The word represented a wide range of meanings that vividly illustrated the importance, to our ancestors, of plans and planning in general.

The *sekher* was not only the plan but was also the actual design of a thing. In the modern sense, *sekher* could be likened to DNA to the extent that it may be seen as the plan of all living things. Contained in our DNA is the plan that when followed to maturity results in the completed thing. In a less concrete way, *sekher* also implied intention, advice, behavior, custom and condition. In the theological sense the word referred to the design and character of destiny. And in that sense *sekher* was understood as the "Eternal Plan". Curiously, it also meant to direct, lead or conduct, and also implied to overthrow or defeat.

To our ancestors then, the plan was eternal and related to the destiny of the people. It was an actual design by which to lead, direct and by extension, the way to overthrow or defeat someone or something.

It should also be noted here that the root *skh* is found in the Kemitic word *sekhem* meaning power. To our ancestors, and since remotest times, plan and power were recognized as being mysteriously linked.

The English derivation of the word plan is also instructive. The word derives from the Latin *planta* which has two root meanings that form cognate words. These are (1) the sole of the foot; and (2) a sprout or twig. The word is also related to the Latin *plantare* meaning to smooth the soil or ground for planting. As used in here the word plan is vitally connected to the three English meanings.

First, the sole of the foot symbolizes foundation. Every structure must have a foundation. It is the strength of the foundation, in large measure, that determines the ability of

Theodicy

the structure to stand. To exist literally means to stand. In a very real sense we exist by our ability to stand. The sole of the foot is, therefore, the quintessential symbol of foundation. The plan is our foundation. It is the collective foot that enables us to stand as a people. We cannot stand, we cannot exist without a plan.

Second, the plan is a sprout or twig. It is a cutting that is ready to be planted in the soil to grow to maturity and bear fruit, after its kind, in due season. This further implies two very important concepts. A sprout or twig is delicate because it is young. It must be nurtured and protected. It must be placed in proper soil, at the appropriate time, and under exacting conditions or it will not grow. It is also at this time in its development that the plant is most vulnerable to attack.

The sprout is a cutting taken from a large, pre-existing plant that it will mirror as it grows. That which the cutting mirrors must exist and must be hardy enough to have survive to maturity itself.

Third, the plan is that by which the ground is prepared for the planting of the sprout. It implies not only cultivation but plowing and agitation of the soil as well. The Latin word for plan is also clearly associated, at least in the last two senses, with tilling of the soil and cultivation which is also, as we have seen, a root meaning of the word culture.

When these concepts are combined we may conclude that the plan is a detailed strategy that forms the foundation upon which we stand and which is comprised of (1) the seed/idea that is the delicate sprout, cut from a hardy stalk, from which our prosperity will grow; and (2) the tactic, technique and technology for cultivation of the soil in which the delicate sprout must be planted in order to grow to maturity at which point it will reproduce both fruit and seed-fruit for today's nourishment and seed for tomorrow's. The plan is both the strategy and the tactic by which its predetermined objectives will be accomplished by the New Body Politic.

Once the plan is in place those who possess the qualifications to carry out its mandate may be selected and trained. For it is an axiom that we ignore at our peril that the plan must always precede the leadership. In the absence of a well-conceived plan leadership is, at best, random haphazard and unguided. Even the leader must be guided by the plan. For this reason the plan must include a leadership strategy as it relates to the qualities of leadership and the quality of the leader.

The plan must also be such that its general contours &re capable of dissemination throughout the New Body Politic that all may witness the transformation as it unfolds. It must also be simple and straightforward enough that even the woman on the street will recognize its value and purpose virtually intuitively.

The first step in achieving any goal, either individual or collective, is to make up one's mind that the goal is, in fact, possible. This may seem a minor, even obvious point but it is fundamental. The New Body Politic and all those who have been selected and trained for positions of leadership must be completely disabused of the notion that the objective of the plan cannot be accomplished or that our efforts will be unsuccessful.

The second step is understanding of the importance of lessons. Most people readily comprehend the notion that lessons are to be learned. But a lesson learned is simultaneously a lesson taught. In life, as in the plan, we must do both. We must learn lessons not only from our glorious ancestral past, but also from our day-to-day encounters in the real world. Such lessons are of maximum importance because they mold our psyche, strengthen our resolve and help us, like feedback to a guided missile, to remain focused and stay on target.

We must also learn to teach lessons to others. We must learn to teach lessons of love, by example, to our children. We must also learn to teach harsh lessons to our enemies and those who would, for any reason, stand in the way of our progress and self-determination.

Theodicy

One of the primary reasons for our current and historical plight is our failure to teach harsh, unmistakable lessons to our enemies that any slight, disrespect or aggression to our people or our collective interests will be met with maximum retaliation, in kind, one hundred-fold in amount and in intensity, swiftly and unerringly. We must know that the plan will be successful and teach harsh lessons to those who would interfere with the plan because they disbelieve. These things having been said let us look at the Elements of the Successful Plan of action.

The Seven Elements of the Successful Plan of Action

The first element of the successful plan of action is the isolation of the objective to be accomplished. This is true whether the plan is long or short term, local or national, individual or collective. This we shall call the mission. A mission is to be understood as an ongoing responsibility and duty that is compelled by one's innate desire to survive and prosper. To the individual eating and drinking are, by our definition, a mission. We must eat and drink to survive but whether we ever truly understand the connection between these acts and survival is irrelevant so long as they are accomplished. We must eat and we know through an innate consciousness that we must eat. The mission serves a similar purpose and must have the same priority.

In developing the plan of action the mission must be, first and foremost, reduced to a *mission statement*. Ideally, the mission statement should be no more than one or two sentences in length. It must be concise, direct and straightforward. Its purpose is to state clearly and concisely the bare essentials of that which is to be accomplished and to focus attention on that which is the planned outcome of the mission. The mission statement must concisely embody the vision that is be made reality by its accomplishment. It must both instill the necessary sense of urgency and inspire the *esprit d' corps* and inflame the collective will of the New Body Politic.

The second element is *situational awareness* and refers to the part of the overall plan that involves *intelligence gathering, background information and reconnaissance* which shall be here referred to as the *Internal Intelligence Function*. It is the stage at which information about the mission and how it is to be accomplished is gathered, assembled and analyzed.

The accurate and effective analysis of information is crucial to any plan if it is to be successful. This stage permits us to learn what we need to know about our situation and circumstances. It covers both internal dynamics and the forces that we can expect to be arrayed against us to prevent the success of our mission. Situational awareness is accomplished by the Internal Intelligence Function and is the knowledge base from which the collective will is informed.

The third element is *execution*. This element involves the detail of the operational methods by which the mission is carried out. Execution is how it will be done. Necessarily, this element of the plan requires several levels of planning and appropriate security measures at each level. Execution is not a matter of public information. It goes without saying that it is often the element of surprise that wins the day. If it is true that forewarned is forearmed, it is also true that successful execution requires that information of the details of the operational methods of the plan of action are to be divulged on a need to know basis only. A telegraphed punch is very seldom effective.

The fourth and fifth elements are combined as *Service and Support or SAS*. This is the element that provides the logistics of the mission. It details how those who are directly involved in the execution of the mission will be serviced and supported. It involves the plans for procurement of necessary equipment, personnel and facilities. It is the lifeblood of the mission. SAS also includes the procurement of funds as they relate to the purchase of materials necessary of the execution of the plan of action.

The sixth element is *control*. This element is the designated chain of command. It is the flow chart that indicates who gives orders, who takes them and designates the various levels of security clearance. It is the voice of execution because the mission cannot be accomplished without a control voice.

The seventh and final element is *communication*. This element details the procedure to be followed and the equipment to be used to insure timely, accurate transmission of the voice of control to all parties necessary to execute the mission. It also includes appropriate security clearance as well as the communications hardware and personnel to facilitate communication.

The importance of this element lies in the fact that even a well conceived plan of action that contains all the essential elements will not be successful if its directives cannot be securely communicated timely and efficiently.

These then are the seven elements of the successful plan of action. *They do not represent the plan itself.* They should be viewed as a skeleton that provides the framework upon which the plan is constructed. A vital element of the successful plan of action is the *Internal Intelligence Function*. Because of the importance of this function a brief digression is necessary to insure that its importance is not underestimated.

The Internal Intelligence Function

The mind is a self-preserving, physical process by which symbols, within a symbol system are stored and manipulated. It is the schematic by which information moves within the brain. The mind is one of the locations of the will and provides part of the information that informs the will. Accurate information is critical to the maintenance of the will. As we have seen the determination of the accuracy of information is made through *Oudja* and intelligence.

Intelligence should be understood here as a technology. It is the process by which information is gathered, assembled and analyzed. Even accurate information is useless if it is not received in timely fashion and constantly updated in real time. It follows that it is the combination of accuracy and timeliness that determines the ability to effectively formulate and enforce the dictates of the will. The acquisition of timely is(.of vital , importance \to the success of the plan of action .. ·and to the functioning of the New Boby Politic. It is the responsibility of the Internal Intelligence Function.

The Internal Intelligence Function operates as a defensive mechanism whose purpose is to insure the survival and prosperity of the body within which it operates. As a defensive mechanism it is best understood as the analysis of reconnaissance information that is organized and systematized for use in military preparedness. It also serves to transmit such information along a pre-determined network organized by chain of command and security clearance.

The Internal Intelligence Function generates a continuous flow of information, recombines it and updates it continuously and in real time. The information is gathered through a network of observation posts, strategically located throughout the Body Politic. Information so gathered· is transmitted to a central processing unit(s) that is, in effect, the brain of the Body Politic. Just as the mind cannot be physically located at a specific place in the brain, the location of the Internal Intelligence Function may not be located.

The power of the New Body Politic to survive and prosper is dependent on its ability to gather accurate, raw knowledge, in timely fashion, on a continuous basis and transform it into useful information. The knowledge must be gathered in three essential categories: (1) knowledge about our past, that we shall call *historical and cultural knowledge*; (2) knowledge about our present state of affairs, that is known as *systemic knowledge*; and (3) knowledge about the world in which we must survive and prosper, this is *environmental knowledge*.

Historical and cultural knowledge are integrated. Each explains and helps make sense of the other. Since they both are comprised of stored knowledge they are properly defined as memory. The memory of the New Body Politic is

Theodicy

then, in a very sense its integrity when integrity is understood as a perfect and unimpaired condition. It is axiomatic that thought is not possible without memory. The combination of historical and cultural knowledge then, is the stock of our *collective memory*. We have examined culture and its importance at length. Let us now look briefly at the importance of history as a separate and distinct component of collective memory as it relates to the Internal Intelligence Function.

History is defined as a chronological record of events that includes commentary on those events. The definition is accurate as far as it goes. It is misleading, however, because of what it does not say. History is much more than a chronology of events. The word history literally means *knowing or learned.* History is primarily knowledge. Secondarily, it is knowledge that has been learned. To learn is to fix in the mind, that is, to memorize. History is, therefore, knowledge that has been memorized or in some way recorded.

Recordation necessarily implicates the past. That which has been recorded can only have previously occurred. But history is not all that has occurred or all that has been recorded. The word history is reserved for something that belongs to the past *and* is important enough to be recorded. Since the determination of what is important is relative and determined by the observer it follows that history exists because someone thought the knowledge important enough to record. It is obvious that observers tend to see as important and therefore worthy of recording, the events and accomplishments of their own people. It is for this reason that history is fundamentally ethnic: Napoleon Bonaparte is credited with having said that "history is a lie agreed upon". To the extent the statement is true the lie is agreed upon by people of the same ethnic background.

The importance of our history is that it is the knowledge of our past. It is the record of events that were import ant enough to our ancestors for them to record. When culture and history are combined they create *cultural history* which is the knowledge of our ancestral becoming and the events that have made our people what they are today.

History is a special form of memory. As applied to the New Body Politic it is collective memory. We are capable of present action mainly because we have the ability to remember. Every action that we take, no matter how minor, requires the use of memory. Even our so-called involuntary actions, like heart beat and breathing, occur because something remembers how and when to do it. We cannot think without memory. If we cannot think without memory we cannot be creative without it.

Creativity is the process of taking old ideas stored in memory and combining them with new information to come up with new ideas that did not exist before. When we are confronted with problems that affect our life prospects we must be creative to solve them. Without memory this vital function is virtually impossible. Without memory we simply stagger through life in mindless forgetfulness and ignorance.

Systemic knowledge is knowledge about us, now. It is current knowledge that is accurate and timely. It must be collected by us and for our own purposes. It is knowledge gathered from our interior reaches. By analogy to the human body it is knowledge accumulated about the body itself. It is statistical information about every aspect of our collective existence. It covers income, occupations, likes and dislikes, proclivities and capacity. It is the systems check of the New Body Politic. It informs us of the state of our health, strength and overall condition. It is constantly updated to insure up to the minute accuracy. It keeps constant watch and records all bodily functions to insure that they are operating at maximum efficiency.

Through systemic knowledge we are constantly aware of internal operations. It advises us of how we are doing now. It is through systemic knowledge that we know at any given moment what the state of our collective health is. This enables us to act swiftly at the first indication of dis-ease or imbalance to take corrective action immediately.

Theodicy

Environmental knowledge is absolutely essential for us to orient ourselves. It is the compass that keeps us on course in our constant effort to navigate the perilous waters of struggle for power and respect in a world that responds to nothing else. The Internal Intelligence Function combines and integrates historical/cultural, systemic and environmental knowledge in a database that is foundational. The knowledge represents the power that transforms. When it is gathered by us, analyzed and transmitted by us it becomes the informational launching pad from which our ascent to our rightful place in world affairs begins. It is the navigational compass by which we direct our ship of state. By the collection, analysis and dissemination of knowledge in the three essential categories the New Body Politic is enabled to preserve, protect and defend itself against attack and insure survival, prosperity and power.

The Development of

Strategy and Tactics

Strategy and tactics are flip sides of the same coin. One cannot effectively exist without the other. Strategy is the thinking process that develops the plan - it is the overall objective to be accomplished. It is necessarily long-term. Tactics, on the other hand, are the set of specific acts taken to bring the strategy to completion. Tactics are day-to-day. Both are essential to a plan of action.

As we have seen the Internal Intelligence Function is the process by which the New Body Politic acquires vital knowledge and the process of analysis by which it is rendered useful. The analysis of the this knowledge and the conclusions distilled from it form the information base from which strategy and tactics are developed.

There are two types of analytical processes. These are the scientific and the philosophic. Scientific analysis is based on experiment and is, therefore, empirical. Philosophic analysis, on the other hand, is based on deduction or the process of reasoning in which the observed effect is recognized to follow necessarily from a stated cause. The history of the development of knowledge informs us that humanity seems to alternate between the two methods in its unending pursuit of knowledge. Theory, general concepts and basic assumptions seem to move, cyclically, between the scientific and the philosophic approaches. The two may however, operate in conjunction.

In the best situation philosophic analysis is used to determine the mission and develops a strategy for its execution. Scientific analysis, in turn, determines the tactics to be employed in pursuit of the execution of the mission. Scientific analysis also serves to alert the Body Politic when a particular strategy is ill-advised based on empirical data permitting such a strategy to be revised or abandoned before resources are committed unnecessarily.

It is instructive to note here that the scientific approach has reigned, in one form or another, for the last two millennia. The approach has been uniquely that of the European. The philosophic approach is the hallmark of Kemitic and indigenous African analysis. When the notion of periodic alternation between the two approaches is viewed in the context of Theodicy and the Wheel of Time the implications are uncanny.

The development of strategy and tactics must be understood as a process by which the strategy is determined by philosophic analysis and the tactics by scientific analysis. In the case of the African American this approach would require us to focus on the observed and indisputable fact of our powerlessness in America. This, in turn, requires us to determine the cause from which the observed fact flows. The strategy to correct the effect that flows from the discerned cause is then formulated.

In order to implement the strategy a specific set of tactics are required. These are developed through scientific analysis. Scientific analysis also provides periodic feedback to assess the feasibility of the strategy and to indicate if or when revisions or even abandonment of the strategy is necessary and appropriate.

Theodicy

The Internal Intelligence Function overlaps with the seventh element of the successful plan of action. It is axiomatic that even knowledge that is accurate, gathered in timely fashion and properly analyzed is worthless if it cannot be efficiently communicated.

Communication is the transmission of messages, ideas and symbols. It is the adhesive that bonds individuals into groups and a group into a New Body Politic. This is true because it permits and encourages the group to see, think and act cohesively because of simultaneously shared information. When such information is shared it immediately becomes the basis of present knowledge and when stored becomes the content of collective memory. Any successful plan of action must include provision for a state of the art communications system to allow the knowledge gathered to be efficiently transmitted expeditiously. In order to fully understand the importance of communication to the successful plan of action we must take a look at the knowledge and its relationship to symbols and symbol systems.

Knowledge

Knowledge is all that has been, or can be, perceived or grasped by the mind. As such it implies *perception*, *registration* and a minimum level of *conscious awareness*.

Knowledge is the body of known facts, and the ideas inferred from those facts through the process of recombination.

Information is knowledge that has been *purposefully gathered* and given special character by inclusion in a particular *system of arrangement* and that has been transmitted or stored for transmission. It follows that knowledge is accumulated information that has been systematized. It is a thing that when activated or put in motion becomes information. Therefore, information is motivated or activated knowledge.

Perception is all the stimuli we receive from the five sense organs and the heart which is the sixth sense organ and the seat of intelligence and intuition. It is through perception that we have knowledge of the world outside of the prison of matter that is the body.

Registration is the process of recordation of knowledge perceived. The word literally means to bring back and refers to a book used to note names and events. It is also the act of recording for the purpose of bringing back at some time in the future. Registration is the process of by which we remember. It is perhaps as important as perception because without it that which our senses have perceived is not stored for comparison. Registration makes comparison and, therefore, thinking possible.

Conscious awareness is distinct from mere awareness. An animal is *aware* of its surroundings. But it may not be accurate to say that animals are conscious of their surroundings. Although it is true that conscious and aware considered synonymous terms their roots are not cognate. Consciousness refers to knowing, or having knowledge regarding one's own thoughts and things inside of oneself. Awareness, on the other hand, involves wariness, being on guard, or alert. By their roots consciousness and awareness are distinct concepts. One relates to the human condition while the other is more characteristic of the so-called lower animals. As used here conscious awareness refers to the combination of the inborn knowledge attributed to human beings and the alertness characteristic of animals whose survival depends not upon their ability to think as much as their awareness of their surroundings.

The Internal Intelligence Function exists to purposefully gather knowledge and transform it into useful information. The process by which this is done utilizes symbols that have been included in a symbol system and communicated.

As we have seen communication is vital to the existence of the New Body Politic. The birth of the New Body Politic is a result of the development of and communication of, an idea. This seed/ idea is then communicated to others to become the vital force that is the soul of the New Body Politic. That which is vital and communicated is knowledge. When knowledge is communicated it becomes information.

Theodicy

The effective communication of knowledge requires ongoing acquisition and efficient and timely transmission. The absence of either leads to stagnation and eventual death of the Body Politic.

Knowledge is the sum of what has been perceived, discovered, intuited and learned. Knowledge must be acquired before it can be communicated. Acquisition of knowledge is a process of discrimination and selection and is inherently subjective. The subjective process of knowledge acquisition is an expression of the interests deemed important by the body that collects the knowledge.

Clearly defined objectives are a pre-condition to the effective acquisition of knowledge. To the extent that the Body Politic, or individual is successful in acquiring knowledge is dependent on its ability to clearly define and focus its search. In order to do so it must satisfy four essential criteria. These are (1) the Body Politic must clearly define its interests and objectives (the mission) in seeking specific knowledge; (2) it must clearly identify the outstanding characteristics of that which is seeks knowledge about; (3) it must determine the methods by which the specific knowledge may be discovered; and (4) it must establish a symbol system by which the acquired knowledge is to be recorded and applied to the situation for which it was gathered.

The quest for knowledge begins with the one who seeks to acquire it. Knowledge itself can be useful or useless depending on the objective of the search. Without clearly defined and focused objectives the search for knowledge will be haphazard at best. It follows that the highest priority must be granted to the formulation of a set of objectives to guide the search for knowledge by the New Body Politic.

When objectives are firmly established the contours of the thing sought to be known must be carefully considered. It seems obvious that the search for a thing is frustrated at the outset if one does not have some idea of what she is looking for. Knowing what you are looking for does not. however. guarantee the success of the search. One must know how, that is by what methods and processes, the knowledge may be acquired. The finest, precision made electron microscope will be worthless in an attempt to ascertain the contours of the Venusian landscape.

Symbols and Symbol Systems

Thought is physical energy. Symbols are the constructs of thought. When thought is understood as energy, symbols become the building blocks of ideation, which is, in turn, the basis of the creativity that fuels the advancement of society toward civilization.

Symbols are literally devices used to store and retrieve thought. We think by use of symbols. We perceive by and through our senses but the data is stored in the memory as symbols. We call on our minds to retrieve data previously stored we do so by the use of symbols that have been coded by the brain. In similar fashion computers utilize symbols to enter, store , retrieve and manipulate data and by the use of symbols is able to "think". The connection between thought and symbols can, therefore, be demonstrated mechanically.

The reader should not be surprised to learn that the first written expression of thought was ideographic and used symbols to represent ideas.

In Kemit, the place to which we must invariably return whenever we seek to discover origins, the use of symbols was raised to the level of the divine. The Kemitic word *medu NeTeR*, meaning letters or writing of the Neter Tehuti, is popularly recognized in its Greek form as hieroglyph. The hieroglyphs are symbols to which specific ideas are connected. Their purpose as sacred writing was to transmit knowledge in the best was to engender the creative thinking process. Tehuti was the *NeTeR* of divine intelligence and the creator of writing. It has even been argued that the word thought derives from his name.

Apparently, more than twenty thousand years ago the Kemites recognized that ideas are intimately connected to and effectively transmitted through symbols. For this reason

Theodicy

they recorded their most sacred notions in the letters of Tehuti chiseled into temple walls and monument surfaces.

The assertion that symbols are the building blocks of the power of ideation is quite accurate. A symbol is literally a concrete idea. The symbol gives the idea substance and renders it capable of manipulation as thought. When symbols are combined they literally build or construct thought. Over time the process of combining symbols results in what may be called a symbol system. It is the symbol system that enforces and transmits culture by its operational control of thought. Symbols and symbol systems control thought by simply and efficiently pre-packaging ideas. A contemporary example will illustrate the point.

Crime is the object of universal fear and disapproval by civilized societies. America is no exception. In America crime and violence are terms that have been used to propel politicians to the White House while simultaneously eroding the cherished constitutional rights of her citizens. The method by which this erosion has been masterfully accomplished if by the ingenious and diabolical use of symbols and symbol systems. The method has worked so efficiently that the average American is unaware of it.

The government and the media are actually *symbol creators,* and *symbol system manipulators*. They have successfully utilized the fear of crime and violence to political advantage. They have done so by making concrete two ideas by joining them in one symbol. The two ideas are each fundamental components of the American psyche and the American culture. They are the fear of crime and racism.

Though racism is no longer current fashion in America, it is still so endemic as to be virtually intractable. The objects of American racism, ore so than any other group, are and have always been Americans of African descent. This fact is played upon by politicians and media alike whenever it suites their purposes.

When the President and the official organs of government at his disposal focus their considerable power of persuasion on the same problem (whether the problem be real or imagined) the result is, invariably, mass acceptance of practically any program or policy that is advocated as a remedy for the problem.

When the media focuses its considerable power of persuasion on the same problem the problem becomes, in short order, the major concern of the American people. The fact that the air time or print space devoted to the problem may be disproportionate to its importance is apparently immaterial.

When the alleged problem is pre-packaged as a symbol and incorporated in a symbol system it will, in time, infect the construction of thought by people who believe it on related as well as unrelated topics.

In the example used here the symbol selected to concretize the idea of crime in America is the African American male in general, and the young African American male specifically. The predictable result is that the young African American male has become the prime example of crime and violence in America. This is, of course, in spite of the fact that African Americans do not commit more crime than their White counterparts. It is the result of the use of symbols to control thought.

A second example is the infamous War on Drugs. As far as symbol systems are concerned the War on Drugs is a classic. It also combines fear and racism as its underlying premises.

The American War on Drugs is actually a war against young African American males based, ostensibly, on the need to eradicate the use of a specific drug - crack cocaine. (The reader should ask at this point if it is possible to eradicate the use of an addictive drug without eradicating the users?)

We need only look at the arrest and incarceration rates of African American males as compared to young White males and the lengths of the sentences imposed to confirm who the War on Drugs is being prosecuted against.

Theodicy

The term War on Drugs is attributed to the late President Richard Nixon. The war began in earnest, however, in the mid 1980's. During that period more than a thousand newspaper and magazine articles and hundreds of hours of television air time were dedicated to exposing the alleged evils of crack cocaine. These articles, news broadcasts and television programs depicted young African American males, almost exclusively, as sellers and users of crack and thereby responsible for all the ills, including violence, associated with it. This in spite of fact that the majority of crack addicts are White and that the raw product from which it is made is manufactured in South America.

In predictable fashion the then President and other prominent politicians rushed before the cameras to assure America that they would rid the country of the scourge of crack cocaine by legislative enactment, posthaste. It was also predictable that during the same period, and for the first time, Americans decided that drugs were the number one problem facing the country. For the first time poverty, education, health care, and racism less important.

In the wake of this deluge of selective and targeted publicity, the most Draconian legislative measure in the nation's history was passed virtually without debate. In one hour and forty minutes the infamous, 100-1 crack cocaine amendment was on the road to becoming law. This disparate and racially motivated law has resulted in the mass incarceration or penal · control of fully one-third of all African American males between the ages of 20 to 29. The explosive incarceration rates that have followed the imposition of the crack cocaine penalty has directly resulted in the United States now having the dubious distinction of being the country with the highest incarceration rate in the world.

This second example of the use of symbols and system systems demonstrates how an idea can be concretized into a symbol and how that symbol can be manipulated. The idea that crack cocaine is a threat to the internal security of the United States has been symbolized by the young African American male. As a result the War on Drugs is freely prosecuted against the young African American male with impunity. Perhaps the most significant piece of evidence is that the War on Drugs has been a miserable failure in all respects but one. The amount of drugs entering the country increased exponentially since the war began. The price at which it is available, both wholesale and retail has significantly decreased and the quality is at an all time high. The only success of the War on Drugs has been that it has accomplished the unprecedented mass incarceration of young African American males and has become the best strategy or the domination and subjugation of our people since slavery.

The reader should also note that wars are fought by the young men of the nation. To incarcerate our young men for the entire course of their youth is to decimate the ranks of our potential warriors. Without warriors our ability to fight our enemies is significantly reduced.

These examples illustrate the negative power of symbols and symbol systems. But, symbols and symbol systems may be used positively. They can become the constructs of positive thought that concretizes the idea of the young African American male as the promise of our future and as the warriors and protectors of our heritage and culture.

Symbols and symbol systems are simultaneously *tools* for the communication of the seed/ideas from which the New Body Politic is born and *weapons* to defeat our enemies in their attempt to disguise the atrocity of their acts by symbolizing the victims of their centuries-old, undeclared war as criminals.

In order to counteract the enemy's negative use of symbols a successful plan of action must include positive, empowering symbols that will be incorporated into a positive, proactive symbol system of our own design.

We have seen that symbol systems are used to construct thought patterns that either enslave or empower. It follows that people require a symbol with which they can identify. The symbol must be immediately recognizable and must

Theodicy

speak, without words, that which its advocates believe is important for the world to know about them.

All free and independent people have adopted a symbol that speaks for them and their cause. The symbol selected always serves to instill, in the people who adopt it, a constant reminder of who they are, of what is important to them and what their individual and collective responsibilities are.

The symbol is the proof of their identification with a cause, an idea, a specific people and a reality that is greater than themselves, but that cannot exist without them.

The symbol must be unique, original and must, above all else, embody the fundamental beliefs that are the golden thread that binds the people together in a New Body Politic.

In our search for an appropriate symbol that reflects who we are and what the world must know about us we must look to the essence of our being, to our *raison d'etre*. When we do so we are forced to conclude that our children and the mothers who give them life and nurture them to maturity are our greatest treasure. We are also compelled to conclude that as a people, perhaps more than any other reason, we have endured slavery, segregation, second-class citizenship, debasement, humiliation and death to insure that our children survived and to insure that their life prospects would be better than ours.

Our children are our future. The possibilities that we envision for the future are really those that we see for our children. Our children are our immortality. It is through them that we live forever. It is for them that we struggle and for whom we have always struggled. In reality, we live and do all that we do for the purpose of protecting and defending them so that they may live long and prosper.

Clearly, the symbol we seek must focus the world's attention and our own, on the fact that we will, at all costs, protect and defend our children. We will die in the horror of war to insure that they survive and prosper. The world must know that no force on the planet will prevent us from our *duty*, *natural obligation* and *right* to save our children from harm.

Our symbol must inform the world, place it on unequivocal notice, that we did not bring our children into this world to be grist for this country's prison mills or to languish in penitentiaries under life sentences for victimless crimes, or to be mindless fodder for the cannons of America's capitalism.

Our symbol must tell the world that our children are no less precious than any others and that we, like every specie on the planet, will defend them in war and in peace, against all odds and all adversaries and to the death.

Our symbol must roar like the proud and courageous lions of our homeland and thunder with a voice as bold as the clouds that gather at the lofty peaks of the Mountains of the Moon.

The question is begged. Is there a symbol that fulfills all of the requirements outlined above and that is also related to our own Authentic Ancestral Culture? The answer is found, once again in our ancient land, in Kemit.

Bes: The Neter of Childbirth and War

We have noted the existence of an undeclared war prosecuted against us for centuries by our historical enemies. The war has been as unrelenting and vicious as it has been devious and disguised. It continues, unabated until this day.

Children are always among the greatest casualties of war. As a tactic whose primary objective is to destroy the enemies desire and ability to wage war, the targets of war are always persons and facilities that are vital to the survival of children. It is no wonder that in time of war the mortality rate of children increases significantly. Our ancestors were intimately familiar with the connection between children and war and demonstrated the fact in the *NeTeR* Bes.

Bes is a Kemite *NeTeR* who possesses two distinct and interrelated characters as *NeTeR* of childbirth and *NeTeR* of war. His antiquity is so remote as to be undeterminable. He is widely recognized as one of the oldest gods of the African

Theodicy

people. He is also, therefore, an authentic, ancient African symbol.

As the symbol of childbirth Bes was always present at the birth of children. He was said to be present to protect with his shield, and otherwise attack, repel and put to flight with his sword, anyone or anything that would in any way harm the child or its mother.

As the symbol of war Bes was armed with a shield and a two-edged sword. He was often depicted with a bow or with knives in his hand. In one example, he has eight knives and the symbol of "millions of years" on his head, indicating that he would wage war for eternity to protect children.

At first blush it may appear that the two characters are contradictory. One does not usually think of childbirth and war as related concepts. When they are combined, however, they form a coherent whole that is a sublime example of synthesis.

Bes is, above all, the symbol of war. But he is not the symbol of the warmonger. He is the symbol of war for the specific purpose of protection and survival of children and mothers. His is the war that must be embodied in the successful plan of action. He symbolizes war that is offensive and defensive.

War is directed against enemies and as such is active hostility that is offensive. Protection is the state of being shielded from danger and is defensive. By the implements of war he carries Bes clearly represents both offensive and defensive capabilities. His two-edged sword is raised and ready to strike. It is an offensive tool with two cutting edges to insure maximum utility in the art of war -- it cuts both ways. His mighty shield is used to protect against attack and is defensive.

Bes prosecutes war. His main responsibility, however, is the protection of children and mothers. In this capacity he protects those who are the future of the nation. He protects against all malevolent forces whether they be mental, physical or spiritual, man or beast, that would, by any means whatsoever, thwart, impede, undermine or destroy our children.

The protection that Bes provides to mothers is linked to the culture because mothers are not only partners in procreation, they are also the first teachers of our children. What the mother teaches our children is, invariably, the culture of the ancestors from whose bloodline the children are born. Bes is also, therefore, the protector and guarantor of the transmission of our Authentic Ancestral Culture.

Bes and the concept of war that he represents may be easily detested, but the necessity of war and the symbol of war is dictated by the law of survival. Interestingly, the Kemitic word for war is *merekh*, a word spelled with the hieroglyphic symbols for weapon, warrior, knowledge, strength and millions of years. *Merekh* is war, but it is also knowledge and longevity.

War is necessary because the survival of a people is predicated on their continuous ability to insure that their offspring will grow to maturity in order to reproduce. The security of children is, therefore, the essence of survival and the underlying principle upon which all First Principles are based.

Bes is the image that best suits our requirements for a positive symbol. He will protect" our children. He will prosecute fierce and vigorous war, to the death, to save our women and protect and transmit our Authentic Ancestral Culture to our posterity. He will give notice to our enemies, without words, that will cause them to understand that interference with our determination to gain that to which we are justly entitled and to secure those entitlements to our children, in perpetuity, will result in maximum retaliation at all levels and by any means necessary. Bes is our only appropriate, ancient symbol.

A final note. In our quest to develop a successful plan of action we must remember that even a plan that includes the essential elements outlined here, and which takes account of the importance of the Internal Intelligence Function, and the use of positive symbols and symbol systems, will not be successful if it relies on tactics that have been developed on the basis of factors that have significantly changed. Because circumstances and people change, tactics too must change accordingly. One of the great failures of the so-called Black Revolution and its well-intentioned plans was that its leaders stubbornly and persistently adhered to outdated tactics. Our historical experience should have placed them on notice that we cannot fight cannons with spear and *assagai*. We must employ the same or better technology than that employed by our adversaries if we are to meet and defeat their unrelenting war against us and our aspirations.

To prevent a recurrence of past mistakes we shall note a general tactic that must underlay all tactics and which must always be considered in the development of any successful plan of action. We shall call it, for want of a better term, Confrontational Politics. We could also call it *aggressive non-violence* or *violent self-defense*. it is the concept rather than the name that is important.

Confrontational Politics as Tactic

Those who find themselves living under undesirable conditions and who have concluded that they no longer desire to endure such conditions are people who have, at least theoretically, decided that change is necessary. But change is a radical concept. It conjures replacement and redistribution. When mixed with the element of the unknown it becomes intimidating and subversive.

Those who profess to desire change but who limit, by their strategies and tactics, the way that change can be effected do not really desire change. They seek greater accommodation with those who they claim as their enemies.

Accommodationists are essentially articulate cowards. They would, while facing a firing squad, looking into the barrels of loaded rifles, counsel their comrades in the necessity for patience, civility and non-violence.

These articulate and dangerous cowards, self-styled leaders all, are people who seek to promote adaptation to, or compromise with, the point of view that opposes what is clearly in the best interest of those who they claim to represent. The train of accommodation upon which they travel is never the express. It stops at every sub-station along the way. It will always be the most time consuming route to reach a destination. The road they travel is the well known, oft-traveled, path of least resistance.

The accommodationist's approach is so dangerous because it misunderstands that that which opposes you is, by definition, against you. Our opponents are against us and can never be accommodated. They have not understood that the synonyms of opponent are antagonist, adversary, foe and enemy not a friend among them.

The approach of the accommodationist is also dangerous because it fails to understand the concepts of adaptation and compromise.

Adaptation is the act of modifying some idea or activity in order to make it fit something else. To adapt is to adjust your position to fit that of your opponent -- you change, that which opposes you does not. In the cultural sense adaptation is a change in behavior in order to conform to the dominant culture. Adaptation, then, is an intentional change to the way of your enemy in order that you may fit in.

Compromise is no better. This brand of accommodation cannot be said to really exist in circumstances where one opponent is overwhelmingly more powerful than the other. True compromise is the result of deadlock. It is the result of negotiation made possible because of the inability of either of the opposing forces to overcome the power of the other. Unless you are the equal of your opponent in power, adaptation accommodation, and surrender are possible outcomes of a confrontation, compromise is not.

Those who advocate adaptation or compromise for African Americans are cowards or traitors if for no other reason than they misapprehend the NaTuRe of the situation they confront.

Theodicy

Confrontation is different. Confrontation literally means foreheads together. It suggests two rams, head to head, horns locked in mortal combat. It is to stand facing and opposing each other in challenge and defiance. Confrontation is a conflict of forces it can also be a conflict of ideas.

Confrontational Politics is both a strategy and tactic that is born of the compelled necessity to change our circumstances - *now*. It is the express train to our rendezvous with destiny. Like power it is a process and an idea that is comprised of two distinctive components: *continuous agitation and relentless demand*.

Frederick Douglass is credited with having said that "those who profess to favor freedom and yet depreciate agitation are men who want crops without plowing up the ground". The analogy is appropriate in the present context. In order to harvest we have to plant; in order to plant we have to plow; in order to plow we must violently and aggressively turn over the ground and shake it up.

The word agitation has two meanings that demonstrate why it is a primary, necessary component of confrontational politics and why Douglass' analogy is so compelling. To agitate is to move violently and rapidly; to shake up; to put in motion; and to turn over in the mind as to contrive or to plot.

To agitate is, at one level, the act of putting something in motion by rapid and violent shaking. It implies a hands on seizure of something and the violent shaking of it back and forth putting the thing is motion by disturbance. To agitate is to disturb, repeatedly, that which is quiet and still.

In the context of the development of a successful plan of action for African Americans the necessity for this kind of agitation is compelled by our present and our historical circumstances. We are a people who have been kidnapped, from our Motherland, our families, our language and our culture. We have been transported, at gunpoint and in shackles to this land of progressive slavery where we have been denied basic rights routinely granted to household pets.

Now, by the passage of time, the descendants of our erstwhile kidnappers and tormentors those who have worked us without compensation for centuries believe, arrogantly, that they have the right, because of the passage of time, to be left alone in their secure and privileged enclaves, and there to be free from disturbances at the hands of "agitators" who simply will not forget the past.

Confrontational Politics ensures that the beneficiaries of our deprivation, the heirs of private and governmental crimes against our humanity, shall never be permitted to rest quietly and still. Always, at every turn, we will confront their hypocrisy, and stir, vigorously, and violently the cauldron of their unspeakable and unpunished atrocities. To that end, the concept of confrontational politics mandates, first and foremost, continuous agitation.

The second component of Confrontational Politics is relentless demand. In law, a demand is a peremptory claim which presupposes no doubt of the claimant's rights. A claim that is peremptory is one that is final and absolute. The peremptory comes from the Latin and means destructive, deadly and to destroy. A demand is more than a mere request. It is more than a claim of right. It is a deadly and destructive claim that may only be ignored at one's own peril. It is, in fact, the claim that destroys all that has gone before and prohibits future claims unless and until it is fully redeemed. In this respect a demand is a manifesto -- a public declaration that reminds all who may be concerned that this claim will not go away -- that it will not subside -- that it will become louder, more strident and vociferous if interposition, denial or delay are attempted. The demand here is final and absolute.

When this concept is applied to the development of a successful plan of action of African Americans the specific demand that must be included is for reparations for slavery; compensation for governmentally sanctioned and administered segregation; reimbursement for lost wages;

Theodicy

damages for attempted genocide, wrongful death and intentional infliction of emotional distress; and redistribution of land confiscated by fraud and chicanery. The list is non-exhaustive. The demand must be relentless.

Given the state of powerlessness of African Americans any plan of action must tend to enforce the overall objective of the acquisition and control of power at least proportionate to our numbers. In this respect it is not dissimilar to politics in general. The distinction lies in the urgency and intensity of the approach. Any plan of action must be viewed against the backdrop of 246 years of forced, uncompensated labor; 100 years of Jim Crow and nearly 400 years of discrimination based on race in every level and area of American society. This urgency must also be viewed prospectively.

Under the prospective view it will take, at the current rate of our annual economic increase, more than 400 years for African Americans to reach economic parity with Whites. Clearly, gradual increase is unacceptable. Moreover, no person exercising true leadership qualities would seriously advocate that we wait for 400 or more years, 20 or more generations, to gain parity or to be fully compensated.

The accornmodationists advocate a plan of action that amounts to "wait and see". They proclaim, apparently with straight face, that "we ain't where we want to be, but God knows we ain't where we been." That, we are told, is a blessing. Be that as it may, it is not a plan of action or a strategy for one.

Our current powerlessness is the direct result of our failure to recognize the urgency of our dilemma. Each generation that waits is a generation that is sacrificed for no apparent purpose. Can we say that if we wait, opt for gradual change, sacrifice one more generation of our precious children, that the next generation will see us provided with that to which we are justly entitled? No one makes that claim because no one can. All they ask is that we wait. This "wait and see" excuse for a strategy also fails to take into account the generational NaTuRe of the successful strategy employed by our enemies. Their approach is simple and quite effective.

Each generation of our enemies are given, by their fathers, one benefit and one command by which they will continue to rule and we will continue to suffer.

First, they are given an inheritance. The inheritance is, in reality, the profit from the slave labor of our ancestors that literally built this nation. It should be pointed out at this juncture that the argument, often intoned by sanctimonious Whites, that "my ancestors were not slaveholders, so I have not benefited from slavery" is utterly specious. History clearly indicates that much of the wealth of this country is illegitimate. Billions, if not trillions of dollars, have been accumulated as a result of slave labor and the outright sale of our men, women and children in open air slave markets from New York to Florida. The entire wealth of the southern states was based on the value of their human property. Even after slavery the Black Codes, forced sharecropping and other methods of preventing the newly freed slaves from leaving the plantation or selling their labor on the open market at competitive prices, conspired to keep them in neo-slavery well into the mid 1960's.

Trillions of dollars of wealth has been transferred by the federal government, exclusively to Whites, through land grants, broadcast licenses and mineral rights. All such transfers were at nominal cost or free of charge. African Americans, of course, were excluded from this government largesse by law, custom and administrative rule.

Although there are certainly many Whites whose ancestors were not slaveholders the fact is irrelevant. Simply by having resided in the United States for generations most Whites have had the unfair advantage of economic and educational opportunities available exclusively to Whites and protection from competition by African Americans through forced and illegal exclusion from the economic, educational and political arenas. There are, as a result, virtually no Whites in America who have not benefitted from slavery and discrimination of the African American whether their forebears were slaveholders or not.

Theodicy

We must also be forced to conclude that, contrary to popular belief, there are no African Americans who have not been disadvantaged (including those who claim to have never "experienced racism"). All African Americans are educationally, economically and politically weaker as a direct result of past exclusions and deprivations. This includes immigrants from the Caribbean and Africa.

This then is the one benefit. Whites collectively are not required to re-invent the wheel. Each generation starts with a leg up. The benefit amounts to trillions of dollars of economic adv ant age and the power that comes with it.

The one command is also simple and straightforward: protect what you have been given, add increase to it and keep the Blacks in their place. Each generation of Whites is enjoined, whether directly or indirectly, to keep African Americans down while increasing their economic, educational and political power. This simple command explains why Whites are overwhelmingly opposed to affirmative action and reparations. A majority of Whites recognize the in justice and unfairness of slavery and racial discrimination. None of the Whites would change places with African Americans and most believe that they would be entitled to some form of compensation for the mere fact of being Black in America. Yet most Whites are opposed to affirmative action and would rather die than discuss reparations. *One benefit, one command*: a successful plan of action by which they rule and we suffer.

It should also be noted that it is the inheritance, the one benefit that make the one command feasible. It is the power that derives from the accumulated ill-gotten gains of centuries of unfair advantage and the control of money, media and the organs of government and war that makes the continued subjugation of the African American possible. The foregoing explains the urgency of this approach. It is urgency that dictates the intensity. Intensity is to be understood as the magnitude of the force that will be unceasingly applied as we confront the political establishment with continuous agitation and relentless demand. Intensity means a heightened degree of force that will stretch to its limits the fabric of the United States Constitution and the limits of law enforcement to contain a people whose will is driven by their Authentic Ancestral Culture and the memory of the greatest unpunished and uncompensated crime in the history of humanity.

Continuous agitation and relentless demand represent the process that is Confrontational Politics. The power that fuels it is the idea whose time has finally come. We must return to the word agitate to help us understand the power of the idea whose time has finally come and its centrality to Confrontational Politics.

We have previously observed that one of the meanings of agitate is to turn over in the mind, to contrive and to plot. That which is turned over in the mind can only be an idea. To agitate also means to think. It refers, however, to a specific type of thinking and a specific kind of idea that is the product of that thinking.

Mental agitation refers to the type of thinking that moves and shakes the conscience, that excites the intellect. It is thinking that turns a coward into a warrior and a pacifist into a martyr. An agitated mind is a restless mind and one that will not be assuaged by strategies that advocate a "wait and see" approach to problems that confront it. When the kind of thinking characterized by mental agitation is present the outcome will always be a plan. Interestingly, to contrive or plot is, in effeet, to think up a plan. Both terms are idea-oriented. Mental agitation is, therefore, a type of thinking that so violently and rapidly moves and shakes the intellect of an individual that it leads to and results in the development of a plan.

The kind of idea that is the product of mental agitation is that which not only excites the intellect of the individual thinker but also the kind that lends itself easily to articulation and written expression. Specifically, it is the kind of idea that is capable of putting into motion the fundamental elements that produce change. It is the kind of idea that when effectively communicated tends inevitably to stir up interest, discussion and support amg people who join forces to

Theodicy

produce the change that is the essence of the idea. The more radical the idea, the more radical the change demanded by those whose intellect has been agitated.

Change, particularly of the status quo, is invariably seen as subversive. Change is a term whose import must not be taken lightly. It denotes the process by which something becomes distinctly different and implies either a radical transmutation of character or replacement with something else.

Confrontational Politics is the process that includes a well thought out strategy and effective tactics to implement it. It is the idea that will excite the intellect of individuals to join forces and develop the plan that will produce the long awaited change. The components of Confrontational Politics are continuous agitation and relentless demand. These will battle against the opposing strategy of benefit and command.

Confrontational Politics is an aggressive concept. it implies action that forces issues important to the initiators into the open. It effectively turns the underdog into the aggressor. it eliminates the possibility that issues will be swept under the carpet or other wised obscured from public attention by those whose primary strategy is to prevent issues from being publicly debated. It allows power, plan and leadership to coalesce creating a force that cannot easily be ignored.

SECTION SIX:

LEADERSHIP

CHAPTER SIXTEEN:

THE FUNDAMENTALS OF LEADERSHIP

We have attempted to outline the contours of an urgent crisis confronting African Americans. The crisis is exacerbated by instability in our political, economic and cultural affairs. Because the crisis arises from a set of historical factors that are unlikely to change in the absence of a well-conceived and aggressively pursued plan of action we have examined the elements of such a plan. But no matter how well-conceived the plan it must be implemented. Implementation requires leadership. To that end we will now examine the fundamentals of leadership.

The Chinese hold that the notion of crisis implies both danger and opportunity. In the case of the African American we have posited that the danger is the real possibility that we may be the victims of government administered genocide. The opportunity is the dawning of the Age of *Hapy* and the new level of consciousness it promises to inspire. This opportunity is perhaps the last one that we will have to marshal our collective energy to launch a preemptive attack that will save us and our children from annihilation.

Our problem is that we are a people who have suffered from a lack of effective leadership that has prevented us from meeting the obstacles that have thwarted our every attempt to secure our rightful share of the power and resources of the world. This is not to say that we have not had an abundance of media-generated, government-endorsed, self-proclaimed leaders. Despite the proliferation of such leaders there continues to be a longstanding vacuum in leadership in the African American community. Note that the vacuum is stated as one of leadership, not leaders. There is a fundamental difference between the related but distinct concepts of leader and leadership. This important distinction has been tragically overlooked in our unplanned and therefore unguided quest for power and self-determination.

A leader is simply one who goes before. The position of first in line does not require talent, intelligence or leadership. The first horse in a team of harnessed horses is the leader but its direction, speed and destination are determined by the crack of the driver's whip. When it is further considered that the horse is arguably the least intelligent animal on the planet the analogy is instructive.

The leader is distinct from the leadership. The suffix "ship" means to create. When it is appended to the word leader it transforms it into a quality. Quality is the essential NaTuRe of a thing. Leadership is, therefore, a creative force that is the quality of the one who goes before. Leaders articulate, implement, facilitate the creative force. But, leadership creates. Obviously, that which creates must precede that which is created. Our failure to understand this distinction accounts, in large measure, for our inability to acquire the power necessary to change our circumstances for the better. Let us look at the concept of leadership to see where and how we have gone wrong.

The ancient origins of leadership are to be found in the first group of humans who, gathered around a favorite watering hole, were illuminated by the understanding of two fundamental principles of survival: (1) that there is safety in numbers; and (2) that when one individual in the group sounds the danger alarm it is better to flee immediately rather than to search for the source of the danger. Thus, it was the threat of predation that gave rise to social groups and, in turn, the reliance upon one person whose visual and hearing acuity provided a reliable, early warning system that maximized the group's ability to survive. Eventually, the experience and dominance of the most savvy individual led to his or her acknowledgement by all as the leader, that is the person to whom all others looked to warn and direct in times of danger.

These principles dictated, over time, that individuals did not leave the group to venture out alone which policy, in turn, gave rise to group cohesiveness. The whole group moved from one place to another or no one did, giving rise to unity of action and simultaneity of movement.

Theodicy

This fledgling social structure required an effective communication system between the persons who formed the group. The system of sounds, probably initiated by the same person who warned and directed in time of danger, became the forerunner of all language.

In time these social groups organized patterns that represented divisions in responsibility such as food-gathering, hunting, defense, child rearing, war and survival planning. The concept of leadership was, therefore, a necessary component of the development of group survival.

It follows that in its formative stages leadership was comprised of an effective early warning system. This survival mechanism was also a defensive mechanism that was based on vision, hearing and the ability to communicate information in an immediately understandable language and in timely manner. The components of the early warning system were developed from the techniques used by the one who marched at the head of the group as they traveled through perilous surroundings in their daily search for food.

The leaders came and went. It was the components, mechanisms and techniques of leadership that were the progenitors and guardians of group survival, evolution and ultimately civilization. Group survival and prosperity are, therefore, leadership oriented.

Leadership is the quality of a leader, that which the leader must have to lead. Among the qualities of the leader would have been the ability to guide or show the way by going in advance, by walking at the head of the group. Therefore, the leader guides by way of example, by becoming a model. In the absence of language she could only teach by doing. Since the leader was always in front she was not only the early warning system incarnate, she was also the first to see the enemy and the first to engage him in battle. When the leader said fight, they fought. When the leader said retreat, they fled with the swiftness of the gazelle.

Because the leader was in front where he could see first and more, was the veteran of many battles, had survived and presumably learned from all of those who had went before him his expertise and eventually his word was valued and he became advisor, counselor and if he lived long enough, revered elder. But, he was all of this because he was out front, had acute vision, acute hearing and courage.

Courage is to be understood here as the willingness to die first in order to protect those who come behind. Because men were generally, although not exclusively, the warriors, the women and children walked behind. As a result men were usually the vanguard. The men also died first. It follows that the leader had to be a person of proven courage. For this reason, and from the remotest times the leader was adorned with a lion's tail that was proudly affixed to his garment.

The ancient Kemites and all other indigenous Africans considered the lion to be the symbol of courage, majesty and pride. A courageous person was one who was, like the lion, both ferocious and dignified. The word courage literally means heart and spirit. Curiously, its ancient definition was mind, purpose and spirit. It referred to the heart as the seat of intelligence and feeling. Until this day courage means the firmness of spirit that faces danger without flinching or retreating. We still refer to courageous persons as having "heart". It is also interesting to note that the Kemitic name for the lion was *maa* which means to see.

We may conclude from the above that there are a set of qualities that define leadership and by which it may be known. It follows also that in the absence of such qualities, leadership too is absent.

The Qualities of Leadership

It is a fundamental premise of this section that leadership is a distinct quality, state and condition that can be known, communicated and taught. A state is an actual form of existence. A condition is something that is indispensable to the occurrence of something else. When viewed as a state and condition we may further broaden the definition of

Theodicy

leadership to a form of existence, essential in NaTuRe, that is indispensable to the occurrence of something else.

To identify the qualities of leadership we must isolate the individual elements or ingredients of which it is comprised. We must also determine the attributes of leadership that cause people to follow. We note here that the relationship between leadership and followership is symbiotic and co-dependent.

We have previously noted that the elements of leadership include, but are not limited to, acute vision, hearing and courage. To these we will add the ability to successfully resolve problems and counsellorship. We should also note here that leadership is a *group dynamic* because in its highest and purest expression it is manifested by a group of people acting together.

The concept of leadership is essentially derived from the notion of the one who goes before. It clearly involves a *forward position*. Leadership is *being* first, *seeing* first and *acting* first.

Being First. This quality is essentially a willingness to be at the front of the line. It is a defining quality because it necessarily implies potential of dying first in battle. The one who walks in front is the first target of the enemy. This may seem a minor requirement but it is not. It affords a process of elimination. The coward, the squeamish, the faint of heart will never elect to be at the head of the line. Persons of that ilk eliminate themselves. There was a tradition in ancient Kemite called the *Sed* Festival at which the leader was periodically required to demonstrate his physical fitness to rule. The *Sed* Festival was a modification of the original ceremony in which the leader was killed and often beheaded after a period of years. We might ask how many leaders would vie for office if they knew that they would be killed at the end of their term of office?

Seeing First. This quality is what we have previously defined as *Oudja*. When we say that a leadership quality is vision we refer to *Oudja* when possessed by one who walks in front. In order to see what is actually before her eyes the one in front must have accurate perception. She must see things as they are. Distortion can prove fatal for her and the group. But she must also know what to look for. Sensory input can be so numerous as to be overwhelming. By knowing what to look for the one in front is able to filter out distraction which is best understood, in this context, as unnecessary information. In order to do so she must know where to direct her attention and what to do in response to the circumstances observed, quickly.

The one who goes in front must know, from experience and training, whether the noise he hears ahead of him is the result of a misstep by a predator laying in wait, or that of a harmless rodent digging in the underbrush. He must know the signs and portents of a violent storm and when and where to take shelter in safety. In short, the one in front must know the NaTuRal order of things in order that he may see when things are amiss.

In the context of leadership, *Oudja* may be defined as the accurate perception of the NaTuRal order and leadership as the ability to guide people through time and space, toward a specific destination, in harmony with that order and to teach others to do likewise, by example. It should be remembered here that the word natural derives from the Kemitic word NeTeR. Both NeTeR and NaTuRe refer to an active power. Order means the condition in which everything is in its right place and functioning properly. In the Kemitic tongue such order is called *Maat*. The NaTuRal order is, therefore, the operation of the active power that is the *NeTeR* balanced by the order of *Maat*.

An essential function of *Oudja* in all persons but especially those who walk in front, is recognition of the fundamental principles of survival whose foundation was characterized in ancient Kemit as the Two Truths or the Double Law. This ancient African concept, stated here with a simplicity that does not do it justice, holds that all facts, statements, assertions, laws, observations and realities implicitly state their opposite. It illustrates, at a basic level, that to the

Theodicy

extent truth can be said to exist at all, it must be two-fold. This two-fold law proves that no singular truth can exist. It is the seminal reasoning in all scientific and philosophical speculations from cause and effect to *yin* and *yang*.

It was this two-fold reality that was perhaps the first quality of the one who walks in front. It was she who saw first and connected first, the fact that a noise was an effect that was invariably the result of a cause, whether the cause was apparent or not. It was she who saw first that a herd of wildebeest running frantically in one direction meant that danger was approaching from the opposite direction.

Acting First. Is essentially the quality of decisiveness. Above all the one who walks in front must be able to make quick, accurate decisions. It is from this person that the group takes its directions for action. In order to be decisive the person must be in a forward position, see first and clearly and have the courage to make a decision whose appropriateness may determine whether the entire group survives or perishes. To act first requires independent judgment that is based on the needs of the group. This implies selflessness. It implies the ability to submerge individual interest in favor of collective survival and advancement.

If all of these elements are present the person who walks in front will be called upon, by virtue of her demonstrated leadership ability, to counsel and advise others in the group. Clearly, one cannot teach what he does not know and he cannot lead where he will not go.

The leader's function then, is to facilitate the process of leadership. She guides and articulates. That which she guides, that which she articulates, is the plan of action. Leaders must have the ability to think for themselves, but they must do so within the parameters established, in advance, by the plan of action. When the plan of action reaches its limit it must necessarily advance to the next level. It must set new parameters in order to avoid stagnation and death. As a result the plan of action cannot be static. Leadership cannot be static either. When a thing arrives at its limit and advances to the next level of development it is being creative, innovative and reproductive. Leadership is also, therefore, the process that facilitates growth.

Finally, leadership is a group dynamic. Because leadership is a quality whose elements can be known it can also be taught. If it can be taught to anyone it can be taught to all. When leadership is taught to all of the members of the group the result is a group of persons who are willing and able to walk in front whenever the need arises. This creates a leadership reserve. The implications of these simple observations are staggering. *A group who maintains a leadership reserve cannot be defeated for the reason that they will never be without carefully selected and rigorously trained leaders who can and will assume the mantle of leadership on a moment's notice.*

Although it is certainly true that the New Body Politic must speak with one voice at a time, it is also true that when all members are trained to speak, the voice of the New Body Politic can never be silenced. To train all the members in the fundamentals of leadership is to utilize the law of power units to elevate leadership to its highest and purest form as collective or group power.

The ultimate objective of the leadership and the plan of action that will implement it is to launch a counteroffensive that will defeat our enemies in their diabolical, undeclared war and to secure the blessings of *freedom, prosperity* and *power* to ourselves and our posterity in perpetuity.

We must digress briefly at this point in our analysis to insure that the reader understands the concept of war and the NaTuRe of the undeclared war being waged against the African American family in order to further understand why African American leadership has been an illusion that has all but guaranteed our continued subjugation and second-class citizenship in America.

Theodicy

The Concept of War

We are in the throes of the longest uninterrupted and undeclared war in the history of the world. It is the unrelenting war against the African people. It has accounted for more deaths then all of the wars of the world combined.

The War Against The African People (WATAP) began with the first outsider who stood awestruck before the majesty and splendor of ancient Kemit, who coveted what he saw and who vowed to take what he saw by treachery or force of arms, rather than learn from those who were responsible for what he saw. Whether the first invaders were Hyksos, Persians or Arabs their intention was the same --to wage war against a peaceful people whose wealth they coveted. This ignoble intention surfaces again when the Romans attacked Carthage and when the Italians attacked Ethiopia. But the Wars of Enslavement (WOE) began when the first Africans were taken, by force of arms, from the sable continent as prisoners of war in 1517 (this is the date that Spanish colonizers were permitted to import twelve Negro slaves each. Apparently, twelve Negroes were required to serve the needs of each Spaniard.) The war continued through the agonizing periods of chattel slavery, segregation, integration and now disintegration. The period of disintegration is that from 1984 to present. Though the weapons of war may have become more sophisticated and deadly its objectives have remained unchanged.

War is generally understood as declared armed conflict between nations or factions within a nation. Of course, war may also be undeclared as in the case of the Vietnam Conflict. War is now a scientific art that is conducted by strategy, tactics and the sciences. War is now considered total war and is prosecuted not only against the enemy's army but also against its economy and population. The purpose of totru war is to defeat the means by which the enemy prosecutes war as well as his will to do so.

Significantly, the word war derives from a German word meaning to *confuse.* War then, is actually a state of *confusion.* When war is understood to imply a double meaning, that is, armed conflict and confusion, it becomes evident that a state of war may exist without actual combat. The notion that war can also be state of induced confusion is best understood when confusion itself is defined.

To confuse is to mix-up mentally and to perplex. To perplex is to disturb mentally in a way that makes clear and critical thinking impossible. It is also the technique and technology of making things so complex that they cannot be readily understood. The end result of confusion and perplexity is bewilderment, that is, to be lost, as in a wilderness. We may deduce from this brief analysis that there are two components of war: (1) declared or undeclared armed conflict between nations or factions within a nation; and (2) an induced state of confusion, or psychological warfare. In this second sense, war may be usefully understood as the elimination of Oudja and Critical Thinking, two of the three elements of the Triad of Visionary Power.

Warfare begins and ends with confusion. In armed conflict confusion is the goal of the primary military tactic of cutting of the head of the enemy so that its body will die. This tactic requires the identification and elimination of the leader so that the troops will scatter in confusion having lost their brain, or more accurately, their ability to think under the pressure of battle. The problem with this tactic is that it is a bloody and inefficient way to confuse the thought processes of the enemy. It also runs the risk of transforming the leader into a martyr thereby making her greater in death than she was in life. The efficiency of the technique lies only in the fact that once armed hostilities have begun it is the quickest way to accomplish the goal.

Psychological Warfare

Psychological warfare can be as deadly and accurate as a bullet. It can also be more effective. Its primary effectiveness lies in the fact that its theater of operation is not a battlefield but the confines of the human mind. Its armaments, though as devastating as a well-placed bomb, are not explosive or incendiary devices. Its soldiers, highly trained killers all, do not wear battle fatigues, unless a double-breasted Armani can be defined as uniform.

The planners and engineers of psychological warfare prosecute war on Madison Avenue, in Hollywood and for the Central Intelligence Agency. They may be executive producers, directors, advertising executives, operations analysts or deep cover operatives. No matter what guise they assume the goal is the same: control the enemy by controlling what he thinks, control what he thinks by controlling the information he receives.

Psychological warfare is the use of mental means to influence and confuse the thinking and morale of the enemy. In this context morale is defined as a condition that is comprised of courage, discipline, confidence, enthusiasm, and willingness to endure hardship for a cause. The importance of demoralization as a tactic of psychological warfare is best understood when the components of morale are defined.

Courage is the heart of the lion. It is the refusal to retreat. It is the core of determination and the backbone of the will.

Discipline is training in orderly conduct. It also entails obedience to orders. Without discipline organization is impossible.

Confidence is firm belief in one's own ability and power. It is trust, assurance and self-reliance. Without confidence humans are shrinking violets whose fortunes are determined by the winds of chance.

Enthusiasm is literally the inspiration of the Gods. It refers to the passion, zeal and fervor that is the hallmark of the visionary.

The *willingness to endure hardship for a cause* is the ability to see the greater good before it has become reality. It is akin to sacrifice. Without it all but immediately apparent and immediately obtainable goals are impossible.

Clearly, a person who is confused about any or all of the components of morale is unlikely to be able to develop the stuff of which warriors are made. They will never fight, join the battle or counsel others to do so. They have been effectively defeated by the subtle tactic of psychological warfare.

Psychological warfare is admittedly long-term but it is also a more efficient way to defeat the enemy by confusion. When psychological warfare is waged against the enemy from his childhood it has the predictable effect of decreasing the possibility that they will ever contemplate, let alone cultivate, the efficacy of revolution as a remedy for injustice.

The ability to control the thinking of the enemy is as important as the soldier and his gun. On one level this control is achieved, most efficiently, by the control of cultural energy. We have discussed the effects of the manipulation and theft of cultural energy and how that theft impacts the development of group cohesion and power. When it is deftly manipulated along with the psychological assault on the nucleus of African American power disintegration and defeat are al1but assured. *The nucleus of African American power is the African American family.*

We have discussed that for African people the family is the nucleus from which all else emanates. It is the concept of nuclear family that is, in fact, the model for the larger society. This fact provides a clue useful to assist us in uncovering another subtle manifestation of the ongoing, undeclared war against African Americans.

War and the African American Family

The family is a Bio-Social Power Aggregate. The Bio-Social Power Aggregate is b6th biological and sociological, but its most distinguishing characteristic is that it is a power aggregate comprised of a combination of power units. When power units having a common objective join together (multiplying themselves) their combined power will exceed the total of the individual power units by a measurable, predictable and exponential rate of increase.

Theodicy

The nucleus of the family is comprised of two or more adults living together cooperatively in the joint enterprise of producing and nurturing off spring of their union or those entrusted to their care by law, custom or circumstance. Family implies blood and kinship and may be nuclear or extended. It can also be an infectious, patently subversive idea.

The nuclear family is a female, a male and the offspring of their union. But it can also be two or more persons who dedicate themselves to the idea of a common, lasting bond with or without children.

The extended family includes grandparents, and all relatives. But it also includes persons, whether or not blood related, who dedicate themselves to a common, lasting bond, and who support and uphold the idea called family.

The idea of family, derived as it is, from the bio-social power unit, serves three primary and indispensable functions that may be called *reproductive, economic* and *cultural*.

The reproductive, economic and cultural functions of the family are interconnected and have been touched on briefly in the foregoing chapter on Stolen Cultural Energy. A further analysis is necessary at this juncture, however, to show why disruption of these three functions is a primary goal of war in general and psychological warfare in particular. We will begin by defining the word family itself.

It is said that the word family derives from the Latin *famulus* meaning servant and by extension the servants of the head of a household and all those related to him by blood or marriage. Of course, the definition is uniquely European and patriarchal because it connects family to the male. This should not be surprising from a people who maintain, common sense and all biological proof notwithstanding, that the woman was taken from the man.

As always we must look to our Authentic Ancestral Culture for the origins of concepts by which our collective actions shall be guided.

The Kemitic word for family is *aut*, which means, under the authority of the female, literally under the hand of the female. As an aside it may be remarked here that in a technical sense the European/patriarchal society has not authority because it is not under the hand of the female. To understand how all this relates to the word servant we must go back to life in a state of NaTuRe.

In a state of NaTuRe we can imagine that whether it was the first male who stayed around after the sex act was over and long enough to bond with the female, or the female who knew she would need him and made him stay, it was certainly the combination of desire and necessity called love that bonded male and female and created the idea of family. It was the birth of the offspring and with it responsibility, however, that made family in the modern sense, a reality.

The first, indispensable function of family is reproduction. But reproduction is more than sex. The birth of the child simultaneously gives birth to the age of responsibility. Even before the birth of the child the chain of reproduction engenders the responsibility to protect the mother during pregnancy and to protect mother and child thereafter. So comes the man to bond with the power aggregate that we now call family.

It must be remembered, however, that reproduction is, first and foremost, a female function. For this reason another definition of family is all those claiming descent under a common ancestor. In ancient Kemit and all matrilineal societies that common ancestor was a female. For the European the only place that this concept persists is in livestock breeding where it refers to the descendent of some outstanding female.

It follows that family can logically be seen as those people, lately including males, who serve the household and are under the authority of the head of the household. In our ancient societies the female was the undisputed head of the household. This was true because, as a practical matter, she controlled not only sex, and thereby the reproductive process, but also the nourishment of offspring. The word

Theodicy

female means to suckle and perhaps, nipple. ncient societies the female was the undisputed head of the household. This was true because, as a practical matter, she controlled not only sex, and thereby the reproductive process, but also the nourishment of offspring. The word female means to suckle and perhaps, nipple.

For the male sex requires a minor investment in time, an overwhelming reward in satisfaction and not much else. It is only under the circumstances of family that he learns responsibility. That which he learns and that we now call responsibility is primarily to protect and provide for the bio-social power aggregate that is under the hand of the female. It should not be surprising that the word responsibility means to promise or pledge and is linguistically related to the word spouse.

Economics, the second function of family, is also closely connected to the female. The household, literally, the things in the hold of the house, that is all the worldly possessions of the family, were also under the hand of the female. Wealth itself was the female's and everything of value was inherited through her, exclusively.

The cultural function of family is primarily educational and entails a two-fold process: socialization and cultural indoctrination.

Socialization is the process of training children to live in society, literally the process of turning a person into a companion. A companion is literally a bread fellow, one who eats from the same bread. From the Latin *com,* with and *panis* bread. It is the teaching of acceptable behavior as that behavior is determined by the members of the group, in this case the family.

he socialization process is informed by the underlying culture because culture dictates what acceptable behavior is. The primary difference is that culture explains while the fundamental educative process merely dictates what is acceptable. Culture tells why it is acceptable for a particular people.

It goes without saying that mothers, and females generally, are our teachers exclusively for the first five or so years of life. Clearly, the cultural value of family should not be underestimated.

The primary reason for the undeclared war against the African American family is that the family is a *power source*, it is literally a *group dynamic*. It is the centrifugal force that causes things to be created and dispersed from the center outward. Family, clan, tribe, nation are the concentric circles of civilization's growth. The family, along with the Temple, form the nuclei of civilization. Its outward, upward spiral is the product of culture.

Where there is a nucleus there is power. It is the release of power contained in the nucleus that is the energetic basis of all life. Properly balanced the Bio-Social Power Aggregate that is the family can drive the engines of civilization and create abundant power and secure prosperity for all because of the creative power contained within it.

Family power is the power of creation. The power of creation is the power of attraction and resistance, it is the power of love, lustful and energetic. All of these latent powers being contained in the family it may be properly called a *dynamo*, that is a power generator, as well. As a dynamic, however, it is subject to *deformation*.

In physics deformation is a change of form that results when pressure or stress is brought to bear on a body. Since the African American family is a dynamic it may be deformed when a sufficient amount of pressure or stress is brought to bear on it. This explains why the African American family is the primary target of an undeclared war.

The measure of strength is the ability to withstand pressure. When pressure is too great or too persistent it begins to change that which it is applied to. In this respect the family may be likened to an atom. Like the family the power of the atom is located in the nucleus. It contains a proton. a neutron and an electron. The atom contains a positively charged nucleus surrounded by negatively charged electrons.

Theodicy

But the atom as a whole is neutral. The total negative charge of the electrons equals the amount of positive charge in the nucleus. It follows that the amount of latent power in the nucleus is revealed by the amount of negativity that surrounds it. The amount of power is directly related to the amount of mass ($E=mc^2$). Nearly all the mass of the atom (99.97%) is contained in the nucleus.

The NaTuRe of the atom is determined by the number of protons in the nucleus and number and arrangement of electrons that are outside of and surround the nucleus. The atom itself is neutral because it is equally positive and negative.

The nuclear family too is equally charged. Ideally it poles are male and female. The female is like the neutron, she is neutral. More accurately, she is uncharged. But like the neutron she has slightly greater mass than proton or, in the case of the family, the male. She also has, as a result, slightly greater potential power than the male.

When the neutron is in the nucleus it is stable. When it becomes a free neutron it rapidly decays into a proton, an electron and finally a neutrino. A neutrino has no mass, no charge and does not interact with matter.

The male, on the other hand, is like the proton. It is positively charged. But it carries only one positive charge. It, must be positive. If it is not positive it is a negative electron. There is no such thing as a negative proton. But, it is the neutron and the proton together that comprise the nucleon.

By analogy then, the female is only stable when she is in the family. When she is unstable, that is outside of the family, she decays and becomes a male. The male is positively charged but he only has one positive charge and he is only positive inside the family. If he is negative he can only be outside of the family because there is no negative charge inside the family.

It follows that the family, comprised as it is of components analogous to those of the atom, is a potent form of nuclear energy. The family, at its center, contains the greatest mass and the greatest potential power as she awaits the influence of the male. Together, and only together, they can release unlimited amounts of power. When the power of the family is properly contained and controlled the effect of the energy it contains can be truly explosive.

The family is also surrounded, at all times, by the negative influence of elements similar to the electron in the atom. The electron is one of the basic components of matter. The atom is surrounded by them and they are negatively charged. Their negative charge ·is in direct proportion to the positive charge at its center. Just like the atom, the family is comprised of the equivalent of a neutron, proton and the electron or negativity that surrounds it. The family is, therefore, the nucleus and the environment that surrounds it. A family cannot exist in a vacuum. It cannot long exist without being part of its environs. Neither families nor individuals can be in the world and not be part of it. In short, the family and its environment are one.

It is worth reiterating here that the amount of negativity in the environment is the unerring indicator of the amount of power latent in the family itself. To the extent that African American communities may be accurately characterized as negative environments they are also indicative of the latent power that they contain.

We have mentioned previously that the period from 1984 to present has been one of *disintegration*. IN nuclear physics the gradual breaking down of the nucleus of the atom is known as disintegration. When the nucleus of the atom disintegrates it becomes *radioactive* as a result of its instability. But the disintegration proceeds at a definite and predictable rate. As the nucleus breaks down the atomic weight of an element is reduced and this process creates an element of lower atomic weight. The process is known as disintegration series. Disintegration brings about change. The change is from that which is susceptible to decay and instability to that which is not. Disintegration is then, the process of change after which the element has lower weight (the dead weight has been removed) and permanent

Theodicy

stability. Disintegration and radioactivity kill, but they kill as a necessary part of the process of transformation.

The period of disintegration in which we find ourselves should be seen, therefore, as a predictable process of transformation whose end result will be purity, refinement and permanent stability. To lament the passing of dross is illogical and counterproductive. Like death itself, disintegration should be understood, in the tradition of our ancient ancestors, as the orderly transition from one form of life to another.

As we have seen psychological warfare has as its main objective the confusion of the thinking of the enemy. The confused thinking is directed at specific and vital functions. Now let us look at the effect of the disruption of the three primary functions of the family to see how and why confusion in those areas relates to the objectives of psychological warfare.

Disruption of the Reproductive Function

The reproductive function is effectively disrupted and undermined in several ways. One way is through the separation of the sexes. The ability to maintain a family when the members of the nucleus are separated is diminished considerably and few families are strong enough to withstand extended periods of such separation. It is no coincidence that the period of disintegration has been marked by the mass incarceration of African American males and to a lesser extent females, in their prime reproductive years, on a scale unprecedented in American history. This mass incarceration strategy is accomplished by racially selective prosecution under Draconian laws that impose the longest sentences for non-violent offenses in the sordid history of this nation.

Disruption of the reproductive function is also accomplished by the mysterious appearance of Acquired Immune Deficiency Syndrome (AIDS) and the proliferation of other sexually transmitted diseases. Aids certainly prevents reproduction by killing off those who would reproduce and by passing the disease on to the newborn. But AIDS has another important function that is wholly psychological. Under the circumstances of the AIDS pandemic, fear of contracting the disease becomes an effective prophylactic. Safe sex also means the avoidance of pregnancy, the natural result of sexual intercourse. AIDS certainly aids someone. The question is who.

Abortion and homicide are also important factors. Abortion does more than prevent births. It diminishes the importance of childbearing and the responsibility that grows from it. The ability to easily abort pregnancies diminishes the value of life and enables potential parents to by-pass the lesson of responsibility that is a secondary and indispensable function of reproduction.

Homicide simply reduces the numbers of males available for reproductive functions. It is no coincidence that homicide is the number one cause of death among African American males of prime reproductive age. We may also question the role played by guns, video and television as well as the criminalization of drug addiction.

Disruption of the Economic Function

Economic disruption of the family is perhaps the most effective and insidious tactic of psychological warfare. Economics is the study (some call it a science) of the production, distribution and consumption of wealth. At base, however, it is the study of the methods of identifying and supplying humanity's needs and as such is little different from the studies conducted by Ivan Petrovich Pavlov.

Pavlov discovered the conditioned reflex in which a response is occasioned by a secondary stimulus that has been repeatedly associated with a primary stimulus now well known by the ringing bells and salivating dogs. Less well known is the fact that Pavlov was a professor at a Russian military academy who had widespread influence in psychology and whose theories of human behavior were considered so politically significant that the Russian government built him an expensive laboratory to conduct his research.

Pavlov was not an economist. He was an experimental psychologist. But his theories were in many ways supportive of those postulated by economists. The connection is subtle but instructive and worthy of a brief digression.

Economics has been defined as the science that deals with the production, distribution, and consumption of wealth. To the extent that this definition is accurate it indicates that economics is the *science of the control of wealth*.

The history of the development of economic theory indicates that at a point in time the term economics was replaced with the term political economy. The replacement was the result of the refinement of the doctrine of marginal utility that asserts that the value of an item is determined by the need for it and by its relative scarcity or abundance, not by the item's intrinsic value. When it is further considered that political science and sociology were originally taught as part of the science of economics the notion that economic theory is used to further political agenda is not farfetched.

It logically follows that political economy is related to the political control of wealth or the control of wealth for political purposes. Economics then, is more accurately defined as the science of the manipulation of value (money) based on human need for the purpose of producing, distributing and controlling political power. Political power is, of course, the primary method by which great wealth is accumulated. This definition implicates the mastery of the disciplines of political science (the science of power); sociology (the science of the laws governing the behavior of human beings in groups, including their values and beliefs); and psychology (the study of how the mind operates).

Classical economics holds that supply and demand are the forces that guide economic life. What is really meant by this is that need controls value. From this simple notion a series of facts emerge that when properly understood evince a most effective method for acquiring and controlling political power. The method is simple and straightforward: identify (or create) perceived human needs; control that which is the object of the perceived need; and thereby determine the market value of that which is needed without regard to its intrinsic value. *Voila!* wealth and the power that follows in its wake are created literally out of thin air.

The sinister genius of this method lies in the fact that need may be psychologically induced so that it becomes the trigger for a conditioned reflex just as predictably as in the case of Pavlov's dogs. Stimulus creates response. Response can be manipulated by stimulus. In Pavlov's experiments he found that a response (the salivating of dogs) was normally caused (created) by the sight of meat. By repeatedly ringing a bell just before the presentation of the meat he could cause (create) the same response by both primary stimulus (the meat) and by secondary stimulus (the ringing of the bell). This discovery was immediately recognized by the military, psychologists and the political establishment. But what is so significant about Pavlov's discovery?

Simply put, Pavlov provided additional insight into the possibility that human political behavior could be scientifically controlled (manipulated) through the application of theories advanced in the science of behavioral psychology, and most importantly, without the knowledge of the subjects.

Psychologists had known about stimulus and response long before Pavlov's experiments. What his work added was something called *hooking*, or the best way to hook the stimulus to the response. He noted, for example, that it was most effective to ring the bell one half second before the meat was presented.

Other behaviorists discovered, at about the same time, that children could be manipulated by this process to become anything from doctors to thieves regardless of race or ancestry. They also discovered that fear could be taught through this process proving conclusively that human behavior could be scientifically manipulated.

Theodicy

People are, in many ways, like animals who are given to herd mentality. In this respect humans are, as a group, very predictable. An adequate period of observation of the herd permits the discovery of patterns of behavior unique to it.

It should be observed here that Southern slaveholders (they called themselves planters) maintained large plantations at which their control of African slaves was absolute for nearly 350 years. The plantations were literally laboratories where African slaves were observed under various conditions in order to develop effective methods to control them and insure their maximum productivity. From these "experiments" theories were developed that are still successfully used today.

Political economists teach that need determines value. Behavioral psychologists teach that stimulus creates response. If need is recognized as a stimulus it too will create a conditioned reflex that is as predictable as the salivating of dogs. But the larger question is, if need can be induced and thereby act as stimulus, is there a predictable response that can be associated with need? The answer is yes.

Need can be defined as a requirement for something essential (food, clothing and shelter immediately come to mind). It is axiomatic that need is closely associated with poverty. In fact, need, want and poverty are synonymous terms all referring to the lack of resources necessary for comfortable living. The predictable response to need is, in a word, desperation. Desperation implies recklessness, lack of hope and even despondency. A person in need is a person without hope and often without courage. It is not surprising that poverty and desperate acts have always been closely related. The acts of desperate persons are, by definition, what society has termed criminal activity. In society the response to criminal activity has invariably been the passage of criminal laws and the development of a massive law enforcement apparatus to enforce them. That this tactic is futile is obvious. That the tactic ignores the cause of criminal activity in the face of its demonstrated futility only proves that the elimination of crime cannot be its true objective.

Poverty is the cause of most crime. The response to crime, however, never employs a strategy that would eliminate the cause. The response is always the passage of criminal laws. It has been said that every law creates an outlaw. An outlaw is a person who has been declared to have no legal rights or protection. Originally, even the murder of such a person was not itself a crime.

It may be seen from this that the creation of poverty is a method of social control. Its effect is to control, by law and marginalization, the victims of economic policies that are themselves politically motivated. Those who are most likely to revolt against the inequitable distribution of the wealth of a society are the ones who are most likely to be criminalized and thereby controlled by the criminal law and the massive law enforcement apparatus. *To create poverty is to create crime. To create crime is to give legal justification to the use of methods by which the populace may be watched, controlled and ultimately deprived of their natural rights by the politically declared necessity to control the crime that is the direct and intended result of the created poverty and need.* In a very real sense then, poverty exists not because of laziness, lack of initiative or act of God because poverty is the absence of wealth. *It is the control of wealth that creates poverty.* Economics is the science of the techniques used to control wealth and, therefore, to create poverty. *Poverty, therefore, is the result of carefully devised, scrupulously implemented and religiously endorsed political policies of governments and private powers.*

But what is the benefit of creating poverty? One benefit is that it permits the top 10% of the population to own 70% of the wealth and the bottom 90% to own 30% of the wealth. It also insures that the unequal distribution will continue because 90% of the population is, as a practical matter, prevented from obtaining any significant amount of disposable wealth with which to launch a war of redistribution, whether by violent or peaceful means. As fate would have it even revolution is impeded by poverty.

Theodicy

Poverty also creates a reserve group of poor persons who can be relied upon to do the bidding of those who control the Wealth. This reserve group will suffer any indignity, sacrifice any cause in return for a pittance of the enormous wealth that actually belongs to them as co-inhabitants of the planet from which all natural resources are derived.

We have said that economic disruption of the family is perhaps the most effective and insidious tactic of psychological warfare. Our digression on economics implies that the statement is true because the control of wealth is a political function that creates poverty of the many to insure the wealth of the few. The poverty stricken many are always the ruled, the wealthy few are always the rulers.

When we relate this to the situation that we, as African Americans, find ourselves in, it is clear that the poverty we endure has been created by our enemies. To work an entire group of the population for centuries without compensation and to deny them economic opportunity by legislation, private act and judicial fiat during the period after is to create their poverty. Since all of this was a matter of public policy it cannot be seriously denied that it was deliberate and planned.

Disruption of the Cultural Function

It is a major premise of this work that culture is fundamental to the development of civilization. We have further posited that culture is specifically created by and for groups of people and passed down by them from generation to generation. In this respect culture is related to religion and the Ancestral Stream.

Our culture has been stolen from us. That which has been stolen is powerful cultural energy. Because the family is the epicenter of cultural transmission the disruption of that function can be devastating. We have noted that culture is transmitted through the educational process and that process begins in and is reinforced in the confines of the family.

If it is true that 80% of what we learn in the course of our lives is learned within the first five years of life then it is easy to see how important the primary educational process is in developing the overall mind-set of the New Body Politic. It is equally true that information imparted at such a tender age is extremely difficult to erase and remains, more or less, indelibly written into the psyche.

Disruption is a term that must also be clearly understood in order to perceive the ramifications and impact in the context of the cultural function of the family. To disrupt means to break apart. In the sense used here it implies two types of breaking apart. The first is to break apart the culture that would be in place in the absence of the disruption, that is, our Authentic Ancestral Culture. The second, is to implant an alternative culture that will itself operate as a disruption of the family function.

In the case of the African American family, the alternative culture has been the American culture, the culture of our enemies. American culture is more accurately described as White supremacist culture and is characterized by violence, professed individualism, sexism and racism. But American culture is, first and foremost, the culture of violence by virtue of the centrality and overwhelming presence of the gun in all aspects of its cultural development and existence. American Culture is also an insidious form of domestic violence in its devastating effect on the development and maintenance of families.

In American culture the gun is a psychological, nearly physical appendage as vital to its existence as the heart is to human beings. The gun has so long been a part of America that it cannot now, if ever, be eliminated, its roots are too deep.

The gun is the symbol of the European heritage of violence, aggression and brutality. It is not coincidental that the great God of the Northern people was Odin the God of War and Valhalla was a place where war was prosecuted every day for eternity and one had to kill in order to gain admittance. If America has a creation myth it is closely related to violence,

Theodicy

the gun and war. Of course, in America the gun is necessary not only to prosecute war but also to defend individual rights. The sacred right of individual freedom, according to the European, also includes the right to control and exercise authority over other so-called inferior races. Rugged individualism combined with racist ideology (the political ideology of America is White supremacy). The United States Constitution is a fundamentally White supremacist document and all of the Founding Fathers were unabashed White supremacists. White supremacy and the gun are the fundamental components of American Culture. When sexism (more accurately the cultural and political philosophy of female inferiority) is added to this volatile mix the potential for the disruption of a family-oriented, matrilineal culture is apparent and overwhelming. When such a culture is implanted as the alternative for our Authentic Ancestral Culture the effect is disruption of the cultural function of the family. Since we have already noted the effect of cultural deprivation we need not revisit the subject here. Suffice it to say that one of the side effects of cultural deprivation is disruption of the family. Let us also note here that when the disruption of the cultural function of the family is also a tactic of psychological warfare its impact is doubly devastating.

It can be seen from the above that the family is the first and lasting manifestation of the existence of an immense, potential collective power base. In a real sense family power is the power of the people that we have ,heard so much about.

It should now be abundantly clear that in a state of war a wise tactic would be to disrupt or destroy the enemies power base. It is also clear that the African American's power base is, and has always been, *the family*. Whether nuclear, extended, by blood or idea, the family is our power base and our secret weapon in time of war. Apparently, it is a secret that is well known to our enemies and ignored by us.

We have demonstrated that African Americans are at war. The fact that the war is undeclared and psychological does not lessen its impact on our lives and fortunes or the life prospects of our children. Nor does it lessen the need for a plan of action and competent leadership to implement it. The plan must include a counteroffensive, a war against war. The understanding of this fact returns us to the fundamental problem that is the focus of this section. We have had an abundance of leaders. But we have had little or no leadership. What we have had, at best, is the illusion of leadership. Let us now look at the concept of illusory leadership to see how it has lulled us into a false and detrimental sense of security that has benefitted our enemies and deprived us and our children of our justly deserved inheritance.

Theodicy

Illusory Leadership

Just as the Sun appears to rise in the east and set in the west, but actually does neither, that which may be most confirmed by our senses may be illusory. Leadership is not an exception. This fact is especially well demonstrated by the history of our sojourn in America. Our experience with leadership is actually the malaise, indecision, cowardice, and accommodation of media-generated, government sponsored "leaders" whose "leadership" has been, by accident or design, an *illusion*.

We can state at the outset and without fear of contradiction, that throughout the entire course of our unfortunate involvement with the European we have been viewed by them as enemies or prey. The confrontations and associations between us have always been that of conqueror and conquered, predator and prey or master and slave. But always, beneath the surface, we have been mortal enemies.

History indicates that the wholesale slave trade was actually an undeclared war against the African people. The result of the war was that African men, women and children who did not fall in battle were taken as prisoners of war. African Americans are, therefore, as a historical fact, descendant of the victims of a multinational, armed, unprovoked attack, who after having been defeated by superior arms (Africans used spears, Europeans used guns) were taken as both prisoners of war and the spoils of war.

During the course of the infamous slave trade virtually all of the European nations descended upon the African continent like locusts. Their intention in doing so was to prosecute war against the African people for the purpose and further intention of extracting every natural resource of value to be found there, including gold, diamonds and especially strong, fertile human beings. Each of the nations dispatched an army, often under the banner of a "trading company" chartered by the "Crown" and blessed by their religious establishments. Among the notables represented in this rogues' gallery were England, France, Spain, Portugal and Germany. Whether the blessing came from the Pope or the

Archbishop of Canterbury, whether directly or indirectly, the sanctioning religion was Christianity.

Africa was invaded by the combined military forces of the entire European nation, all with one overriding motivation -- to enslave the African and control the wealth of her homeland. It is in this context that so-called African American leadership must be viewed because we are the descendants of a people against whom a vicious war was waged and continues to be waged. We are, even today, the prisoners of that ongoing war. Since war is waged against us, we must wage war in return. In war those who lead are those who are trained in the art and science of war.

If it is true that we are a people who survive in a perpetual state of undeclared war and who are prisoners of that unprovoked war, it seems clear that our strategy, that is our plan of action must be, at least in part, a *military* strategy. It must also include psychological and physical training for war. At very least, we must view our life circumstances for what they are, sometimes open, sometimes covert, hostilities and perpetual conflict between mortal enemies.

It is in this light that we must look, critically, at the history of African American leadership. Through the entire course of our history in this country those who have been our leaders have been of one type --preachers. We have been led, some would say led astray, by men who believe or at least profess they believe in reward in the hereafter; who turn the other cheek when slapped; believe in non-violence as a strategy; and love and pray for their enemies even when being raped or killed. Even Malcolm X was a religious man, a minister of Islam. Though Islam lam speaks of jihad, Malcolm X never called for a holy war.

Two exception may be made. The first is Marcus Mosiah Garvey one of the true visionaries of our struggle. He recognized the necessity flag, pomp and ceremony. He proudly wore military uniform and even carried a sword. But he did not call for war and as far as is known did not prepare for it.

Theodicy

The second example is the Black Panther Party, a group of courageous young African Americans who played soldier for the media. Those young men, potential warriors all, rapidly became labeled as the greatest threat to the internal security of the United States and were, literally, hunted down and *exterminated*. It was not there strategy, training (they had little of former and none of the latter) or military preparedness that made them so threatening. It was the *powerful symbols* of the clenched fist, the gun and their *revolutionary rhetoric* that made them the target of virtually every police force in the nation.

To the extent that politicians may be placed in the category of leaders (a highly doubtful possibility) they have always been and will always be woefully ineffective. Unlike preachers whose oath and allegiance is to the God of the European, politicians are sworn to *uphold* and *defend* the government, Constitution and laws of the United States. In short, politicians are the ultimate accommodationists. With few exceptions (Adam Clayton Powell, Jr. comes to mind) politicians are *elected traitors*. This is because they cannot be both part of the struggle and part of that which we struggle against. If a politician advocates the overthrow of the government she violates her oath of office. Unless a politician is actively attempting to destabilize the government (an unlikely possibility) she is actively working to advance its interests. Perhaps this is why we have never seen a preacher or politician who has as much as advocated revolt. Clearly, a person who believes loving and forgiving his enemy or one who openly joins the enemy by swearing allegiance to his enemy's cause, can never be considered a leader of the forces that oppose the enemy. More importantly, warriors are led by generals, not preachers and certainly not politicians.

Illusory leadership is leadership that is unreal or deceptive and for that reason is the equivalent of no leadership at all. Where leadership does not exist true leaders cannot exist. Without leadership even a well-trained army becomes an unguided mob. But the most detrimental effect of leadership that is illusory is that it deceives those who might otherwise develop leadership to believe that they already have leaders who are exercising leadership on their behalf. Even the person mired in the time consuming pursuit of life's necessities will recognize, in time, that if no one does anything, nothing will be done. Change requires initiative.

The illusion of leadership is not only equivalent to no leadership at all, it also operates to cause people to rely on the professed leadership of people who actually have none. This is why the necessity for true leadership should never be underestimated. We are, as a people, in our present state of powerlessness partially because we suffer from the debilitating effects of illusory leadership. In this respect illusory leadership should be seen as a tactic of warfare. The point requires a brief elaboration.

A people who believe themselves aggrieved may logically be expected to take collective action designed to relieve them of their affliction. It may also be logically expected that they would elect a person or persons to formulate a plan of action and to implement it. They would necessarily place their trust in the hands of the person(s) elected having come to believe that she is not only capable of leadership but also has their best interests at heart. Having made such preparations they will assume that their interests are being protected and return to their normal pursuit of life's necessities. But what if the elected person(s) has only the appearance of leadership? He speaks well but has no plan. He talks war but has the courage of a coward. He speaks of great vision but is actually blind. He has none of the abilities necessary to make the change that he has been elected to effect. He is no more than an elaborate illusion. Blue smoke and mirrors. The little man behind the curtain in Oz. As bad as this scenario may seem it is not the worst aspect of illusory leadership.

The illusory leader becomes, wittingly or not, a tool of the enemy as well as a traitor to his people and their cause. He does this in two ways. First, because he is virtually guaranteed to be completely ineffective in whatever he undertakes to do (except perhaps in getting elected leader) he presents no threat to the enemy and represents to them

Theodicy

the equivalent of a white flag of surrender. Second, and at the same time, he serves the important function of making the aggrieved people believe that he is actively doing something to alleviate their affliction. As a result of such false belief they will, in turn, do nothing themselves. They will wait on the one who is, unknown to them, incapable of solving their problems.

Illusory leaders lead astray. The incalculable expense of their incompetence is to be viewed as time lost and opportunities missed. Had African Americans had genuine leadership at any point in our unfortunate history in America our present condition would be quite different and our enemies would not be laughing because we continue to follow preachers and politicians whose allegiance is not to us but do the God and government of our enemies.

Illusory leaders are traitors. They should be treated as such. Those who presume to call themselves leaders must be held accountable for their lack of success. In any event, we must not continue to give support to those who have not been selected and trained by us to implement our plan of action.

The illusion of leadership has been detrimental to us. It has caused us to forego the development of leadership qualities among our people as a strategy for change and has aided our enemies by that failure. What we have done is to simply wait for persons to appear whose only qualification was that they were articulate enough to intone the magic phrase "vote for me and I'll set you free". None have delivered and most have been rewarded for their failure. The illusion of leadership is no leadership at all.

In order for the plan of action to succeed it must have carefully selected and rigorously ,trained leadership to implement it. For the leadership to carry out its mission it must be protected. We will conclude this section with an examination of the concept of *Redundant Leadership* and *Multiple Centers of Control*, as the method by which the leadership may be protected and the success of the plan of action assured.

Redundant Leadership and

Multiple Centers of Control

There is an ancient and apparently effective military tactic that provides that if you cut off the head of the enemy its body will die. More specifically, it states that in war you first locate the enemy's command center, kill the leader or otherwise disrupt its ability to communicate with the troops and they, unable to coordinate actions or exercise leadership, will scatter and cease to resist. Hence, the most efficient way to destroy the enemy's ability to resist is to destroy the leader or, more accurately, the ability to exercise leadership. It is indeed astonishing that this simple tactic has been successfully used against us for so long. It also speaks volumes about our inability to learn from our mistakes. We may distill from this a maxim that we ignore at our peril: *the lifespan of the leader and of effective leadership is proportional to the length of time required for the enemy to locate and destroy her ability to exercise leadership.*

In order to implement the plan of action and to protect the leadership we must, at all costs, effectively counteract the enemy's "cut off the head tactic". The concept of Redundant leadership and Multiple Centers of Control provide the answer.

We have previously indicated that the New Body Politic, the organism of our collectivity, is modeled on the structure and vital components of the human body. In the human body the brain is the apparatus that processes information from the senses and, in turn, communicates commands to the rest of the body. This process is operative at leisure and in situations of imminent danger. The brain is also the locus of the body's command center and the seat of its leadership function.

Through the process of its development the brain has been endowed with a mechanism that provides the example of a contraposition that frustrates and neutralizes the possibility of disruption or destruction of its leadership function. The

Theodicy

mechanism is known as *redundant representation* and it functions as a method of *multiple control*.

The brain is organized in a unique way. It has developed an organizational structure that permits it to shift vital control functions from damaged or destroyed areas to unimpaired areas in order to maintain continuity of control. The brain abounds with redundancy. It contains numerous areas that replicate the functions of other separate and distinct areas. The mechanism for control of a particular function is often found in several areas of the brain and electrical impulses carrying the same message travel along different neural pathways creating multiple control centers.

These configurations are biologically purposeful and result in obvious advantage to the body. By these mechanisms the body is guarded against the otherwise devastating effects of damage to the brain. Of equal importance is the fact that these mechanisms create an organism that is highly adaptive to the ever changing circumstances of life in an environment where peril is perennial.

One prominent example will suffice to illustrate the point. It is now known that damage to the left hemisphere of the brain (where verbal communication is controlled) will often result in *automatic transference* of the speech function to the right hemisphere. Apparently, the brain counterbalances the damage by moving the function to an unimpaired area where it can utilize pristine brain cells. Redundant representation and multiple control in the brain provide the model for Redundant Leadership and Multiple Centers of Control .in the New Body Politic.

In order to counteract and neutralize the "cut off the head and the body will die" military tactic that has been the mainstay of our enemy's ongoing undeclared War Against the African People our leadership must e diffuse and amorphous. Although it is true that the One Who Goes Before provide a beacon and an early warning system for the people in times of darkness and danger, her function is essentially titular and symbolic. The One Who Goes Before is the voice that articulates the plan of action and the will of the New Body Politic. If necessary she becomes a living diversion sacrificing herself as the target of the enemy's failed attempt to prevent leadership by killing a leader. Leadership must, therefore, be redundant.

Redundant leadership is accomplished by the selection and training of a cadre of persons who become enriched and proficient in the exercise of leadership. These persons, thousands strong, spread throughout the width and breadth of the land and will be *invisible* because publicly unnamed and unknown. Each will share in the intricacies of the plan of action. Each will be qualified to assume the titular and symbolic position of the One Who Goes Before on a moment's notice and in an orderly, pre-determined pattern of succession.

Redundancy creates a *Hydra Effect* that serves to neutralize the effectiveness of the "cut off the head" tactic. The Hydra was the many-headed water serpent of Greek mythology who was difficult to kill because each time one of its heads was cut off, instead of dying, it grew two new heads in the place of the severed one.

The concept of Multiple Centers of Control, like that of Redundant Leadership in the New Body Politic, is the functional equivalent of a mechanism of the human brain. After catastrophic damage, whether the damage is environmental or genetic, the brain has the ability to "reorganize" itself in a unique way.

The brain contains several centers that are either symmetrical or whose functions are represented, to a greater of lesser degree, in other areas of the brain. The arrangement is such that each of these areas are capable of assuming various configurations and levels of activity to facilitate "reorganization" after an injury has occurred. By this mechanism the brain continues to function by the simple expedient of a paired area instantaneously reconfiguring itself to assume the activity of the damaged one and thereby continue the flow of information vital to the overall functioning of the body.

Theodicy

We have noted that in order for the enemy to "cut off the head" it must first locate the command center before it can paralyze the New Body Politic by disrupting the flow of information and preventing it from communicating commands to its parts. Of course, the this goal is considerably complicated, if not frustrated entirely, if the command center cannot be located. The concept of Multiple Centers of Control embodies several elements that effectively frustrate the enemy's ability to locate and paralyze the command center.

First, the control centers represent a network of databases at various locations each of which contains the encrypted information necessary to facilitate "reorganization" of the chain of command and flow of information to all body parts, instantaneously in the event that any control center is compromised. This national network serves to coordinate all information and direct its flow. It also serves to dispatch personnel and materiel to damaged areas and either repairs them on the spot or rebuilds them at a new location.

Second, the cadre of persons who have been carefully selected and rigorously trained in the fundamentals of leadership and the intricacies of the plan of action are on 24 hour call to spring into action and direct the operation of the control center under their sphere of authority or to be dispatched to any damaged area of the national network to direct repair or relocation. In any event, no control center can be compromised for any length of time and even the death of the One Who Goes Before cannot disrupt or paralyze the New Body Politic. When those who exercise leadership and the control centers in the national network are both multiple and self-regenerating like the Hydra they will be capable of replication ad infinitum. Any attempt to destroy either will be an exercise in futility and the ancient military tactic of "cut off the head" will have been effectively neutralized.

We have said a great deal about leadership. We have seen that illusory leadership operates to the decided advantage of our enemies. But its operation is the result of illusory leaders who, lacking true leadership qualities, merely play into the hands of our enemies and assist them in the furtherance of their nefarious objectives. We have not, however, looked at leadership from the point of view of our enemies. From their standpoint the development of true leadership qualities by African Americans must be prevented at all costs.

We have seen the swiftness and brutality with which the Black Panther Party was exterminated. Their ascendency to the dubious distinction of being the greatest threat to the internal security of the United States focused attention on the threat of the symbol represented by young Black men armed with revolutionary rhetoric and guns. We might also add here, the assassination of those who demonstrated the potential for true leadership by virtue of their popularity such a Martin Luther King, Jr. and Malcolm X. And the political assassinations of Marcus Garvey and Adam Clayton Powell, Jr.

We have also seen how the "cut of the head" tactic has been effectively used against us and how Redundant Leadership and Multiple Centers of Control will neutralize its effectiveness.

In order to fully understand the importance of leadership, however, we are required to go one step further and examine the underlying reason for the enemy's apparent obsession with preventing the development of true leadership qualities among African Americans and why it is seen by them as a clear and present danger.

In the summer of 1967 amid the turmoil and tragedy in America's rebellious inner cities, the Federal Bureau of Investigation, under the direction of an avowed White supremacist, established a counterintelligence program, code named *Cointelpro*, was to neutralize Black nationalists and to *prevent the rise of a Black messiah*. The program sought to counter enemy intelligence by use of any means that would neutralize their activities. The program was entirely outside the realm of the authority granted to the FBI by its charter and was thereby patently illegal. The question we shall attempt to answer here, in order to complete the discussion of leadership, is why the United States

Theodicy

government would be so interested in preventing the rise of a Black messiah as to adopt and employ ruthless, criminal means to do so?

The Rise of the Black Messiah

The answer to the question that we have posited is discovered in the subtle connection between messianism and nationalism. We have discussed earlier in this work that the concept of nationalism is seen as revolutionary and subversive when championed by a separate group within a larger society and that the term is synonymous with self-determination and collective will. Let us now examine the concept of messianism that the connection between the two and their relationship to leadership may be illustrated.

The ideological movement known as messianism teaches the belief in a messiah. The messiah is the anointed one who will come, presumably from God, to establish righteousness. The word messiah is apparently of Hebrew origin but the concept is universally recognized. It is well-known in nations such as the United States that profess a Judeo-Christian heritage. The concept is reflected in the savior-kings of many religions and cultures. The Hindu has Vishnu, Buddhists, Zoroastrians and Confucians have their Holy One, the Muslims their *Mahdi* and the Christians their Christ. Though the concept is most often associated with an individual it may also be an idea that is the messiah. The messiah is often associated a nativistic or revivalistic movement. Nativistic movements are those in which a visionary leader offers salvation to a specific group of people by the destruction of the control and culture of foreigners. Revivalist movements, on the other hand, seek to return a specific group of people to a golden age when an Authentic Ancestral Culture brought stability and prosperity to its adherents.

Whether nativistic or revivalist messianism embraces two intricately related concepts. The first is the restoration or establishment of righteousness, the fundamental mission of every messiah. The second concept is the destruction of foreign culture and control by it over the lives and destinies of the people to whom the messiah brings her message of righteousness. The culture that is the target of destruction is, more often than not, not only foreign but also inimical to the interests of those who would receive the messiah's message.

Theodicy

It seems only NaTuRal then, that those who represent or advocate the continuation of foreign culture and control, for whatever reason, necessarily find the idea and fact of a messiah intent on altering their present and privileged status troublesome and subversive of their authority. It is for this reason that nativist and revivalist movements are viewed with extreme suspicion and contempt by host governments. But the case of the illegal program to prevent the rise of a Black messiah in the United States as envisioned by J. Edgar Hoover is unique.

The reasons that motivated America's most powerful White supremacist are lost in the catacombs of his bigoted mind. we may speculate, however, as to the reasons underlying his fear of a Black messiah. Two reasons, among many, may be isolated for analysis.

The first is the concept of righteousness and its implied dependence on balance and fairness which as we have seen is part and parcel of the messianic mission. The second is the umbilical connection between African Americans and Africans of our Motherland. Let us remember that revivalism is, in essence, a cultural/political movement that is based on the determination of a specific group of people, within a larger society, to create, resuscitate or resurrect a culture that is their own and that better suits their collective requirements for survival and prosperity. When such a cultural/political movement has as its additional aim the restoration of a perceived golden age when ancestors of the group fared better than their descendants do now it invariably proclaims the advent of a messiah who will usher in the new age and its culture. It is by and through this messiah that the predicted and anticipated transformation of society will take place. Such a transformation necessarily portends a redistribution of weal th or power or both. Not surprisingly, most movements of this type are suppressed rapidly, brutally and by force.

Revivalism is then, a basic component of messianism. Together they represent a significant threat whether the movement is the brainchild of a self-proclaimed messiah or of a predetermined, well focused plan implemented by a person anointed with the mantle of leadership by the collective will of the people. The key aspect of the threat, however, is the combination of culture, righteousness and the belief that the revived culture will inaugurate a new period of righteousness.

Righteousness is itself a fascinating and even intriguing concept. Unfortunately, it is honored more in the breach than in practice. Be that as it may, it is, at least, a term of historic popularity. It has found its way into the celebrated writings of the Judeo-Christian bible and has been proclaimed as the benchmark and aspiration of all those who walk with God. Perhaps more interestingly, the concept of straightness and right, from which the concept of righteousness derives, predates the plagiarized and diluted biblical notion by thousands of years. By examination of the origin of the concept we may better understand why the call for righteousness, particularly by African Americans, has been received with such disdain by those currently in power.

The oldest known concept of righteousness is to be found, not surprisingly, in ancient Kemit, where it was known as *Maat*. Although the concept of *Maat* is multi-dimensional, we will here only address the facets of it that deal with the mundane level of righteousness.

Maat is the female *NeTeR* of justice. She represents accuracy, honesty, truth, authenticity, legitimacy, integrity and legality. She is a state of balance between opposing forces and the equilibrium of the Two Truths. Her symbol is the feather of perfection that counterbalances the heart of the deceased at the weighing of the soul. *Maat* also represents the harmony that counteracts dissonance. Most importantly, however, *maat* implies unerring, unswerving straightness. It is more than mere coincidence that the words straight and right are synonyms and both imply that which is aboveboard, true and legitimate.

In ancient Kemit Kings and judges were sworn to observe and uphold not the law but *maat* simply because she supersedes all law because it is the only true law and obligation. It was said of her that even the *NeTeRs* existed

Theodicy

because of her and that she inhabits and governs everything that exists. When it is considered that the ancient Kemites preserved order, harmony and peace without revolution or rebellion from within for thousands of years, we see the only real example of a civilization in which righteousness actually prevailed. Subsumed in the concept of *maat* is its antithesis, namely that discrimination, maldistribution of wealth and resources cannot be suffered to exist where *maat* is strictly, unerringly observed. *Maat* is the enemy of political corruption, usury, unfair labor practices, unjust laws, manipulation and deceit. She exists to keep balance, order and harmony and does so without fear or favor. Slavery, starvation and abject poverty cannot exist is her presence.

Those who have secured and maintain their hegemony by methods and means contrary to righteousness will always rally against the philosophy or person who calls for the restoration of righteousness. Only those who are unjust fear justice.

One is reminded, in this context, of the massacre of the innocents recorded in the Jewish New Testament in which Herod, whether in actual fear of the coming of the messiah or just to hedge his bets, sought to destroy all male children of the Jews of a certain age to prevent the rise of the anticipated messiah.

A ruler or government intent on maintaining its position of power keeps abreast of what people believe will occur in the future on the off chance that what is predicted might actually come to pass. Whether he believes it or not is not important. It is the fact that the people might believe it and by the force of their belief make it a reality.

The ruler intent on maintaining his power also keeps track of, and, suppresses when necessary, those who seek to restore righteousness whether they claim messianic calling or not. It is not whether the reformer will actually restore righteousness, it is the unsettling implication that the current state of affairs is unjust or corrupt that must be avoided. Nothing can be more devastating to the power of the status quo than the widespread belief that ruler or government is unjust, corrupt or dishonest. This insidious belief forms the seed/idea of revolution. Such a belief, if not extinguished rapidly, has the tendency to spread like wildfire and consume everything in its path.

In America there remains, until this day, a historical rift between the races. There is, on the one hand, the underclass of African Americans, young and violent, who grow increasingly aggressive and strident in their call for righteousness and who have nothing to lose. On the other hand, there is the class of Whites who are older and whether privileged or not have a great deal more to lose and who are intent on maintaining and improving their status. This group is no less violent than their counterparts. They have, however, the imprimatur of the laws, that they have written, and the law enforcement apparatus that they control to disguise their violence with a cloak of legitimacy. These two groups are on a collision course and neither is likely to give way.

African Americans, because of sheer numbers and location at the hub of the nation's industrial, financial and commercial centers are like so many incendiary devices set to detonate at the slightest disturbance. Our explosive force and the sobering impact it can have has, thus far, been contained because lacking true leadership we are unorganized and without an effective plan of action. Our enemies have concluded mistakenly, but not without some justification, that we will only move from potential to actual threat upon the occasion of the rise of a Black messiah to lead us. Their conclusion is mistaken because the messiah may also be an idea. Messianism may be predicated on nothing more than an idea whose time has finally come. In this context we find not only an explanation for the tactic examined here but also proof of why it is now doomed to failure.

The second connection is born of the first. While the first is local the second is global. It is the umbilical connection between African Americans and Africans of the Motherland. It has long been understood by Europeans that the rise of an

Theodicy

African power must be avoided at all costs. The reasons are not difficult to ascertain.

First, the wealth of Europe derives, by and large, from the resources, both natural and human, stolen from Africa during the War of Enslavement. In fact, the primary reason for the War Against the African People was, and remains, to subdue them so that their resources could be raped at leisure. The planned result of this has been that while Europe and America has grown rich Africa, the richest continent on the planet, has been mired in poverty.

Second, the historical record of the status of the African people as the light and leaders of the world, though periodically disputed by Europeans, is indicative of the potential power of the African people to lead the world against the forces of the unseen hand of capitalism. The rise of an African power would focus the attention of the people of the world (the vast majority of whom are people of color who are also avowed enemies of the European) on their own ability to better their condition by disavowal of an allegiance to the European and his decadent way of thinking.

The rise of an African power would lead, over time and inevitably, to the economic displacement or ruin of Europe and America as well as a reverse domino effect that would cause the nations of the Third World to rise and join forces against their common enemy.

African Americans represent a key factor in the rise of an African power. The destinies of African Americans and Africans are bound by a genetic umbilicus. African Americans are literally the children of the African Motherland. Whether we, at present, recognize this fact is irrelevant. We are the kidnapped children of mothers who long to have us returned to their bosom. We have matured but our genetic makeup has not changed and can never change. We have adopted new ways and adapted to new conditions but we are still, and will ever be, offspring of the African womb. Even the child adopted at birth longs to know its mother and with the onset on maturity invariably seeks to find her. The mother who places her child for adoption always, in her heart of hearts, regrets the choice.

We have noted that Africa is without friends. But she has no need of friends when she has family. When the familial connection between us is truly understood we will recognize that as children in the land of wealth we are obligated to assist in every way possible, our relatives who find themselves impoverished through no fault of their own.

Our enemies recognize this all important connection even if we do not. They have discerned long ago that the power of the African is the power of family. To the extent that we fail to recognize our familial and ancestral connection to Africa we unwittingly serve the interests of our enemies immeasurably and disserve our own interests.

Our enemies concluded from the simple facts that they must prevent the rise of a Black messiah among African Americans as well as Africans. They have undermined or assassinated Africans with the same swiftness and ruthless brutality as they have African Americans. They have been successful in preventing the rise of a Black messiah because the "cut off the head" tactic has been successful. When the fundamentals of leadership are taught to all of our people, and when the concepts of Redundant Leadership and Multiple Centers of Control are known and employed our enemies will no longer be able to thwart true leadership or undermine our plan of action.

We have looked at *power*, *plan* and *leadership*, three indispensable components in our preparation for the coming age. We have seen that we must understand power, develop a plan and train the leadership to implement it. But none of these will avail us much if we do not have the will to make our vision a reality. To that end we next examine the function and importance of the *power of the will*.

Theodicy

SECTION SEVEN:

THE POWER OF THE WILL

CHAPTER SEVENTEEN: WILL

Will Defined

The title of this book has been carefully selected to underscore the cosmic connection between the unfolding of Theodicy and the Power of the Will. An appreciation of function of the will in its relationship to power and their relationship to the New Body Politic is essential to that end.

Will is essentially a form of power. Will and power are so closely related as to be inseparable. Will is ineffective without power to effect its intentions. Power, on the other hand, is random and inefficient without will to give it direction and focus. Will is, therefore, a power in its own right. It is a power that is expressed by all living things.

To the single cell amoeba will is the instinctive determination to divide and reproduce. To the plant will is the instinctive determination that thrusts its roots downward and it branches to toward the sky. To the individual human being will is the power to make decisions and act on them in spite of opposition. To the New Body Politic will is the collective power of the group to make decisions and act on them in spite of opposition or resistance.

Will is a combination of power and action. It is the singular and characteristic determination of all things to reproduce, and by so doing to survive. Whether purposeful or instinctive, will is energetically enacted.

The will is also the character of the mind. It is that which gives the mind shape and texture. If the mind may be likened to a loom on which the fabric of thought is woven, the will may be likened to the dye that colors the yarn and gives the finished product its distinctive character.

The will consists of two primary elements. The first is mechanical and is the result of the Internal Intelligence Function. It is fed by the stored data and images provided by the individual's life experiences. It is, in effect, the *hardware* of the will. The second element is the power that motivates the will. It is that which fuels it and which has its own

Theodicy

measurable intensity. It is peculiar to the individual and is the *software* of the will. The hardware of the will is provided by culture and is learned. The software of the will is evoked by the cosmic age and is intuited.

The will has been variously perceived as the part of the soul that interacts with the intellect to create reasoned choices. It has also been seen as the part of the mind that balances thought and feeling to create action. More accurately, however, the will functions through both intellect and emotion. It is both rational and non-rational, conscious and unconscious forces acting with the individual to determine choice, action and emotion. Will, then, is also *power coupled with intuition*. The will is also the collective determination of a group either when all are agreed or as determined by an interplay and elimination of divergent and conflicting viewpoints.

Curiously, the concept of mind has been perfunctorily dismissed from the canons of modern psychology. It has been boldly proclaimed to be an unscientific principle. Psychologists now use concepts like personality development to explain what was once understood as the function and domain of the will. They have also dispensed with the concept of mind.

The unceremonious removal of will and mind from the lexicon of psychology is curious because psychology is purported to be the study or science of the mind. Perhaps this apparent anomaly exists because mind literally means spirit or soul and the concept no longer fits with psychology's newly acquired scientific status. The ancient connection between spirit and soul was based not only on cultural traditions but also on philosophic analysis. Since psychology is now proclaimed to be a full-fledged scientific discipline it is no longer in need of philosophic analysis. We have already seen the results of the use of scientific analysis when it divorces spirituality from the search for ultimate reality. The result is decadent complexity and science without soul.

We have also noted that there is a treasure trove of ancient teachings known as Sacred Science that is the fruit of our

Authentic Ancestral Culture that can be accessed to learn what our ancestors believed before the confusion that now dominates and undermines Western civilization.

In the land of our ancient beginnings the word for will was *nu*, a word that also implied thought and intention. When the letter "n" was added at the end of the word it became Nun and referred to the celestial, cosmic ocean from which all things were thought to emanate. Emanation refers to the concept that a sacred essence flows from the *Neter Neteru*. This essence never lessens of ceases and flows eternally back to the source of its origin.

When the last letter is doubled The resulting *nuu* means guide, leader or director. In our ancient language a doubled letter indicated that that which it defines is activated, it comes to life.

To our ancestors the *nu*, was the mind energy that guides, directs and perpetually emanates from the cosmic ocean *(Nun)* and the Ancestral Stream flowing within it. Here they have explained a simple yet profound concept that psychologists in their new found scientific status dare not acknowledge or even investigate. The notion that the will not only exists but is related to the soul and is projected from a common, perhaps otherworldly source is for them, untenable. But our ancestors knew that scientific analysis alone will never discover this reality. Only philosophic analysis permits the abstract investigation of ultimate reality.

While dismissing the will psychologists still manage to agree that children as young as three years old have a basic idea of a private self that no one else has access to. They seem to recognize an inner self and can define it. By seven years of age they recognize mind traits such as how they feel. Apparently, there is an innate spirituality that is common to all human beings. It appears as awareness of some higher power and a connectedness to other human beings and NaTuRe.

Psychologists evade the question that is begged by this apparent, innate spirituality. Where is its place of origin?

Theodicy

Could it be the cosmic ocean of *Nun*? The possibilities are worthy of further investigation.

Our ancestors characterized the body as the prison of the soul. Other people, particularly Europeans, have concluded that the body is the temple of the soul. Let us assume that our ancestors were correct. If the soul is imprisoned its natural reflex would be to escape. In order to do so the soul must, on some level, be aware of its imprisonment and it must, in some way be motivated to escape. If the force that motivates the soul is seen as an affinity it would be forever attracted to that which it was captured from. This affinity can be further likened to the will in human beings.

From this we may speculate that the will derives from the cosmic circumstances of our capture and that it drives our innate determination to be free from imprisonment as well as our plans for escape and return to our place of spiritual origin. It follows that the will to freedom is innate in human beings. At each end of the continuum that is life we find the will. It is ever present and has always existed.

The will is also influenced by the color given to it as a result of the movement from one cosmic age to the next. The effect of the current age colors the will. Each age, therefore, has its own characteristic will. It is the power and influence of the specific will of the age that drives the course of human events in each age. In a real sense, the will of the people, in any given age, is evoked by the age itself. The will of the age may, therefore, be determined with relative certainty, by the characteristics of the age itself.

The coming age is the Age of *Hapy*. The character of the age will determine the NaTuRe of the will of the people that is evoked by it. The Age of *Hapy* will be governed and influenced by Saturn, Uranus and its complement Leo. Let us review briefly, how *Hapy* may be expected to mold the collective will of the New Body Politic.

Saturn is the ruler of change and the controller of governments and nations. It is also the Lord High Governor of the Wheel of Time. The influence of Saturn in *Hapy* indicates a change in the governance of nations as well as change in the form of government. Because it is the ruler of change in general it also influences new experiences, new associations and new ways of thinking that help to effect change. As a result Saturn also governs the urge to change. In this respect it is the initiator of change because the urge precedes both thought and action. The urge is like the initial impulse that is sure to impel action. By extension it also profoundly affects those who have the desire to start over, to begin again or to renew that which has previously existed.

Uranus is the planet of extremes, intuition and will. For these reasons it is the planet of revolutionaries and inventors. It governs revolutionaries because they are, at base, extremists while great inventors are endowed with intuition and insight. It is also the planet of electricity which is itself emblematic of energy and power.

Uranus is also a higher octave planet and as such will tend to elevate the overall level of consciousness of the age. It indicates that a quantum leap in consciousness that will propel humanity to heights never imagined in preceding ages. It is the planet of the Sixth Sense, of the Intelligence-of-the-Heart. it is by and through this intuitive influence that the sudden move to higher consciousness will be communicated.

As governor of the will Uranus provides the most important element of revolutionary change. It provides disciplined, focused motivation to implement change. When it is remembered that the will is derived from and is part of the cosmic ocean and the specific Ancestral Stream that flows within it and that it functions as a guide, leader and director, we are forced to see the contours of change that will mark the age. But the age only guarantees the end result. The character of the age is also defined by the choice of methods by which the end result shall be accomplished. To a great extent the choice of methods are determined by courage and daring.

Leo is indicative of the *majesty, pride* and *courage* of the lion. The King of Beasts is noted for its refusal to retreat in the face of danger. Its family is known as its pride. It is also the symbol of heart as that word is related to courage. Leo, as complement of *Hapy*, brings indomitable courage and pride in family to the age. The influence of Leo will insure that the methods chosen will be courageous, radical and revolutionary because they will be in defense of our families, our only true pride.

The Age of *Hapy* is the age when all of the elements necessary to set in motion the cultural/political chain reaction will be present. To the extent that we are aware of the NaTuRe of the age and actively prepare for it we will insure a safe, efficient and expeditious transformation in accord with Theodicy and the Wheel of Time. Whether we do so *en masse* or only on the level of Critical Mass the change is inevitable. Although a sufficient amount of lubrication may reduce the friction as the wheel turns it cannot be stopped or reversed.

In summary the Age of *Hapy* will be governed by a triangular influence (Saturn, Uranus and Leo) that indicates abrupt, revolutionary change dictated by heightened consciousness, direct spiritual insight and intuition, and indomitable leonine courage that will result in the incitement of an unparalleled, resistance that will subvert and undermine prevailing thought, authority, religion and culture to the end that our Authentic Ancestral Culture will overtake our thinking and usher in two millennia of peace and tranquility during which the African perspective and world-view will return true civilization, marked by harmony and peace, to a beleaguered world weary of the domination of *science without soul*. Having reviewed the characteristics of the age that will evoke the will let us return to the will itself.

The will then is the motive power that drives individuals and groups toward their destiny. It is the determination of the soul to fulfill its mission. Its ultimate mission is the return to origin. But the will operates on at least two prevailing thought, authority, religion and culture to the end that our Authentic Ancestral Culture will overtake our thinking and usher in two millennia of peace and tranquility during which the African perspective and world-view will return true civilization, marked by harmony and peace, to a beleaguered world weary of the domination of science without soul.

Having reviewed the characteristics of the age that will evoke the will let us return to the will itself.

The will then is the motive power that drives individuals and groups toward their destiny. It is the determination of the soul to fulfill its mission. Its ultimate mission is the return to origin. But the will operates on at least two distinct levels. It governs the drive toward reunification with the sole-singular cause from which all life emanates. It is also the impetus to human survival and prosperity.

The will to reunification is spiritually controlled and may or may not involve conscious effort by individuals. The will to survive and prosper, on the other hand, is spiritually driven but rationally executed. The first can, and often does, exist without our knowledge, while the second is virtually impossible without it. It is for this reason alone that the body may be seen as a temple. But it is not the temple of the soul. *The body is the Temple of Knowledge in which the soul is imprisoned.* In it we must learn in order to gain our freedom and be reunified with the sole-singular cause.

Our spiritual and sacred essence will, eventually, and inevitably return to its source. The time that it takes to complete the experiential journey that is our destiny is irrelevant because the destination exists outside of time. Whether two or two thousand life times we will endure until all fetters have been loosed and we are free to return.

Our survival and prosperity in each life, in each age, is another matter entirely. Confronted with the seemingly insurmountable obstacles placed in the survival path of life, it is the determination or will to overcome obstacles (the very definition of survival) makes continued existence possible. This aspect of the will is the result of reflection on the circumstances of life and the necessity to overcome obstacles to survival. This aspect of will also motivates the desire for prosperity which is the level above survival.

Theodicy

The will is the power of self-determination. It is the driving force of life. It is that which makes purposeful activity possible. It is itself a stimulus that seems to originate action based on thought.

The power of the will is an unlimited force that can change the course of human events and give back to us the youthful vigor that once made us great. It has always been the power of our will that has kept us strong and motivated our unparalleled accomplishments. We are in need of symbols to constantly remind us of the power latent in our collective will.

We have at our disposal a symbol that has stood the test of time and that is recognized throughout the world. It is one of the Seven Wonders of the ancient world and stands today as a constant reminder that no feat is beyond our ability to accomplish if we will it. The symbol is the Great Pyramid of Khufu.

The Quintessential Symbol

of the Power of the Will

The Great Pyramid of Giza is the only one of the Seven Wonders of the Ancient World left standing. It has been linked to various and sundry fads and fallacies from pyramidology to the miraculous sharpening of razor blades. It has given rise to pyramid hats and has been called everything from a tomb to a landing marker for extraterrestrial travelers. Be that as it may, it is still an architectural and mathematical marvel and the greatest tribute to the ingenuity of humankind.

The pyramid exists, in its true form, only in ancient Kemit. The pyramids of Giza are the largest and finest examples of the architectural style in the world. The Great Pyramid of Giza, constructed during the reign of Khufu, is the largest ever constructed. It is a solid mass of limestone and granite blocks covering more than 13 acres and was originally 756 feet square and 482 feet in height. Its triangular face the points of the compass and slope at a 50° angle to the ground. It is believed to have taken a period of twenty three years to build. When it is considered that there are nearly two and a half million stones, each weighing approximately five thousand pounds, this gargantuan feat required the lifting, perfect placement and alignment of one stone every five minutes.

Over the four thousand five hundred years since its construction Khufu's vision has fascinated the world and raised two questions: (1) what was the purpose of the pyramid?; and (2) how was it constructed?. By focusing on these two questions the world has missed overwhelming message of the pyramid simply because, like the forest obscured by trees, it is so patently obvious.

It is now confirmed that the Great Pyramid was not built by Hebrew or any other slaves. There is no technology on Earth today that is capable of constructing such a massive structure. As a tomb it would be colossal waste of manpower and resources and even the mammoth ego of a Hitler or Napoleon would not embark on such a massive project to create a mere mausoleum. Of course, the notion that it was built by visitors from another planet as a landing marker is both preposterous and insulting. It implies that a structure so clearly evincing a high level of architectural, mathematical and astronomical science could not be the creation of the indigenous people who happened to be Black Africans.

The Great Pyramid of Khufu, like all the cultural components of the great Kemitic civilization, was the product of the genius of the indigenous Black Africans based on their ancient Sacred Science. But how they built the pyramid is, not nearly as important as why they did.

In 23 years the Kemites created a monument to something that has stood for more than four millennia. Its symbol is recognized the world over. Its mere existence has generated a massive amount of research including literally thousands of books, articles about every aspect of it. It is clearly a universally recognized symbol that has fascinated the world since its erection. But what is the Great Pyramid of Khufu a symbol of?

Theodicy

We have discussed the general importance of symbols to our ability to think and communicate. We have also noted that Kemitic symbols were always carefully, purposefully and precisely selected to concretize an important idea. The idea concretized was selected because it was deemed to be vital to survival and either physical or spiritual existence. The Great of Khufu is no exception.

Egyptologists have concluded that the pyramid is linked in some metaphysical way to Ra, the *NeTeR* of sacred essence symbolized by the disk of the sun. They do not explain, however, how their theory can possibly be gleaned from the pyramid itself.

Symbols may be conventional or universal. Conventional symbols result solely from convention. The Nike symbol, for example, stands for the corporation or its product merely because it is accepted as such. Archaeologists discovering a Nike symbol in the future would never surmise that it symbolized a running shoe. The Nike symbol is conventional. The connection between the pyramid and the sun, if there is a connection, is likewise, conventional.

The massive undertaking involved in constructing the Great Pyramid seems to render ludicrous the notion that it is a symbol of the sun. Even dressed, as it originally was, in polished limestone capped with a golden pyramidion, gleaming in the African sun it would not bring to mind the sun. Compare this with the *Aten*. The *Aten* was symbolized by a disk with rays radiating from it with hands at the end of each is clearly symbolic of the sun. The pyramid, especially that of Khufu, cannot be a mere conventional symbol. A symbol on such a massive scale would never be conventional. Only universal symbols are constructed on the scale of the universal.

A universal symbol is one in which the idea and the symbol are related and discernible, intrinsically. Such a symbol speaks a language that transcends the spoken tongue, time and culture. Universal are those that derive their effectiveness from that which is thought to be timeless.

At first glance the pyramid is a triangle. it is the simplest of the polygons and has the least possible number of sides. The triangle manifests the number three on sight. The importance of the number three has been noted by sages and mathematicians since time immemorial and we need not belabor the point here.

The pyramid also sits on a square, the four-sided geometric figure that is itself the first product of multiplication. It is, therefore, a triangle that appears to rise out of square. It immediately forces upon the observer the existence of two numbers each of which is fundamental to the understanding of reality. When contemplating the pyramid, the numbers three and four are unavoidable. The pyramid then, through its expression of number is the sacred scientific symbol of reality and the key to the understanding of the universe and all things, animate and inanimate, contained in it.

It will serve us well to remember here that Pythagoras studied in the temples of Kemit and under the tutelage of the sages and priests there for more than 20 years. Thereafter he returned to Italy where he founded a mystery school at which he taught that *all is number*. This oft-repeated maxim clearly implies that number is the key to all knowledge because it is the essence of all things. But the profound message embodied in the symbol of the pyramid could be and was, with far less effort and expense, inscribed in less grandiose ways. One does not need to construct an edifice covering 571,536 square feet, containing two million, three hundred thousand stones weighing five thousand pounds each and standing nearly fifty stories tall to make the point. We must look elsewhere for the true symbolism of the pyramid.

There is one universal response, one overwhelming impression experienced by everyone who sees the Great Pyramid --its massiveness. Following swiftly on the heels of the forced observation is the fact that it is not a natural structure. Human beings, at least 4,500 years ago, constructed the only one of the Seven Wonders of the Ancient World still left standing.

Theodicy

We may also observe that the pyramid was constructed without the aid of modern technology. The only tools used seem to have been copper chisels and saws, mallets and wedges of wood. All of the tools were what would now be called primitive and unsophisticated. It is equally true, however, that there is no equipment or technology presently available, anywhere on the planet, to recreate the structure. No one seems to know how it was constructed although theories abound. One thing is certain, however, all seem to agree that the single most important element in the construction was good old fashioned manpower. The suggestion that the stones were put in place be slave labor has been repeatedly discredited and may now be dismissed as a factor.

The Greek historian Herodotus reported that it took 100,000 men working exclusively during the flood season twenty years to complete the Great Pyramid. Modern observers have settled on 23 years as the length of time required to complete Khufu's vision. The implications of this give us the key to the true and universal symbol that the pyramid represents. Given the number of blocks that were placed (2.3 million) and the amount of time allotted (23 Years) the Kemites had to place one stone, weighing five thousand pounds, with precision unparalleled in any man made structure or the time, every five minutes. There is only one power on Earth that would enable such a monumental task to be accomplished -- the Power of the Will.

Whether the Great Pyramid was a tomb or a massive public works project it was an undertaking that the mind of man would be hard pressed to conceive, let alone seriously consider, without vision and the power of the will go accomplish that vision.

We have before us today, 4,500 years later, the greatest tribute to, and symbol of the power of the will ever conceived. The implications of that fact should not be underestimated.

A nation of Black, indigenous Africans struck upon an idea. But the idea was so far beyond that of any idea ever conceived that they had to shudder at the mere thought. Someone, an architect, a sage, a follower of Imhotep, the Council of Thirty or Khufu himself, struck upon an idea so massive, so advanced as to be the essence of insanity. Undaunted, that person whose name is forever lost, would have had to next sell the idea to those who would have to approve it, carry it out or both. We can almost hear the conversations and debates in council, the derision, the laughter, the predictable incredulity. "She proposes to build a structure 500 feet tall. We will have to quarry two million stones in one place and transport them to another miles away." No doubt the naysayers proclaimed that it was impossible and to what purpose even if it was possible. Apparently, it was an idea whose time had come.

The enormous size of the project required an even greater task than selling it to those who had the power to approve it. The people, those who would actually do the work, those who would supply the manpower had to be inspired, convinced to support the project with their blood, sweat and tears, with their time, effort and backbreaking labor. But to what purpose?

The Great Pyramid is a demonstration of the power of the collective will. It is the unique example of the ability of a people to accomplish a goal against seemingly insurmountable odds. The Great Pyramid stands as a silent monument to the colossal power of the will of the African people. It stands as a reminder of the greatness of our ancestors and a testament to the quality of their Sacred Science.

The Great Pyramid is the symbol of the latent power and potential of the New Body Politic when it is energized and actualized by the determined, motivated, collective will and sustained action. It is by this symbol that we visualize the power that lays just beneath the surface of our collective psyche. By creating this grand symbol of the power of the will our ancestors directed our attention to the three fundamental collectives: *collective thought, collective action*

Theodicy

and collective power. Those who are of one thought, and one action on create for themselves unlimited power.

The power of the will symbolized by the Great Pyramid is not unlike other forms of power. It may be used to accomplish goals in the same way all other power is used. Whether the goal is political, economic or cultural it is the will that makes it happen.

The power of the will is directed and focused. It is power that has been imbued with sacred purpose. Its distinction lies in the fact that it is power that has been infused with purpose intuited by and through the *Intelligence-of-the-Heart*. It is like a ray of sunlight that has been focused and directed through a magnifying glass that gives the intensity of fire.

The power of the will is the instrument of divine justice, it is part and parcel of Theodicy. Because it derives from the cosmic ocean and the Ancestral Stream it carries with it not only the purpose of the age but also the collective memory of the ancestors expressed and modified through the influence of the particular age and for a specific people.

The power of the will is the determination that creates the awareness of the necessity for the development of a plan to meet the exigencies of the age and dictates a course of action to carry it to completion by any means not destructive of the goal itself.

PYRAMID POWER

Much has been said recently about a curious phenomenon called pyramid power. Though we cannot and do not subscribe to the outrageous claims made for it there remains a great deal in the symbol and concept of the pyramid that may be accurately described as powerful.

Pyramid power does not sharpen razor blades but it does hone the determination that turns dreams into reality. It does not preserve food but it does preserve an Authentic Ancestral Culture.

Pyramid power is the power latent in the symbol of the pyramid. It perpetuates the concept of accomplishments achieved by the sheer force of the will. It is the power of determination. It instills the example that the will not only moves mountains, it can also build them.

The power of the pyramid lies in its use as a powerful symbol. A people who are destined to guide the world for the next two thousand years but who now find themselves in the unenviable position of servants and second-class citizens require powerful symbols to guide them to their destiny and actual power to make that destiny a reality.

Pyramid power is the power of the symbol. It symbolizes the power of the will. The Great Pyramid of Khufu is the symbol of the great power of the African people. To the extent that we draw upon the power of this great symbol and use it to inspire and motivate we too shall be great.

Theodicy

CHAPTER EIGHTEEN:

TOWARD NEW WASET

Theodicy establishes, through the Precession of the Equinoxes and the Wheel of Time, that the New Age is actually a result of a movement and cosmic re-orientation from one house of the Zodiac to another.

We have concluded that this movement is always predictive of a radical culture shift that will itself cause a cultural/political chain reaction that is explosive in its impact and effect. The current movement is from Pisces (a Northern constellation) to *Hapy* (a southern constellation).

We have also concluded that the necessity for this radical, cultural metamorphosis is evident in the unenviable state of powerlessness in which African Americans find themselves. We have been under the subjugation of a northern European patriarchal culture for the better part of the last two thousand years. It seems obvious that our deliverance from this unfortunate state of affairs must at least include a change from this northern European patriarchal approach to the governance of human affairs.

Our ancestral history indicates that our collective resurgence has been invariably marked by a return to the south which is the place of our ancestral birth. These epic resurgences have always been precipitated by a brutal assault from the north that has caused the disruption of our sacred and ancestral way of life. In the face of such disruption we have always returned to the south in order to revivify and marshal power, plan, leadership and will to defeat those who have usurped our land, traditions and power.

The south has always represented the place of our birth and of our re-birth. It is for this reason that our ancestors turned toward the south when in need of assistance and to the south when they were laid to their eternal rest. The south is the place where the spirit of our ancestors resides and is most strong. The south is the location of the power of our ancestral will.

In the Age of *Hapy* our vision and power will be in the south. In the context used here "the South" shall mean (1) *Hapy*, the southern constellation that will govern and influence the coming age; (2) the region of the continent of Africa below the equator where our ancestral roots are to be found; and (3) the southern United States where the majority or our people reside and where the New Body Politic will be born.

Our vision for the future necessarily requires of to see a picture of that future. We must have a psychological as well as physical location upon which to focus our attention and toward which to direct our collective thought energy. We must have a mental picture of our destination. We must visualize a city standing high on a sacred mound, bathed in Ra's life-giving light. We need a place of mind and spirit that radiates the life force of the *NeTeRs* from a powerhouse that is its energetic epicenter. We must be able to see a thriving sacred metropolis where the life force of the *NeTeR NeTeRu*, the power generated by our Authentic Ancestral Culture in action, and the unique power of the will evoked by the New Cosmic Age combine to create the cultural/political chain reaction that will revolutionize our thinking and change the course of human events.

Waset:

The Sacred City of a Hundred Gates

Our vision of the future must have a psychological as well as a physical location that serves as the focus of our endeavor, the aim of our enterprise and the height to which we aspire.

The highest level attained by our ancestral culture was represented by the civilization of ancient Kemit. The highest level reached by the civilization of ancient Kemit was that which flourished during the Eighteenth Dynasty of Upper (southern) Kemit. The capital of this great civilization was *Waset*, known to the ancient Greeks as "Thebes of the Hundred Gates". The memory of the resplendent city that was the capital of Kemit, the place of the royal residence, the location of the necropolis and the seat of the service of Amun, provides an unparalleled picture upon which to focus

Theodicy

our vision of the future. *Waset* is also a perfect picture because it is the place to which our ancestors returned repeatedly when attacked. It was to *Waset* that they returned when the land and its people were under attack. It was from this sacred city that our ancestors were rejuvenated, regrouped and launched the attack that drove the foreigners and their culture from the land.

The return to *Waset* has occurred at least two times in Kemitic history. Each return demonstrated the importance of a return to our southern ancestral moorings as a prerequisite to the type of thinking and vision that is the harbinger of cultural and political revolution.

A Brief History of Waset

Just as the Sun preceded from Taurus (*mentu* in the Kemitic tongue) to Aries (Amun) the Middle Kingdom of ancient Kemit began. This period, marked by the Eleventh Dynasty, was led by a a strong family of Black kings from the area of Upper (southern) Kemit called *Waset*. The family was known by the prenomen *Mentu* which means bull in Kemitic. The period was simultaneous with the astrological Age of Taurus the bull. At that time *Waset* was a small group of villages in Southern Kemit. It was from this area and under the leadership of the family *Mentu* that the land was unified under the Golden throne of Heru and the new capital was established.

In the Twelfth Dynasty, and under the leadership of the kings of *Waset*, the power of Kemit was solidified and two hundred years of prosperity and *hetep* (peace) ensued.

In the Fifteenth Dynasty the infamous *Hyksos*, the so-called "shepherd kings" seized the administration of the country at *Men-Nefer*, the northernmost boundary of Kemit marked by the "White Wall" constructed to keep foreigners our of the land. Rescue came from the south. Prince *Ahmeses*, after the death of his father *Kamose* rallied the forces of Kemit at *Waset* and drove the *Hyksos* out of the land forever. Prince *Ahmeses* and his beautiful wife *Nefertari* became the first king and queen of the Eighteenth Dynasty the most glorious of any in Kemitic history. The world renown *Tutankhamun* was a minor king of that dynasty.

Prior to the Eighteenth Dynasty the Kemites had no navy standing army. They had been content to live peacefully in their luxuriant valley for millennia without interference from outsiders. They became a warrior people as a direct result of the actions of others who sought to take by force or destroy their peaceful way of life and appropriate their abundant wealth.

It was also in the Eighteenth Dynasty that *Amun* became the Great *NeTeR* of the Cult in recognition of the precession of the Sun from the Taurus *(Mentu)* to Aries *(Amun)*.

Our ancestors learned two important lessons from the events of the Twelfth to Eighteenth Dynasties that we will be well served by remembering. They learned the need for strong, centralized leadership was ignored at one's own peril; and (2) that protection of the land and people requires a standing and use of *preemptive attack* to prevent enemies from growing strong enough to attack.

This brief history of *Waset* illustrates two factors important to the survival and prosperity of African Americans. First, our ancestors have always retreated to the south, to our ancestral homeland when under attack in turmoil or danger. The purpose of the retreat was to return to the place where our spirits and our strength could be rejuvenated amid the spirits of our ancestors and the wisdom of our elders. Second, our strength has always come from the power generated by that return and rededication to our Authentic· Ancestral Culture and the Sacred Science taught by it.

The New Cosmic Age

The New Cosmic Age requires a new perception, a new way of looking at reality and a quantum leap in the level of our consciousness. It requires a new way of *thinking* about the problems that confront us. Our problems will never be solved with the same level of thinking that created them. It requires the immediate abandonment of all methods and

Theodicy

tactics that have proven counterproductive or that have simply not worked. It requires that we begin, posthaste, to *restructure* our thought patterns and actions to insure that we begin to live and interact in harmony with the age and not attempt, foolishly, to act in opposition to it.

In the long history of humanity there has only been one nation tithe experience to instruct a fledgling nation how to stand on its feet and establish itself upon the principles of Sacred Science. Only one nation that has raised its people from the dead level of savagery to the living perpendicular of civilization. Only one nation from whose example we may see the end result of our unique ancestral plan sublimely illustrated.

At *Waset*, the capital and epicenter of our great Kemitic civilization, we see indigenous African culture, undefiled by European influence, thriving at its resplendent best.

We see African people free, independent and feared by the world not because of their brutality because of the willingness to fight against seemingly insurmountable odds to protect and defend their women, children and sacred way of life.

We see old people revered and protected for their wisdom as well as for the great contribution they have made to the progress of civilization just by having lived and blessed us with their presence for so long. To our people the old people were "Elders" not the elderly. They were the ones who had gone before and upon whose shoulders the present generation stood so tall.

We see women in positions of authority for authority was always under the hand of the woman. They stand as priests, scribes, administrators, sages, teachers, queens and kings. The administration of the home, the education of children and the disposition of all world possessions were in their hands. And they executed their responsibilities to ably that no man could ascend the throne unless we was married to a woman who was rightfully heir to it. No woman was inferior and none was mistreated. All women were mothers and sisters and all were protected.

We see children, the essence of our future and our immortality, free to mature under the watchful tutelage of an entire nation in which no child was an orphan, no child unloved, no child without mothers and fathers as numerous as the nation itself. All children were free to reach the greatest heights to which their individual potential could carry them. And every child's best friend was an "Elder".

We see a nation of people possessed of a collective mind driven by a collective will that made obstacles unheard of and that removed defeat for the lexicon of their lives.

We see a cultural and educational system so advanced that it turned out scholars that literally taught civilization and the useful arts to the world. And so important to the progress of the world that upon the destruction of it the entire world was plunged in a period of nearly one thousand years of darkness and ignorance.

We see a governmental structure and approach to governance that was recognized as the most perfect that the human mind had ever devised. A government that served the people, protected them and provided that which was requisite and necessary to their advancement and progress. It insured food for all and beneficial labor at tasks suited to the talent and aspiration of the individual.

We see a civilization in which when the collective work was done the party was on. In which everyone was free in the spirit of festival to let done their hair and indulge their wildest fantasies for it was the ancient command of our ancestors that we "eat drink and be merry for tomorrow we die".

We also see the Temple, the powerhouse par excellence, the repository and dispenser of Sacred Science, as the center of the life of the nation.

The Temple was the place where scholars, teachers, philosophers, sages and artisans received their education

Theodicy

and training. It was the place where the service of the *NeTeRs* was performed daily on behalf of the nation. But it was not religion foisted upon the people. It was the obligation of the state to be wholly responsible for the maintenance of peace, prosperity and harmony which included the performance of religious functions in the name of the people. The people themselves were guided in their dealings with each other by the teachings of our ancestors but they never so much as saw the performance of the ritual and were not permitted in the inner sanctum of the Temple, nor did they care to be.

When we envision *Waset* we see through the lens of our glorious, ancestral past the future that can be ours in the coming age. But seeing it is only the first step. We must prepare for its arrival with diligence and care. We can not doubt the corning of the New Age. We cannot avoid its end result. But the future, as we have seen, is a network of possibilities. Only our active dedication to a plan of action will insure that the coming age will benefit us our children and our cause.

The concept of Theodicy and the movement of the Wheel of Time indicate that it is time for us, once again, to direct our attention southward. We must return to a *Waset* where we can revivify and rejuvenate our people that they may become *not a unity but a harmony* of purpose and will.

In our southward trek we will reclaim that which we were forced to abandon. The south is the land where the bones of our ancestors who were brought to these shores in chains and as prisoners of war, are buried. By the presence of those bones and the blood, sweat and tears interred with them, the land of the south is our sacred burial ground. We cannot and will not go back to the Motherland unless and until we bring honor to our ancestors who have been laid to their eternal rest knowing that some day we would come for them, and so we shall.

Our ideological journey, the destination of our ambition and pride shall be a *New Waset*. A shining metropolis build upon a sacred mound where the beacon of enlightenment and courage will signal all of our people that time to advance is now. The vision of *New Waset* must become the reality of our future, and so it shall.

Theodicy

EPILOGUE

This has been a long, arduous journey of discovery with many stops and digressions along the way. It has been so not to needlessly prolong the journey but to insure that the reader arrives at the intended destination with the full complement of knowledge and information to make understanding and enlightenment possible.

This is the dawn of a new millennium and a new age that seems, in some mysterious way, to add urgency to the already perilous times. We are a people who fervently believe that God is just. We have been taught to wait on that justice based on the promise that it is inevitable. Of course, we have not been provided a timetable for that justice and perhaps one is unnecessary since death obviates the need for it. Surely justice prevails in God's heavenly abode.

For other, namely those who breath the fire, and who are possessed of a radical mind, something more than promise is required. It is for the latter group of people that this book has been written. This is not to say, however, that persons of the former group may not receive enlightenment by this journey and by so doing become members of the latter. We can always hope.

In any event, we have concluded what we began. *Theodicy. The Wheel of Time. Cultural Revolution. Change. Critical Mass. Power. Plan. Leadership. Will. Culture.*

Theodicy assures a basis for prediction. It is the foundation upon which to construct an analysis of the past and a view of the future that confirms the existence of divine justice even in the face of the existence of an evil that is unprecedented in history.

Theodicy allows us to see that God's justice is non-judgmental and operates according to universal laws from which it cannot deviate. As unfair as that may sound it is, nonetheless, balanced and impartial.

The Wheel of Time is the self-regulating balance of Theodicy. It is the ineluctable movement that guarantees that God's justice will not sleep forever and that it will be carried out predictably and without malice of favor. The Wheel of Time moves constantly forward in time toward its set destination. As it moves it elevates and castes down in regular succession. It does not stop or falter. That which is on the top cannot hold on to its position any more than that which is at the bottom can prevent its ascendency.

As the wheel turns it creates disturbance and friction in its wake. The disturbance is revolutionary by definition and is manifested as change. The change is effected in culture, politics, religion and economics. The inevitability of change is not the same as the conditions brought on by change. For example, we may be sure that within hours night will change into day. The change is inevitable and therefore predictable. But the change does not guarantee the conditions attendant upon that change. The dawning of the new day may bring happiness or sorrow, life or death. And we may not be prepared for the conditions brought on by the change. It follows that change may occur to find people affected by it who do not benefit from it or even recognize that it has occurred. In order to capitalize on change we must recognize it before it comes and make necessary preparations for its arrival.

In all societies the masses are so involved in the unending pursuit of life's daily necessities that they are prevented from acting decisively as a group. It is for this reason that mass movements are never the impetus to change. It is always a small group, of persons, we may call them visionaries, who implement change. It is only after they have taken decisive action that forces the masses to choose sides that the mass movement begins. The small group of persons endowed with vision are, in effect, a Critical Mass. It is the Critical Mass, therefore, that initiates change on the scale of the mundane. Their success is determined by their ability to recognize the signs and portents that change is imminent as well as their ability to prepare, in advance, to take advantage of the movement of the Wheel of Time. In order to do so they must understand power, develop a plan, select and

Theodicy

train the leadership, and above all, they must have an unconquerable will to succeed.

To understand power is to know God because God is power. In all its attributes, in all its myriad manifestations power and God are one. It is power that must be understood in order to understand Theodicy. We cannot fathom God or its Justice unless we have decided what God is. The understanding of power is a threshold matter. It is absolutely essential to the development of a plan of action because the acquisition and control of power is the number one objective of all political and cultural movements. That this fact is often disguised by the use of lofty sounding terms like freedom, justice and equality does not change the objective. *The bottom line is always power. Not Black power or White power but raw, unadulterated power.* The poor do not have power so they remain poor. The rich have power and remain rich. The poor get poorer and the rich get richer as a direct result of the amount of power they control. A plan that fails to account for this simple fact is doomed to failure from the inception. To the extent that a plan or a mission may be said to be blessed by God it still must have the power that is God to succeed. A people without power are a Godless people.

Even the well conceived plan is no more than a worthless curio if it never gets off the drawing board. A plan conceived is not necessarily a plan achieved and the best laid plans of mice and men not only go awry --the often go nowhere. It is leadership that brings the plan to fruition. The scarcity of leadership has been the bane of our existence in this country.

Since NaTuRe abhors a vacuum, the presence of one guarantees that it will be filled. Our failure to actively cultivate leadership qualities among our people has caused the vacuum to be filled by leaders. Even well-intentioned leaders cannot help but be mis-leaders without proper training in the fundamentals of leadership. Leaders may be born, but leadership is cultivated.

In every contest it is the most committed who wins. Commitment is dedication to a long-term course of action and as such is a primary function of the will. People succeed in their endeavors by the sheer force of their will. Collective will is no different. A group of people set upon a course of action must first have the will to succeed. The will itself is evoked by the cosmic age.

Theodicy teaches, through the Precession of the Equinoxes, that the coming age is one of radical change, revolution and a quantum leap in consciousness that will clarify our vision and change our collective way of thinking. The collective will evoked by the Age of *Hapy* will reflect these precise characteristics.

The reason that it is said that the people perish without vision is because vision is our power to see the possibilities and potential of times, places and people. Without vision the people are literally blind. But the vision must be well-informed. We must have not only vision but also clear vision. All thought, all plans, all action and all leadership must be informed by accurate unbiased knowledge and information. *Oudja* makes clear vision and accurate perception possible. Oudja is clear vision. When it is assisted by Critical Thinking and the Intelligence-of-the-Heart they comprise the Triad of Visionary Power.

We have spent a great deal of time on culture. This is because culture may very well be the most important concept for us to understand if we truly seek to change our circumstances and avail ourselves of the benefits inherent in the cosmic re-orientation that will usher in the Age of *Hapy*. A people without culture are doomed to exist as the servants of another and foreign culture, if they exist at all. A people who abandon their culture and adopt the culture of their enemies are not worthy of existence.

Culture is not only the technology of survival, it is also an operator's manual formulated for a specific group of people by their ancestors. It contains all they need to know to survive and prosper in a hostile and calamitous world. Without our own Authentic Ancestral Culture we have no mooring. We are a rudderless ship of state whose destiny is

Theodicy

to sink in the turbulence of the political storm that rages around us.

By resuscitating our Authentic Ancestral Culture we can avail ourselves of the Sacred Science that made our ancestors great. We must not overlook or forget our glorious ancestral past or the civilization that was created in it. The highest level of that civilization was attained in ancient Kemit. In Kemit is to be found the perfect model for our future. In its majesty and wisdom it has demonstrated and recorded for us the supreme example of the perfected nation. From the perfect form of government to the rearing of children, to the service of our ancestral Gods, our ancestors have addressed every issue vital to our survival and prosperity as a people. The answers and methods they have provided have stood the test of time and maybe easily modified for application to our present circumstances and needs.

Our ancestors knew when they created their Sacred Science that they were preparing the blueprint that would be used by their descendants to rise, like the *Bennu* Bird, from the ashes of the conflagration that would result when ignorance triumphed, for a time, over enlightenment. They inscribed the blueprint upon the walls of their temples and in tombs where they were laid to rest. They constructed the Great Pyramid as the quintessential symbol of the power of the will to demonstrate to us that nothing is beyond our power when we are driven by an indomitable will and to show that ours is a culture perfected for eternity.

Our ancestors left, as their legacy, all that we need. All we are required to do is avail ourselves of their instruction. All roads lead to Kemit. At the end of each road, at the crossroads of destiny and fate we shall find, standing high on a sacred mound, resplendent in the rays of Ra's life-giving energy, the Temple of *Hapy* sitting at the.,, center of the city of *New Waset*. There the spirit of our ancestors awaits us with open arms to embrace us with the wisdom and power that will change our lives and change the course of history.

We have now come full circle and arrived at the place where we began. *Theodicy and the Power of the African Will*. A crisis of danger and opportunity is before us. Will we sit idle and permit our enemies to effect their final settlement or will we launch a counteroffensive against the undeclared war that now threatens genocide. Will we adopt the tactics of confrontation and preemptive attack or wait until we no longer have the strength or numbers to fight?

One final note: Our children have been kidnapped and imprisoned. We will not rest until they are returned. The mass incarceration of our children as a tactic of the so-called war on drugs is a travesty. Let the word go out to all the world, to friend and foe alike, we are coming for our children and no force on this planet or in the heavens above will stop us. Our children will be safe and they will be free. Those who doubt our will shall feel our wrath. *So let it be written. So let it be done!*

Theodicy

APPENDIX

"The Night of the Teardrop"

At a time before history began, when the world was new and the *NeTeRs* were young, a man of exceptional distinction was occasioned upon the Earth. It is said that at the moment of his birth the voice of the *NeTeR NeTeRu* was heard to proclaim that the Lord of Created Things had been born. The arrival of this "great soul" marked the beginning of the ascent of humanity from savagery to civilization.

This exceptional man, born of exceptional woman, was given the name Asar, whispered by his mother at the moment of his birth. It is said that his goodness and mercy surpassed that of any who had come before. It is for this reason that he was revered as the Great Ancestor of the people of Kemit the land o   f his birth.

Through introspection and selfless pursuit of the innate spiritual consciousness that is the Intelligence-of-the-Heart, Asar gained wisdom and spiritual power far beyond that of any who had walked the land before him. Those who knew him recognized that he was destined to be the first communicator of wisdom.

As the young, precocious *Asar* grew to maturity and surveyed the condition of those born of his blood and bound by the lineage of common ancestry, his heart grew heavy with the weight of their suffering.

The people were uneducated, given to acts and lifestyles representative of their lower instincts alone and fettered by a profound lack of spiritual development.

By the *Intelligence-of-his-heart* Asar knew that it was his unalterable destiny to uplift and harmonize his people. He became, instantly, teacher, organizer and administrator of civilization.

Now *Asar* had a younger brother whose name was *Set*. *Set* was the opposite of his brother in all things. Where *Asar* was kind, generous and compassionate, *Set* was rude, parsimonious and egotistical. *Asar* was pragmatic and viewed life holistically, while *Set* was impulsive,

Theodicy

discriminatory and fascinated with minutiae, *Set* believed that all things should be separated and segregated to each its own individuality. He believed in competition.

Asar, on the other hand, knew in his heart, that all things, all people are interdependent, that separation, segregation and individualism encourage and foment dissension and disarray. He knew that cooperation led to efficient accomplishment of the objectives of society while competition led to inequality and discord.

Set believed that it was better to be feared than loved. He believed that education was wasted on the people because they were not educable and in any event education only served to make the unsuitable for manual labor which was their inevitable lot in life. Never have two brothers been so diametrically opposed.

Undeterred by his brother's incessant nay saying, *Asar* pursued the path of spiritual development and by his deeds brought culture and civilization to his beloved people. *Asar* taught the people, by example, agriculture, cultivation of the vine, weaving, architecture and construction. He established a code of fundamental laws and a system of courts to mediate disputes between. individuals and clans. He established national service to the *NeTeRs* and encouraged the continuation of service to tribal *NeTeRs*. He established and educational system that permitted the people to improve themselves that each might rise to the highest level of his potential. The people were content and *hetep* reigned in the land. By virtue of his deeds and the power of his words, *Asar* became loved and respected throughout the land of Kemit as a selfless benefactor of the people. As his fame grew fare and wide, security and prosperity flourished in its wake.

Now *Set*, always jealous of his brother became more so in light of Asar' s accomplishments and the unstinting adulation he received from the people. On the day that Set watched his brother's coronation, by acclamation, as "'*Suten* of Kemit, he could no longer contain, his hatred. It was at that precise moment that he began to plot his brother's downfall.

Asar's achievements were many, his skill and leadership the pride of the nation. Yet, personal happiness eluded him. One day Asar sae a lovely maiden in a court procession. He knew immediately why personal happiness had eluded him. He berated himself for not having recognized it sooner. He who had done so much for the people had neglected his own happiness. In his zeal to bring the people the understanding of holistic necessity in life had failed to recognize his own need for it.

Asar and *Aset* fell in love almost immediately and after a brief courtship that was closely watched and admired by the entire nation they were married amid the pomp and ceremony only a grateful nation can bestow on its universally acclaimed leader and his beautiful bride.

Aset was a woman of unparalleled beauty, refinement and wisdom. Together they led the people of Kemit to a level of civilized prosperity and progress unknown in history. Their names and the report of their accomplishments traveled to the far corners of the Earth.

Having made Kemit a land of peace and prosperity and upon invitation from the leaders of the nations of the world, *Asar* set out with an entourage of professionals in the useful arts, to instruct the people of the world in the science of civilization.

During his absence Asar's good wife the beautiful *Aset*, the First Lady of Kemit, the Mistress of Charms and Enchantments, the Divine Mother, ruled the land with benevolence and compassion. It is said that the efficiency of her rule during this period equaled or surpassed that of her illustrious husband.

Now *Set*, who hated his brother and was always jealous of him, became even more hateful. He attempted to spread rumors about his brother and sister-in-law to undermine the allegiance of the people. All attempts failed. Soon he became convinced that the love of the people for their "good king" was too deeply felt and too sincere to be undermined and began to plot his brother's assassination instead. It is said

Theodicy

that envy is the handmaiden of treachery. With the assistance of seven-two co-conspirators and *Aso*, the Queen of Ethiopia, Set formulated a plan to assassinate his brother upon his return from the triumphant world tour.

In furtherance of his dastardly plan *Set* secretly secured information regarding Asar's bodily dimensions. He took these and had a lavish, bejeweled sarcophagus constructed out of precious cedar from the Lebanon. The plan was simple but ingenious. He would induce his brother to lie down in the sarcophagus which would be presented to him at the grand celebration to be held at the good king's residence on the night of his return.

Set calculated that because of the ancient tradition of passing around a miniature sarcophagus to viewed by the guests at a banquet to emphasize the fleeting duration of life and the imminence and eternity of death, he surmised that his brother would not be able to decline an offer to "try it on for size".

On the evening of the celebration, after a sumptuous meal and all manner of lively entertainments, *Set*, as planned, presented his brother with the lavish gift.

Asar thought the gift, the most beautiful sarcophagus he had ever seen, extravagant and in poor taste. But because he did not want to embarrass his brother before the hundreds of guests in attendance he graciously acceded to his request. No sooner had *Asar* reclined in the sarcophagus then the seventy-two co-conspirators took armed control of the banquet hall closed the lid, nailed it shut and sealed it with molten lead.

Aset and the assembled guests watched in horror as the sarcophagus was taken from the hall by *Set* and his cohorts who took it to the mouth of the River *Hapy* and weighted it to the bottom. The "Good King" did not survive.

Having assassinated his brother and now in control of the seat of government by force of arms, *Set* proclaimed himself ruler of Kemit and immediately instituted policies to restore "law and order". All administrators of the land appointed by the "Good King" were discharged and replaced by handpicked lackeys who swore allegiance to *Set*. Taxation was introduced. Religion was imposed in the place of Sacred Science. Mercantilism supplanted socialism. A massive law enforcement apparatus was installed. Laws were codified in ever-increasing numbers which exacted severe punishment for minor offenses. Government became oppressive and the people sullen and restless.

Aset, now dethroned and without the aid of her husband fled the capital. Her valiant search for the sarcophagus led her to the Phoenician city of Byblos where she retrieved it and brought it back to Kemit where she hid it.

One evening, while hunting by the light of the moon, Set discovered the sarcophagus, removed the corpse of the dead king, dismembered it and scattered the fourteen pieces at different locations throughout the land.

Aset, having discovered what her brother-in-law had done searched for and found the pieces of her husband's dismembered body. At each location where a piece was found she erected a tomb.

The annual overflow of the River *Hapy* is the life-blood of the Land of Kemit. During the period of Set usurpation of the throne the overflow ceased to occur as usual. First the flow diminished, finally it ceased altogether leaving the land barren with widespread famine in its wake.

The union of *Asar* and *Aset* produced a son who was called *Heru*. Heru had been instructed, in the tradition of his ancestors, that it was the obligation of a son to avenge his father's death. The son of the king was also obligated to reclaim the throne and reinstitute the policies and government in the fashion of his father.

Having come of age, *Heru* challenged his uncle *Set* to mortal combat, in order to fulfill his obligation to his father's memory. Many battles ensued over a period of many years. In each battle neither *Set* nor *Heru* was victorious. The result, however, was that *Set* and his harsh rule remained in

Theodicy

place during the seemingly interminable stalemate. no matter what tactic *Heru* tried he was unable to defeat his uncle. In one battle *Set* succeeded in dismembering one of *Heru's* eyes. Her left the battlefield half blinded, taking with him the pieces of the dismembered eye. He immediately went to the elders to seek their advice.

The elders informed him that there was a person who knew the sacred words of power that could, if properly employed, restore his vision, defeat *Set* and end the mortal combat.

Tehuti was known by many names. He was called the Master of Divine Intelligence and science; the Reckoner of Time; the Righteous Judge of the cycle of the *NeTeRs*; Lord of Writing; Creator of Sacred Letters; the Sweet Tongued Voice of the *NeTeR NeTeRu* and the Chief Judge of the Ten of Upper Kemit, the Kemitic Supreme Court.

Heru consulted Tehuti who restored his vision by making the dismembered eye sound again. The restoration of *Heru's* vision represented the turning point in the conflict between *Set* and *Heru*. Tehuti also instructed *Heru* in the *hekau* or words of power by which *Set* could be defeated. Much to *Heru's* surprise the method suggested did not rely on military strategy. *Heru* was directed to bring his claim to the Kemitic Supreme Court where Tehuti was chief among the ten judges. *Heru* did as he was instructed and filed suit to regain his lawful right to the throne and for the wrongful death of his father.

Set was judged by the law that he had imposed to maintain "law and order" after the assassination of *Asar*. *Set* argued that he was, by virtue of the sovereign immunity of a ruler, exempt from the laws that he had so hastily enacted and brutally enforced. This novel argument was unanimously rejected by the court which held that no one was above the law.

One of the laws enacted under *Set's* reign by Royal Edict provided that conspiracy to assassinate, attempted assassination and assassination of the ruler were crimes punishable by death. The Court found that the law could be applied retroactively. *Set* was found liable and the death penalty was imposed as required by the law he enacted.

Set appealed to *Aset*, whose influence with the people of Kemit was still considerable. He pleaded with her to use her influence to spare his life. "After all," he argued, "killing me will not bring back my brother". Upon hearing those words *Aset* began to weep. It is said that at that precise moment the River *Hapy* began to overflow. The life-blood of the nation was restored. The day is commemorated as the "Day of the Teardrop" when prosperity and *hetep* returned to the Land of Kemit.

Being compassionate of heart and not wanting to shed more blood, *Aset* requested that the Court spare the life of her husband's brother and murderer. Tehuti and the Supreme Court proclaimed *Heru* the legitimate heir to the throne of Kemit and *Aset* the Queen Mother of the nation.

As for *Set* the court ruled that because he had intentionally caused the death of the "Good King" and thereby deprived humanity of his leadership and wise counsel, *Set* would, henceforth and forever, serve as the "wind that propels the boat of *Asar*". *Set* was sentenced to actively, aggressively and eternally disseminate the wisdom of *Asar* to all people in all lands.

www.ingramcontent.com/pod-product-compliance
Lightning Source LLC
Chambersburg PA
CBHW021116300426
44113CB00006B/172